Under the Radar Michigan
The First 50

Written by
Tom Daldin

Photographs and stories
about episode names by
Jim Edelman

Contributing prose by
Eric Tremonti

Scribe Publishing Company
First Edition

Under the Radar Michigan: The First 50

Published by Scribe Publishing Company
Royal Oak, Michigan
www.scribe-publishing.com

Copyright © 2015 by Under the Radar Productions, Inc.
www.utrmichigan.com
Cover photo by Caryn Taylor Photography
Cover and interior design by Miguel Camacho

ISBN 978-0-9916021-0-0

Publisher's Cataloging-in-Publication data

Daldin, Tom.
    Under the radar Michigan : the first 50 / Written by Tom Daldin ; photographs and
stories about episode names by Jim Edelman ; contributing prose by Eric Tremonti.
    p. cm.
    Includes index.
    ISBN 978-0-9916021-0-0
1. Under the Radar (television program). 2. Michigan –Description and travel. 3. Cities and
towns –Michigan. 4. Natural history –Michigan. 5. Wilderness areas –Michigan. I. Edelman,
Jim. II. Tremonti, Eric. III. Under the radar Michigan : the first fifty. IV. Title.

F566 .D35 2015
977.4 –dc23   2014942256

Printed in Michigan

TABLE OF CONTENTS

Each chapter follows the Under the Radar adventure, from the first episode to the fiftieth.
Use the **index** in the back for quick navigation.

Season 1

Season 2

Season 3

Season 4 (To be continued...)

How it all started...
Our story in a nutshell.

Like so many worthwhile endeavors, Under the Radar (UTR) was born out of necessity. In 2010, Jim and I both lost our livelihoods and had to literally reinvent ourselves to survive. Jim was head of national sales for a big radio conglomerate, and I was flying around the country producing automotive videos for the Big Three car companies in Detroit. When the auto industry took a serious slide, I lost most of my income and was slowly going broke. On President Obama's inauguration day, the company Jim worked for laid off half their workforce nationally, including Jim. There we were, two longtime friends, up the financial creek without a paddle. And when I say long time, we met in 1982 when we were both getting our work feet wet at 101.1 WRIF radio. To this day, we still play in a rock band together.

About ten years ago I attempted to produce and host a TV show for kids called "Bob's Job." The program was a career series that showed kids different jobs and what it's really like to be a grownup. I produced three episodes that were aired on Detroit Public Television, but the project eventually faded away due to lack of funding. Jim and I decided to see if, together, we could resurrect the show with PBS.

Five minutes into the meeting with Detroit Public TV, they informed us that they weren't looking for more children's programming and asked point blank what else we had to propose. Well, Jim and I are both huge fans of where we live, and of any and all types of travel shows. So after a few blank stares, dramatic pauses and a couple swift kicks back and forth under the table, we "Seinfelded it." We said, "How 'bout a Michigan exploration program, where we travel the state discovering and uncovering cool people, places and things that people don't (but should) know about?"

Well, their eyes widened. They said, "Make it, fund it, bring it back, we'll broadcast it and they will come." Or something like that. So we went off, and while I was producing a pilot episode, Jim found the funding necessary to get us off the ground and running around the state. Eric Tremonti was a producer we absconded from a local video post production house because we realized that his tremendous talents would be a great addition to the mix. Eric's contributions have transformed the show. The resources and different qualities we all brought to the table made for a perfect partnership. So we got the party started, and it's been an amazingly fun and rewarding adventure ever since.

Author's Note...
Important Reading.

Please remember that books are timeless, but people, some places and things are not. Some of the many places we feature in this book may have, over time, changed, moved or simply ceased to be. So we can't stress enough that you always need to check ahead and contact any of these places before setting out to visit them. It could save you a long drive there and a very frustrating and disappointing drive home.

Another very important thing to keep in mind is that many resort community businesses and attractions are seasonal, and their open and close dates may fluctuate due to any number of reasons, including the weather. For this reason, we did not list dates, and you should always call ahead before setting out on your adventure.

Contact information for each location has been provided in this book, but given how easy it is to change phone numbers and email addresses, please be aware that this may have occurred. We have given you the best and most accurate contact information we had at the time this book was published.

> Be sure to use the index in the back if you're trying to quickly locate something we've featured in the book. You can search by city, category or name.

Additional note: You may notice that a few of the people, places or things we featured on the TV show are missing from this book. This is simply because, at the time of publishing, we became aware that a person, place or thing may have moved, changed or ventured into a different business. Also, a few of the people, places and things featured on the show wish to remain private or are not open to the public. For reasons of respect and privacy, they have been excluded from the book as well. Thanks for your understanding.

For more information on all the people, places and things we feature in this book, please go to www.utrmichigan.com. There you can find maps, watch episodes, see when we're broadcast in your area and even get cool UTR wearables.

Have fun. Explore Michigan.

Dedication

To be honest, there are so very many people to thank for helping us get this far that we could probably fill the pages of this book with their names. The scariest thing about thanking people is no matter how hard you try, you always seem to forget someone. Ugh… that's a horrible feeling. So, to those who have touched us, influenced us or helped us in any way, shape or form, please accept a humble and sincere thank you.

One person in particular we do need to recognize is Gary Heidl from the Michigan State Housing Development Authority (MSHDA). Back when Under the Radar Michigan was just a concept, Gary sat down with us, understood what we were trying to do, saw the power and value in our program and has ever since been our biggest supporter by helping us spread the good word about Michigan. Actually, we can't say enough good things about all the people at MSHDA and their marketing partner, Pace. They have helped us, believed in us and continue to make our mission of turning Michigan around possible.

Bob Fish, owner of Michigan's own Biggby Coffee chain, has also believed in us and supported us for some time now, and for that he deserves a sincere mention here.

We'd also like to thank the Detroit Public Television team for helping to bring UTR to the air. We are proud they think of us as more than a TV show on their station and that they include us in station events and allow us to report from the Mackinac Policy Conference every year. Rich Homberg, Dan Alpert, Dan Gaitens, Jeff Forster, Jamie Westrick and Lauren Smith are the people who regularly touch the show and keep us moving forward.

A special thanks also goes out to the many people we have featured on the program over our first three seasons. Without their inspiring stories of perseverance and success, these pages would be blank.

Thanks to all the great people who never gave up on Michigan and who are helping make it better, brighter and more braggable every day.

We'd also like to thank our incredibly talented team of "UTR Super Associates" who work so hard to make our show shine. Chris Randolph (editor in chief), Howard Hertz (lawman), Mike Sorrentino (who we account on), Marty Peters and Chris Hugan at Ozone (a sound decision), Jeremy Anderson (spins our web), Augie Fernandes (the wind in our sales), David Wesch (groovy graphics), with additional awesome edits from the likes of Cristin Trosien, Elaine Danielian, Eric Carlsen and Dyan Bailey. And we can't forget to thank Jennifer Baum at Scribe Publishing for giving us this incredible opportunity.

And last but not least, a heartfelt thanks goes out to our families. Without their love and support, none of this would have happened.

Forward

W̲e all work hard in life. We struggle to grow up, get through school, get a job, pay our bills and provide for our families. This is noble work because it helps you and the people you care about survive and thrive in this crazy, confusing and complicated thing we call life.

Jim, Eric and I have worked hard all our lives to provide for those around us. But I have to tell you that never before now have we felt so fortunate. We've always wanted to do something that really meant something, and UTR has given us that chance. In all the different things we've done over the years to support our families, this is the first time we've had the opportunity to really give back and help so many people and businesses that need and deserve the exposure and support. Countless people we've featured on the program have told us what an incredible difference it has made in their lives and their businesses. To us, that kind of thanks is priceless. I can't even begin to tell you how lucky and thankful we are to be producing this program. We count our blessings every day.

> Whatever you do for a living, if it doesn't reward you emotionally or feed your soul, get involved with a group or organization that does.

In your spare time, take the time to volunteer and do something that will make a difference in someone else's life. Help your neighbors, your community and, most importantly, those less fortunate than you. It feels good to do things that mean something, and it would mean a great deal to those who really need it.

Thanks for working hard to support those you love and for the continuing contributions you all make to the great State of Michigan. I've said it before and I'll say it again: I've been around the world, but there's one place I keep coming back to, because it's the place to be.

Have fun and explore your state. Read on...

Chapter 1

Season 1, Episode 1

Royal Oak
Detroit
Kalamazoo

In the 70s it was a tired, forgotten town, but ingenious Michigan entrepreneurs with a vision turned it into what it is today, 'the' place to be. If you're looking for unique, funky local shops, cool eclectic restaurants, hip nightspots, a great place to spend a weekend or an even better place to live, put your foot on the brake, because you're in Royal Oak, Michigan. Let's face it, when friends come in from out of town, Royal Oak is where you take them. It's a small town that's got a really big metropolitan feel. There are great downtown condos and loft living, beautiful neighborhoods and a great diversity of people to bump elbows with.

R oyal Oak is known for many great things, but my favorite is its incredible range of restaurants. Whatever your dining pleasure, it's there. So in this chapter, we have a "dine-amic-duo" for you.

You've heard the old saying, "If you want something fast, cheap and good… you'll have to pick two." Well, here are two casual Royal Oak eateries where you can get all three and leave laughing like a pirate.

Second Street Sub Shop
108 W. Second St., Royal Oak, MI, 48067
(248) 543-7474

Located on 2nd Street just west of Main, **Second Street Sub Shop** is a funky little place that claims to have the world's best subs. As far as we know, Second Street also holds the title of Royal Oak's smallest restaurant, with seating for only eight. Owner Scott Perry hand-picks all his ingredients; there are no bulk food service deliveries happening there. The place has a ton of character, and Scott is a bit of a character himself.

When Scott's not entertaining his regulars with witty barbs and thoughtful banter, he's making colossal subs with hand-picked, local ingredients. To make sure he gets the best of the best, Scott gets his meats from nine different places, including Detroit's Eastern Market. He even goes all the way to Dearborn to get his bread from a hundred-year-old, family-owned Italian bakery. There's a real sense of community in his subs.

I got to make a sub with Scott, and I have to tell you, after watching the master at work, I was pretty intimidated. Scott was extremely patient and an absolute blast. No matter how you slice it, Second Street Sub Shop is a great place for a quality meal. Just make sure you bring your appetite and your sense of humor.

Zumba Mexican Grille
(248) 542-1400
304 N. Main St., Royal Oak, MI 48067
www.zumbagrille.com

My second place for a fast, cheap and good meal in Royal Oak is a fresh-Mex place the locals absolutely swear by. **Zumba Mexican Grille** has a great feel with traditional Mexican art done up in cool, modern, funky materials. It's upbeat, it's casual and all the great tastes of Mexico are served up at a single counter. Brilliant!

Owner Tim Castaneda is the reason this place is the real deal. He grew up in his family's Mexican restaurant and took all his recipes right off the family tree. It's real Mexican food that's fast, fresh and affordable. Zumba is also a place where Royal Oak's movers and shakers like to connect. Not only does Tim serve up some incredible Mexican chow, he's also involved and engaged in his community, and that's a flavor I love.

I'll be honest—Zumba Mexican Grille is only about a half hour from my house, so when I feel the need for the fresh flavors of Mexico, I zip down to Zumba for my favorite three amigos of food: fast, cheap and good. Heck, if it was twice as far, I'd probably still go there.

S ay you're in downtown Detroit and suddenly your right brain gets a craving for some culture. Head straight for the creative, cultural and educational center of the city, **Midtown Detroit.**

The Inn on Ferry Street
(313) 871-6000
84 E. Ferry St., Detroit, MI 48202
www.innonferrystreet.com

If you're ever in Midtown Detroit, there's an under the radar hidden treasure you've just got to experience. **The Inn on Ferry Street** is a collection of beautifully restored historic homes that have been turned into an outstanding, first-class bed and breakfast. You won't believe the experience you'll have when you're there.

Sue Mosey heads up the University Cultural Center Association, and when she's not running the inn, she's helping put the spotlight back on Midtown. Sue is an incredible urban visionary who continues to help support, develop and promote the new Detroit. You won't meet a more fascinating, involved or passionate person in the city.

As for the inn, these homes are incredible. Every home and room is different and uniquely appointed, and the location is perfect. You're literally steps away from the Detroit Institute of Arts, the Detroit Public Library, Wayne State University and all the major medical centers. Midtown is also exploding with new shops, restaurants, breweries and bakeries, so a weekend at the inn would be a fun way to discover some of these cool new places. If you're looking for a wonderful way to reconnect with the city, the Inn on Ferry Street is an outstanding start.

Kalamazoo is an awesome city that's big enough to have that urban feel, but still small enough to be totally walkable. In 1959 Kalamazoo opened the first walking mall in America right downtown. Now it's a collection of cool businesses, shops and great restaurants. K'zoo also has some incredibly beautiful and historic neighborhoods that are very welcoming. What give the city its intellectual energy are Western Michigan University and Kalamazoo College. The city is also covered with some of the coolest and most creative building murals I've ever seen. They give the city a funky urban soul and a really inviting sense of place.

Air Zoo
(866) 524-7966
6151 Portage Rd., Portage, MI 49002
www.airzoo.org

The main reason we went to K'zoo was to explore a place just south of town. It's called the **Air Zoo**, and it's a one-of-a-kind destination. It's an absolutely mind-blowing aviation museum that was voted the best place to take someone who's visiting Michigan. Don't let the word "museum" scare you away. This just might be one of the funnest places I've ever been.

The Air Zoo is an experience like you've never had before. They have over fifty rare and historical aircraft, full motion flight simulators and a breathtaking 4-D theatre that takes you right back to WWII. There are indoor amusement park rides, and the Guinness World Record™ largest indoor mural ever painted is located there (and believe it or not, it was painted by one person).

One of my favorite rides was the 3-D Space Shuttle Ride. It's a simulator where you blast off from Planet Earth and travel all the way up to the International Space Station. The experience was incredible and oh-so lifelike. After a successful landing, I decided to try one of the full-motion flight simulators. It's like you're really flying, and you can pick from a number of different airplanes. You know me; I picked the fastest.

The 4-D theater is a total trip on the senses. You get to see, smell, hear and even feel what it was like to fly a bombing mission during World War II. This experience was outstanding. The Air Zoo is a great place to take the family. You'll get lost in both the history and the future of flight. You'll also learn a ton along the way. The Air Zoo and K'zoo were both well worth the trip.

Story behind the name:
Take Me to the Pilot

Show number one of a series is always the pilot episode. In our very first episode, we look back on an ancient Elton John song to ingeniously inject the word PILOT into the title of the show. This also sets the tone for odd titles that, on many occasions, only mean something to the crew. Sometimes it's only known to Jim why he named a show a particular way... These "Story behind the name" features will let you peek in Jim's head.

Chapter 2

Season 1, Episode 2

Grand Rapids
Cadillac
Port Huron

When we pulled into Grand Rapids, I couldn't believe how much it had grown. It's alive with new business, tourism, nightlife and tons of culture. There's a real modern and progressive feel there that makes it one of the greatest places to live in the U.S. today. Everywhere we looked, there were young professionals engaged with their city.

The B.O.B.
(616) 356-2627
20 Monroe Ave. NW, Grand Rapids, MI 49503
www.thebob.com

We came to Grand Rapids to experience a building called **The B.O.B.** It's a classic 70,000-square-foot four-story red-brick building that was built in 1903 as Judson's Grocery Warehouse. It stood vacant for decades and was destined for the wrecking ball until a local group called The Gilmore Collection transformed it into a cool complex that features everything you need for a great time in the city. B.O.B. stands for "Big Old Building," and it sits right in the heart of downtown. You'll find great restaurants, bars, night clubs, entertainment venues and meeting spaces all rolled into one very cool environment. The range of establishments is amazing, and there's something there for everyone.

The B.O.B. creates a great space where urbanites can relax, visit, enjoy live music, have an elegant dinner, a casual bite or just unwind from the day. It's a great place to connect with other people who live and work downtown. It's also a great place to check out even if you're just visiting. We had a blast.

A ton of young people are reconnecting with Grand Rapids and living in the city. The B.O.B. creates a real sense of place and community for the people who live there, and that's important. When the sun goes down, The B.O.B. comes alive with the beat of the big city. If you haven't been to Grand Rapids in a long time, it's time for you to go.

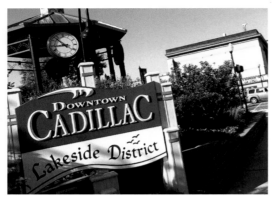

Not only is **Cadillac** a great boating, skiing and golfing destination, the downtown has been completely renovated. Mitchell Street is the main shopping district, and it's alive with great new shops, restaurants and awesome spaces to just kick back and relax. Without forgetting its past, Cadillac is another Michigan city that's moving into a bright future.

When I was a kid, we took tons of family vacations in northwest Lower Michigan. And whenever we traveled up Highway 115, we'd always stop for gas just outside Cadillac by **William Mitchell State Park**. It's a beautiful park that sits between Lake Cadillac and Lake Mitchell. The road passes through a narrow strip of land that gives you a beautiful panoramic view of both lakes. I can remember all five of us saying to my mom, "Why can't we just stay here? It's awesome." But we always headed up to the sand dunes. Well, now, thanks to UTR, we stayed in Cadillac and loved it!

Toy Town
(231) 775-TOYS
122 S. Mitchell St., Cadillac, MI 49601
www.toytowncadillac.com

When we shot this segment, Ryan and Nicole Schultz owned **Toy Town**, a progressive and really cool toy store right downtown. Their mission is to provide families, young and old, the opportunity of adventure, imagination and discovery inside, outside and everywhere in between. This is a really cool place that will thrill your youngins and totally make you feel like a kid again. At Toy Town they're always searching for new products to engage, entertain, educate and enlighten your little ones. Just walking through the store is fun. I spent about $60 at the store (partly for me) and loved the experience. If you've got little ones at home, or there's still a little one in you, check out Toy Town. Okay… it was mostly for me. :-)

We also stumbled upon something very cool called **The Sound Garden**. It's a rustic musical art sculpture that's not only fun to look at, it also makes music. It was a community art project created by local artist Frank Youngman for all to enjoy. It's located at the headwaters of the Clam River Greenway and is an art installation with built-in musical instruments like a log drum, xylophones and chimes created from recycled brake drums. Very unique and very cool. When you're there, you should really check it out. Just ask a local. They'll tell you where to find it.

After a full day of exploring, the crew was getting tired of my antics, so we decided to look for a great place to eat and a comfortable place to sleep. This is where the story gets good, because we found both at the same place right downtown.

Hermann's European Café
(231) 775-9563
214 N. Mitchell St., Cadillac, MI 49601
www.chefhermann.com

What we found was **Hermann's European Café**. Now get this: it's a gourmet restaurant, a casual deli where the locals meet, an expert butcher shop, a fantastic wine shop, and upstairs from all of this is a four-star, European-style hotel.

If you're wondering how this concentrated slice of European culture came to downtown Cadillac, it's all the doing of Chef Hermann Suhs. Chef Hermann lives by the motto, "You're only as good as your last meal." He's an incredibly bigger-than-life personality with an absolutely fascinating history. He was born and raised near Vienna, Austria, spent five years as an apprentice to learn his trade and got his first certificate in a Vienna Konditorei Shop, where he learned European and Viennese pastries. Next he apprenticed in the famous Hotel Sacher in Vienna with the finest European Master Chefs. From Vienna, he cooked his way around the world. In Sweden, he earned his Master Chef certificate. In Nepal, he was Executive Chef at the Hotel Annapurna and also served as a personal chef to the King of Nepal. He's worked in Thailand and in the Caribbean Islands, giving his international dishes a rare authenticity.

I actually had the chance to cook with Chef Hermann, and this guy is the real deal. He's a chef in the truest sense of the word and an absolute old-world gentleman. All his establishments on the block are impeccable and his staff first rate. Hermann's Hotel is right upstairs from all his shops and is awesome as well. The rooms are very European in flavor and way convenient. There aren't many places in Michigan where can you dine in a gourmet restaurant and then climb the stairs to spend a luxurious night.

If a ticket to Europe looks a little steep to you right now, give Cadillac and Hermann's a try. Not only will it be way cheaper, they speak Michigan there. Bonus!

 It was early in the morning when we rolled into **Port Huron**. I was just about to ask if anyone wanted to stop for coffee when I heard someone on the crew say, "Wow, this is pretty cool." Well, I happen to agree. I've always liked Port Huron for the way it feels. It's a great mix of old and new, it's just the right size and it's on the water. I love the water. Good thing I'm in Michigan.

The city of Port Huron is the maritime capital of the Great Lakes and stretches seven miles along the shore of the St. Clair River at the base of the second largest of the Great Lakes, Lake Huron. The boardwalk there goes on forever and provides excellent views of the St. Clair River, passing freighter traffic and one of my favorite bridges in the whole world, the Blue Water Bridge (the majestic gateway to Canada).

Besides the beautiful waterfront scenery and boating activities, Port Huron has even more to do when you're off the water. The historic downtown shopping district has tons of interesting and funky shops and very cool restaurants.

Studio 1219
(810) 984-2787
1219 Military St., Port Huron, MI 48060
www.studio1219.com

There's also a thriving art community in Port Huron. Next time you're there for a stay, you gotta check out **Studio 1219**. I've never seen anything like this place. They took a furniture store built in 1882 and turned it into a really cool art cooperative. Over one hundred local artists display their art there, and it's always changing. I even bought a cool necklace for my daughter.

If you want to have an experience in Port Huron that's totally nautical, try spending some time (or even the night) on a real U.S. Coast Guard cutter.

The U.S. Coast Guard Cutter Bramble
(810) 982-0891
Port Huron Seaway Terminal, Port Huron, MI
www.phmuseum.org/drupal/about/bramble

The U.S. Coast Guard Cutter Bramble is part of an incredible Port Huron museum program. This is an absolutely fascinating 180-foot seagoing ship. It was commissioned in 1944, and following World War II, it participated in "Operation Crossroads," the first test of an atomic bomb's effect on surface ships at Bikini Island in the South Pacific. In 1957, along with two other ships, the Bramble headed for the Northwest Passage, traveling through the Bering Straits and Arctic Ocean. It traveled for sixty-four days through 4,500 miles of uncharted waters. The three ships finally reached the Atlantic Ocean. They were the first ships to circumnavigate the North American Continent. See what I mean?

Now, get this. If you have a special group of twenty to thirty people, you can actually spend the night on the Bramble. This is an outstanding experience. You get to see what all aspects of military life at sea were like. We toured the entire ship from the galley to the massive engine room and had a blast. Contact the museum for tour times and days the ship is boardable.

Next time you're looking for a medium-sized Michigan city to explore, try Port Huron. I guarantee it will float your boat. Ha!

Story behind the name:
Piece of Cake, er Strudel

After just two shows, we had this TV thing DOWN. We knew what we were doing and we were confident. That could be the source of the title… or it could be that Chef Hermann made us a mess of Apple Strudel and we were in a carb coma.

Chapter 3

Season 1, Episode 3

•Detroit
•Lansing
•Battle Creek

No city in America has more heart and soul or is making a stronger comeback than Detroit. Market-making entrepreneurs and modern urban developments are cropping up everywhere, and for good reason. Detroit has a tremendous amount of history, culture, entertainment and unique shopping to offer. It's like any big metropolitan city. If you know where to go, your experience can be richly rewarding. Believe me; there's a ton to discover.

As we all know, Detroit has a long and rich history of manufacturing automobiles. It literally put the world on wheels. Detroit also has a rich heritage in music. We all know about Bob Seger, Kid Rock, Eminem and of course all the Motown greats. But did you know that in the 1930s and 40s Detroit was one of the premier jazz cities in America? All the jazz greats from around world came to play the dinner clubs in Detroit, and one of those historic clubs is back.

Cliff Bell's
(313) 961-2543
2030 Park Ave., Detroit, MI 48226
www.cliffbells.com

Cliff Bell's is one of Motown's original classic jazz clubs. Today it's a fully and authentically restored art-deco nightclub in the heart of Detroit's historic entertainment district. Cliff Bell's is all about live jazz, great food and classic cocktails. When you're there, you can almost feel what it must have been like to be a jazz fan in the 40s. The original bar is amazing, and the atmosphere there is almost seductive. You can't help but feel cool just being there.

In the mid-80s the club closed for twenty years and fell into complete ruin. Then in 2005, three young entrepreneurs had a vision. Paul Howard, Scott Lowell and Carolyn Howard put their blood, sweat, tears and cash into making Cliff Bell's a great jazz club again. If you go to the Cliff Bell's website, check out the full history of the club; it's fascinating. You can also see photos of what the club looked like while in ruins. The restoration they did is absolutely amazing.

Not only did Cliff Bell's come back, Detroit is coming back in a big way, and it's up to you to rediscover it. I'm having a blast doing it!

When you think of **Lansing**, what do you think about? Most of us think of the capitol building, where state legislators work day in and day out to keep Michigan moving forward. We also think about the great halls of justice like the Michigan Supreme Court, where people are protected and our rights are preserved. Yes, Lansing is a place where noble minds work tirelessly to make Michigan a great place to be. But if you haven't been to Lansing since that last school field trip, you're in for a big surprise. Tons of young people and cool new businesses are reconnecting with the city and making Lansing one of the best places in Michigan to make a great future.

Elderly Instruments
(517) 372-7880
1100 N. Washington, Lansing, MI, 48906
www.elderly.com

While we were in Lansing, we made our way over to Old Town to a place I'd heard about but never been to. Every time I mention **Elderly Instruments** to anyone who knows anything about music, their eyes light up. So we decided to find out why.

Once we got inside the building, we were wonderfully overwhelmed. I had never seen so many stringed instruments before in my life. Everywhere you look, you see different things with strings. And the policy there is, "Everything is okay to play." If you're looking to buy something to pick, stroke or strum, Elderly is a musician's Mecca. Even their repair department is mammoth. The atmosphere is relaxed, welcoming and filled with spontaneous melodies erupting around the store.

Elderly is probably the world's most trusted source for new, used or vintage stringed instruments. They've got everything from acoustic and electric guitars, steel guitars, dobros, banjos, mandolins, ukuleles and violins, to auto harps, dulcimers, bouzouki, psalteries, zithers and even the occasional Egyptian oud. If it has strings, they'll buy, sell, trade or repair it.

Elderly has become a destination that attracts an international clientele. On any given day, you might see Vince Gill, Ricky Skaggs, John Mayer or Lyle Lovett hanging out at the store. They've got a string for every pick and an expert for every instrument. The passion for Elderly is amazing, and if you spend an afternoon there, you'll see why. If you own a stringed instrument, you owe it to yourself to visit Elderly. You'll be pickin', grinnin' and wishin' you lived in Lansing.

The people of **Battle Creek** have done an outstanding job combining history, nature, commerce and entertainment to make it an awesome place to live, work and play. Battle Creek has a downtown on a mission, and I'd say mission accomplished. There are great restaurants, unique shops, great places to stay and a winding river walk that brings it all back home. And like many metropolitan areas, people are moving back downtown to enjoy the ease and convenience of city living.

Binder Park Zoo
(269) 979-1351
7400 Division Dr., Battle Creek, MI 49014
www.binderparkzoo.org

Now, say you're in Battle Creek and you get a sudden urge to do something wild. I mean really wild. Just ten minutes south of town is **Binder Park Zoo**, one of the Midwest's premiere wildlife parks. It was voted one of the best zoos in America, and it's right here in Michigan. My sister Vicki told me it was a must see, and she's a veterinarian who's been to just about every zoo there is.

This is the closest thing you'll find to exploring wild Africa in Michigan. The park is 433 acres of forest and wetlands that have been turned into an authentic wildlife experience. You'll see some of the world's most exotic animals roaming free on a recreated African plain. And thanks to an incredible elevated boardwalk that takes you through the park far above the jungle floor, you'll see the animals up close and personal.

This really is a cool family excursion. When you get to the park, there are tons of great exhibits and activities to partake in. Then, when you decide it's time to visit wild Africa, you hop on a tram that takes you on a short transformative trip through the Michigan jungle. When you get off the tram, you're instantly transported to an authentic African village where you're surrounded by all the sights and sounds of Africa. It's an amazing immersion experience that makes you feel like you're really there. And you don't even need your passport.

There's nothing like exploring Africa and seeing giraffes, gazelles, ostriches and zebras all roaming in their natural habitat. Especially when you're doing it in Michigan, just ten minutes south of downtown Battle Creek. Bonus!

Battle Creek and Binder Park Zoo are two places that will surprise you when you get there. Both feature lots of happy land mammals in an awesome environment. The only difference is it's okay to feed the ones in town. Ha!

Story behind the name:
My Guitar is Worth $12.50

Tom was convinced his guitar was a relic that was going to be the ticket to his retirement and an escape from the idiots on the crew. As it turned out, the experts at Elderly had other plans. $12.50 doesn't even buy a round of beer at Founders. Nice try, Tom. You're stuck with us for a while.

Chapter 4

Season 1, Episode 4

•Marquette
•Alpena

If you've never been to Marquette before, it's really worth the trip. Not only is the city home of Northern Michigan University and the Upper Peninsula's largest city, it also sits in one of the most beautiful spots in the U.P. The downtown is very cool (and hilly... I like that) and there are cool restaurants, funky shops and lots to explore. It's also a great port city with some very cool places to live and play right by the water.

Lagniappe Cajun Creole Eatery
(906) 226-8200
145 Jackson Cut Alley, Marquette, MI 49855
www.marquettecajun.com

L et's say you're in Marquette and you get a sudden craving for some authentic Louisiana, Creole and Cajun cookin'. It's 1,400 miles down to New Orleans, so that's not an option. What do you do? Simple! You get yourself over to **Lagniappe** and get your voodoo on.

Lagniappe is an awesome Creole, Cajun eatery, and when you step inside you won't believe your eyes. It's like you were instantly teleported to Bourbon Street in New Orleans. This place is the real deal because of Chef Don Durley. He's a master chef who fell in love with Louisiana cooking and brought it all the way up to the U.P. for you and me. Everyone has the same reaction when they walk in the front door. Wow! And they have the exact same reaction when they taste the food. From the Gumbo and Jambalaya to the Alligator Bites and Red Beans and Rice, it's all made with Don's own blend of Louisiana love.

Chef Don said that the first time he cooked Cajun, it felt second nature to him. He loves it because of its incredible array of rich flavors and because of the great history and culture connected to it. It's a uniquely American cuisine that's custom made for foodies who live to eat. Chef Don also explained that a lot of people avoid Cajun cooking because they think it's all spicy hot. Nothing could be further from the truth. 'Flavor' is what it's full of. You can get it hot if you want, but that's totally up to you.

When we were there Chef Don filled us up with incredible food, amazing stories and a real appreciation for what he's accomplished. He also poured us an adult beverage called a "Cat 5 Hurricane." I knew it was strong when the umbrella on top came pre-crumpled. Don's daughter Nicole is now helping to create more incredible Creole masterpieces, so expect good things from Lagniappe. If you do go, check out the voodoo shrine behind the bar. It's full of good juju for your gris-gris.

Hotplate
(906) 228-9577
153 W. Washington St., Marquette, MI, 49855
www.hotplatepottery.com

Our next stop was called **Hotplate**, a cool, colorful and eclectic paint-your-own-pottery studio that's bringing the whole community together. You go there to connect and share, and while you're there, express yourself on cups, plates, wall hangings—you name it. It's an absolute blast, and the staff there will totally bring out the artist in you. They also offer the art of glass fusing, and you can even purchase pieces created right there.

Owner Sue Kensington is the Hotplate lady, and she has more creative and positive energy than anyone I've ever met. You feel inspired just talking to her. She and I sat together and designed a UTR plate that, in spite of my lack of even one artistic eye, came out awesome. This is a place that's great for kids, adults and anyone who wants to relax, express and create. Their mantra is, "We take your good times seriously," and it's absolutely true. Even if you think you have absolutely no artistic ability, when you leave Hotplate, you will. You'll also feel better about yourself, and that's priceless.

Bike Furniture Design
(906) 361-2483
P.O. Box 11, Marquette, MI 49855
www.bikefurniture.com

In the afternoon we met up with Andy Gregg from **Bike Furniture Design**, a U.P. bike enthusiast who makes very artistic and very functional furniture out of used bicycle parts. At first I didn't know what to expect, but when I saw his stuff I was impressed and amazed. This isn't junky stuff; it's modern, high-design furniture that Andy is selling around the world. When you first see his work, it's not immediately obvious that the components are elements from bygone bikes, but when you look closely, his pieces instantly bring a smile to your face.

When Andy was a young bike mechanic, he would gaze at the piles of bike parts that would accumulate in the corner of the shop and wonder what he could do with all the discarded stuff. Well, he brainstormed while riding and came up with his calling. While we were in town, a number of his pieces were on display at the Marquette Public Library. There were stools, chairs, loveseats and coffee tables, all tempered from timed-out two-wheelers.

If you want a coffee table that people will admire more than the books you put on it, get in touch with Andy Gregg. I wonder what he could make out of Pee Wee Herman's bike?

Lakenenland
(906) 249-1132
108 Timber Lane, Marquette, MI, 49855
www.lakenenland.com

As we drove out of Marquette that day, we stumbled onto something the likes of which we'd never seen before. It's called **Lakenenland**, and it's just east of Marquette on M-28. This is a whimsical and wonderfully bizarre place that's great for the entire family. From the small to the very huge, every sculpture in the park was constructed from machine pieces and industrial scrapyard junk. The word "junk" is kind of misleading though, because these creations are amazing.

Here's the best part. It's a drive-through art exhibit that's absolutely free to the public. It is without a doubt one of the most unique places I've ever been. Tom Lakenen is the inventive and talented artist who's made some of the coolest and strangest artistic things imaginable. Some of the art is funny, some of it is very strange and some of it is absolutely huge.

If you're ever anywhere near Marquette in the U.P., you really have to experience Lakenenland. There's nothing else like it anywhere. It's hard to miss because of the thirty-foot-tall green dinosaur fishing in the little pond right out front.

When we drove into **Alpena**, the first thing I noticed was how nice the town is and what a great, walkable size it is. There's a huge selection of places to shop and lots of great eateries to pick from. Alpena is also an awesome place to live. There are some wonderful neighborhoods and historic homes that are right within walking distance of a beautiful Lake Huron shoreline. Imagine, after work, being able to walk one block to the beach and put your toes in the sand. I could totally live with that.

For lunch we went to the oldest historical saloon in Alpena. The scary part was that paranormal researchers have spent many nights there and discovered evidence of an actual ghost. At first I was kinda scared, but then my tummy growled, and that's even scarier.

John A. Lau Saloon
(989) 354-6898
414 N. 2nd Ave., Alpena, MI 49707
www.johnalausaloon.com

The John A. Lau Saloon is right in downtown Alpena, and for years they've been serving up great meals, cold beverages and I guess some pretty good ghost stories. The original saloon was built back in 1893 and during prohibition became a "candy store" (hmm…). Today it's a very cool, authentic-looking saloon and restaurant that's full of old-time knickknacks and great memorabilia.

The saloon has great food and friendly people, but it's best known for its resident ghost. As the story goes, the original owner's wife died in childbirth and, to this day, inhabits the saloon. They say if she likes you, she leaves you alone. But if she doesn't, she can be a bit mischievous.

Nothing malicious, just the occasional tap on the shoulder or glass rattling. There's a spot at the top of the stairs where they say her soul likes to linger. I went up there and came back down pretty quickly. I'll admit it; I was a little spooked.

The big scare of the day happened while I was sitting near the fireplace. I looked in it and actually saw the face of a child. It really, genuinely scared me… until I found out with great embarrassment that it was a two-way fireplace, and it was just a family sitting on the other side waiting for a table. A ghost hunter I'm not. But food? That I can handle, and we handled a great lunch that day.

As we drove out of town a bit, I had a sinking feeling I was about to learn something, and when I met up with Ty Black, I did. Ty is a geologist and a complete expert on all aspects of the **Alpena Sinkholes**. They're like a mound, turned upside down, and they're absolutely fascinating.

These giant sinkholes happened a long time ago when water flowing hundreds of feet below the earth's surface washed away the gypsum deposits and the ground collapsed. My favorites were what are known as the Stevens Twin Sinks. They're so close together that there's only a narrow strip of land that runs between them. There's a path you can walk between the two that's a very cool experience.

Alpena Sinkholes
caves.org/conservancy/mkc/preserve_tb.html

You have to be careful around these sinkholes because you don't want to fall in. But to be honest, if you're mindful, that's pretty hard to do. If you want to see them, do a little research, make the drive and make sure to look down. Remember, they're upside down mounds.

Thunder Bay Marine Sanctuary
(989) 356-8805
500 W. Fletcher, Alpena, MI 49707
www.thunderbay.noaa.gov

Another thing I didn't know about Alpena was that they do tons of shipwreck research there. At the Thunder Bay National Marine Sanctuary is a place called the **Great Lakes Maritime Heritage Center**, and they have everything there to educate you on Michigan's incredible maritime history. Alpena has become an international dive site for shipwreck research and shipwreck dive enthusiasts from around the world. There are over two hundred historical wrecks right off the coast at a variety of depths. From giant, multi-masted sailboats to paddle wheelers and steamers, there are tons of wrecks to discover and explore.

At the Heritage center you'll also find really cool replicas of many of the ships that lay at the bottom just off shore. You can see what they looked like, read their stories and get lost in the mysteries of their demise. They even have underwater videos of the wrecks you can view.

My favorite exhibit is the life-sized replica of a great lakes schooner you can actually get aboard and walk on. Even though the boat is indoors, with lights and sound, they simulate what it must have been like to be out on the lakes in a tremendous storm. You can even go below and see what cabin life was like. I'd say this is big fun for kids, but I think I liked it even more.

They also do serious research at the center. While we were there, Sarah Waters showed us some of the artifacts they had retrieved and were studying. They had hundreds of them from hundreds of ships resting hundreds of feet below the surface, and some of them were hundreds of years old. Very cool to see!

Of course by this time we were hungry. And luckily, one of our UTR Facebook friends suggested a place for us to have dinner in Alpena called the **Court Yard**. I have two words for that friend: thank you very much! Oops…

Court Yard Ristorante
(989) 356-9511
2024 U.S. 23, Alpena, MI 49707
www.courtyardristorante.com

Chris and Lora Bauer-Carlson own the Court Yard, and their love for good friends and great gourmet food makes this place a must stop. The experience we had was warm and friendly, the food we ate was off the hook and the owner Chris was so cool, so casual and such an engaging guy, we dubbed him The Food Dude.

Not only are Chris and Lara wonderful people, they completely and passionately believe in their town, their staff and the incredible food they serve. They've got everything from beautiful, beefy burgers and specialty pizzas to escargot (best I've ever had) and something called Black & Blue Salmon. These are two true foodies who travel the world looking for the very best food ideas. Then they bring them home, add hometown ingredients and home make'em. The Court Yard is also a great place for cocktails and live entertainment. It's fine dining meets fun and casual.

When you go, kick back, relax, soak in the ambiance and get ready for a good meal and some friendly people. Oh, and if The Food Dude comes up to your table, get ready for a good time. We love those guys!

On our way out of town the next day we ran into a place I just have to tell you about. What would you say if I told you there are some folks just outside Alpena who have over twenty-five dinosaurs on their property? Yeah, I thought the same thing until I saw it with my own eyes.

Dinosaur Gardens
(989) 471-5477
11160 U.S. 23, Ossineke, MI 49766
www.dinosaurgardensllc.com

It's called **Dinosaur Gardens**, it's just south of Alpena and it's an absolute trip… back in time. The park is a walking tour that lets you see what dinosaurs must have looked like as they roamed the earth millions of years ago. It's set in a forest, so as you walk through, you get the feeling of what it would be like to see these giants doing their thing in a natural environment.

It's so awesome to walk right up to life-sized, realistic replicas of all kinds of dinosaurs. They even have some really cool caveman exhibits that show what their lives must have been like. My two favorites are the T-Rex and the Triceratops. They have them squared off across the path because apparently they used to fight, and believe it or not, the triceratops would win a good percentage of the time. Dinosaur Gardens is a wonderful family excursion, and it's something the kids will never forget. It's like going to Jurassic Park, only you'll have no trouble getting away from these dinosaurs. They don't move.

Our trip to Alpena was action packed and packed full of fun. If you haven't been there yet, put it on your A list, because that's where it belongs. It starts with A.

Story behind the name:
Does it or Does it NOT?

As the saying goes, we're lovers, not fighters. So in the back alley behind Lagniappe, we encountered a couple local Marquette boys who wanted their Sunday evening to end in fisticuffs with the six UTR crew members.

One of the locals proclaimed, "Stuff happens. Does it, or does it not?" Jim calmly replied, "It does not."

For the next six months we kept repeating the line, "Does it, or does it not?"

It still does not.

Chapter 5

Season 1, Episode 5

Traverse City
Port Austin

Traverse City is consistently listed in the top ten for best beach community, best food town and best wine destination. AOL Travel News even named it one of the top ten coolest cities in the United States. TC is definitely one of the most beautiful places in Michigan. The wineries are exceptional, the boating is the best and downtown has tons to offer. There's every kind of shop imaginable and tons of incredible restaurants that serve the great wines that are produced in Michigan. But wine isn't the only fun liquid that's made in Traverse City.

Grand Traverse Distillery
(231) 947-8635
781 Industrial Circle, Traverse City, MI 49686
www.grandtraversedistillery.com

Did you know that one of the top six rated vodkas in the world is made in Traverse City? I'll drink to that (responsibly of course). In a totally unassuming location just south of town is a little place called **Grand Traverse Distillery**, and they're making heads turn around the world with their True North Vodka.

Kent Rabish is the man behind the still, and his mission is to end our dependence on foreign alcohol. He went on vacation a few years ago, tasted some great vodka and said, "I can do that." Now his vodka's aroma, flavor and finish are winning multiple gold medals in competitions everywhere. Here's the best part: all the wheat, rye and corn he uses in the process are grown within seventy-five miles of the distillery. Home grown potent potables, yes!

Even though True North Vodka has made a huge splash around the planet, Kent is now producing incredible whiskies, gin and even rum. He set out to change the perception that fine spirits are only produced overseas, and he's done exactly that. Not only can you purchase his awesome adult beverages at the distillery, they're showing up in retail locations everywhere, so keep an eye out. Kent Rabish is a Michigan man, using Michigan resources to make a Michigan product to sell to Michiganders in Michigan. My kinda guy!

Cherry Festival
(231) 947-4230
250 E. Front St., Ste. 301, Traverse City, MI 49684
www.visit.cherryfestival.org

Next we jumped in the car and headed across town to an event I just had to go to. It had been 'on' my radar for years, but for some reason, I'd just never made it there. **The National Cherry Festival** in Traverse City attracts over half a million people every year. It's been going strong since 1926, it's all about cherries and there's tons of fun stuff to do there.

Traverse City is the Cherry Capital of the World, so every year the entire town gets together and celebrates all things cherry. From cherry pies and candies to cherry wines and even cherry Bar-B-Q sauce, if you can make it with cherries, it's there and it's good. The festival also features food from tons of local restaurants and live entertainment, and it's more kid friendly fun than you can shake a cherry popsicle at. I even entered a cherry pie eating contest. I lost miserably, but who cares? I got a free piece of cherry pie. Bonus!

If you like cherries and good family fun, all wrapped up on one of Michigan's most beautiful bays, check out the National Cherry Festival. It's a slice of pure Michigan life.

Village at Grand Traverse Commons
(231) 941-1900
1200 W. 11th St., Traverse City, MI 49684
www.thevillagetc.com

Where we went next blew my mind. It's another great story that totally reminds me why I live in Michigan. It's called the **Village at Grand Traverse Commons,** and it's now a beautiful village community that offers everything you need for a great way of life.

It's become an awesome place to live in the Traverse City area, but believe it or not, it was once the Northern Michigan Asylum. In 1989 the asylum closed down and the beautiful buildings fell into complete ruin. It looked like this entire sixty-three-acre complex was destined to just decay away.

Thanks to Ray Minervini and The Minervini Group, this village is turning into one of the coolest places to live, work and play in Michigan. It's also one of the largest historic preservations and adaptive reuse redevelopments in the country. They're actually turning the entire complex into a self-contained community. The historic century-old Victorian-Italianate buildings now house restaurants, a bakery, winery, cool shops, new businesses and there are incredible living spaces available for a variety of income levels.

Living there would almost be like living in a small European village where everything you need is a short walk away. The bonus here is you're living in Michigan just minutes south of Traverse City. Spending the day with Ray gave me a real appreciation for what he and his family have done. If you're looking for a fun and fascinating place to live, work, shop or eat, visit the Village at Grand Traverse Commons.

Before I got to **Port Austin**, my complete knowledge of the town was, "I think it's somewhere up in the thumb on Lake Huron." Well, I was in for a huge surprise with the cool people, places and things I found there. The town is small enough to get to know in a day, but it's nice enough to make you want to stay. If you like living on the water, this is your town. Everyone was friendly, and it's a great family destination. A lot of the beautiful and historic buildings have become really cool inns and very nice restaurants.

The Lake Street Manor
(989) 738-7720
8569 Lake St., Port Austin, MI 48467
www.lakestreetmanor.com

If bed and breakfasts are the way you like to stay, try the **Lake Street Manor**. The rooms are very nice and the backyard has a great place to sit, relax and reflect. The location rocks, as does the owner.

Little Yellow Cottages
(248) 760-7696
114 Union St., Port Austin, MI 48467
www.portaustincottages.com

If the cottage life is more your style, you'll want to stay at the **Little Yellow Cottages**.

This place is a Port Austin favorite. They're five little cottages all in a row, located right downtown just a block from the beach and public park. You can rent just one or bring all your friends and family and rent them all. I've done that, and it's a blast.

Each of the Little Yellow Cottages features a screened-in porch, a living room with a TV, a full kitchen and a private bath with a shower. They also come with both one and two bedrooms and can accommodate up to six guests. These cottages have all recently been redone and are very nice. Staying there totally reminded me of the fun family vacations we had as kids. I'll be surprised if you don't smile when you see them.

Port Austin Kayak and Bike Shop
(989) 550-6651
119 E. Spring St., Port Austin, MI 48467
www.portaustinkayak.com

Port Austin is quickly becoming one of the best places to kayak in the Midwest, so I met up with the man who could show me why. Chris Boyle owns the **Port Austin Kayak and Bike Shop**, and he rents everything from beginner kayaks to some pretty cool state-of-the art stuff. If you're into kayaking or want to learn, he's got everything you need.

Until we hit the water, I didn't realize just how much fun kayaking could be. The water was clear, calm and unbelievably warm. And the views were spectacular, but according to Chris, we hadn't seen anything yet. About a half hour into the trip we paddled around a rocky point, and what we saw was unbelievable. It was a huge rock formation called Turnip Rock, and I had no idea this kind of shoreline existed on Lake Huron. Turnip Rock is like a giant upside down triangle with trees growing on top. I'm not even sure how it stays upright.

We pulled into a little bay surrounded by cliffs and some pretty outrageous rock formations and took a few minutes for lunch. Chris lived in the Detroit area and vacationed in Port Austin as a kid. He started kayaking up there as an adult, fell in love with it and moved on up. I have to say that Chris is one of the nicest people you will ever encounter, in or out of a kayak. He made my first time experience a blast. If you've got it in ya, get to Port Austin and get in a kayak. Just promise not to turn turnip rock right side up. :-)

Joe's Pizzeria American and Italian Restaurant
(989) 738-8711
8725 Lake St., Port Austin, MI 48467

After a long day of extreme kayaking, there's nothing like an Italian pizza, hand tossed by an authentic Italian. So we went straight to **Joe's Pizzeria American and Italian Restaurant**. It's casual, comfortable and a lot of fun. Owner Sal Cucchiara is the real deal. He came to Port Austin thirty years ago straight from Italy and brought all his pizza-tossing skills with him. If you're wondering why Joe's Pizzeria is owned by a guy named Sal, I'll tell you exactly what he told me. After a quick wink, he said, "Believe me, you don't wanna know."

Sal and his wife Maria are absolutely wonderful people who bend over backwards to make sure your meal is exactly the way you want it. They're so nice, they even let me back in the kitchen to toss some dough. I made a mess, got flour in my eye and had a blast. They don't only serve pizza; they've got a full menu that will fill you up. If you want good old fashioned Italian (and American) home style cooking, get to Joe's and get to eatin'. Just make sure to bring some green, because last time I was there, it was cash or check only.

Dave Thuemmel
(989) 738-8772
2090 Grindstone Rd., Port Austin, MI 48467
www.woodbowls.homestead.com

When I was in seventh grade I made a cutting board in woodshop, and it lasted almost a year. I was very proud of that cutting board, until I met **Dave Thuemmel**. Dave is an incredibly talented artist and wood turner who takes scrap, fallen or just plain useless chunks of green wood and turns them into beautiful and very useful pieces of art. He creates bowls, vases, boxes and even pieces that are just pure art. His designs are unusual, organic and every one is one of a kind.

Dave is a dairy farmer turned Port Austin's premier wood turner. He spent years perfecting a technique of handcrafting greenwood into usable, unique art. While Dave was a dairy farmer, he got the creative itch clearing fence rows, repairing buildings or splitting wood. He retired from the dairy business, went back to the basic woodturning skills he learned in high school shop class and is now creating masterpieces. If you get a chance, find Dave and check out what he's doing.

In one visit, Port Austin went from being totally off my radar to being one of my new favorite places in Michigan. The day I got home I even made plans to go right back up kayaking with my kids. Port Austin was simply awesome!

Story behind the name:
Shut Your Pie Hole

Challenge accepted. Tom and a junior crew member really went at it in a pie-eating contest. The crew member proved he had a bigger mouth than Tom by crushing him in the pie-eating contest. But if you watch the show at all, you know that when it comes to a big mouth contest… Tom takes first place every time.

Chapter 6

Season 1, Episode 6

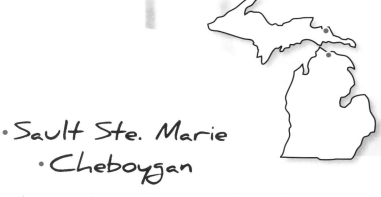

• Sault Ste. Marie
• Cheboygan

One of the coolest parts about coming up to Michigan's Upper Peninsula is you get to drive over one of the longest and most beautiful suspension bridges in the world, The Mackinac Bridge. Every time I drive across it, I'm amazed.

The drive into Sault Ste. Marie is pretty cool. You'll need to do a bridge or two, because you've got the incredible Soo Locks on one side and a canal on the other, so the entire city sits on an island. Another cool thing is that the town sits right on the locks, so at any given time you'll look up and see a giant freighter pulling in. The downtown has beautiful tree-lined streets, and there are tons of great shops and restaurants to choose from.

Karl's Cuisine
(906) 253-1900
447 W. Portage Ave., Sault Ste. Marie, MI 49783
www.karlscuisine.com

We stopped and had lunch at a great place called **Karl's Cuisine**. It's a gourmet restaurant that the locals absolutely swear by. Karl and Paula Nelson have put their heart and soul into this place, and you can really taste it. They serve comfort food that's good for you because it's made with fresh, local ingredients. Even the desserts are to die for.

For years Karl and Paula dreamed of having their own gourmet restaurant, and now that dream has come true in a big way. From incredible salads and sandwiches to some dinner entrees that will knock your wool U.P. socks off, these two are doing it right. They're on a first name basis with the local farmers, and they take extreme pride in everything they serve.

Another great thing about the restaurant is that it's really close to the Soo Locks. So while you're enjoying your meal, you can watch the giant ships going up and down in the locks. Great views and even better chews with Karl's Cuisine.

Riverstone Gallery
(906) 635-6033
321 W. Portage Ave., Sault Ste. Marie, MI, 49783
www.riverstonegallery.net

If you're fond of the old expression, "One man's trash is another man's treasure," you'll totally love the next place we found. It's called **Riverstone Gallery**, and not only do they feature incredible, one-of-a-kind local art, photography and jewelry, they also have some very unique vintage recycled treasures. They actually make jewelry, clocks and even little robots out of used computers, radios and cell phone parts. Very fun, original and cool!

Since 1980 owner and artist Greg Steele has been turning discarded "stuff" into stuff you just gotta have. My two favorite pieces were actual working clocks made out of an old Zenith radio dial and an old Brownie Camera. It takes a very talented and inventive eye to create these cool collectables, and Greg's got two of them. If you're looking for the unexpected, expect to see some awesome stuff at Riverstone.

Soo Locks
(906) 632-6301
P.O. Box 739, Sault Ste. Marie, MI 49783
www.soolocks.com

While you're in Sault Ste. Marie, be sure to go see the **Soo Locks** in action. It's fascinating to get up close and watch these gigantic ships from all around the world go through. They pull in and are either raised or lowered twenty-one feet. If they go up, they're heading north into Lake Superior. If they go down, they're heading south into Lake Huron.

Standing on the observation platform, I had a conversation with a deckhand on board one of the giant freighters. When we started talking we were looking eye to eye, and when we were done, I was yelling down twenty-one feet to him. A very strange sensation. Then the lock doors opened on the south end, and the ship powered out and onto its destination. The cargo on the ship was grain headed to ports all over the world. Believe it or not, more cargo goes through the Soo Locks than the Panama and Suez Canals combined.

S.S. Valley Camp
(906) 632-3658
Corner of Johnston & Water, Sault Ste. Marie, MI 49783
www.thevalleycamp.com

If you've always wanted to go aboard a Great Lakes freighter, check out the **S.S. Valley Camp**. It's a five-hundred-foot freighter that sailed the Great Lakes for over fifty years. Now it's a floating maritime museum, and it's an outstanding experience. Up on deck you really get a feel for what it must be like to spend time on one of these great ships. Every detail of the ship has been left exactly as it was when it was retired.

Below deck is a completely different story. The entire cargo bay of the ship has been turned into a fascinating maritime museum with some very cool exhibits. The most notable thing on display is one of the actual lifeboats from the ill-fated Edmund Fitzgerald. All hands were lost when a huge storm took it to the bottom of Lake Superior in 1975. Standing next to this life boat really gives you reason to pause. It's tough to put into words.

The Tower of History
(906) 632-3658
326 E. Portage, Sault Ste. Marie, MI 49783
www.saulthistoricsites.com/tower-of-history-4

Another cool thing to check out in town is **The Tower of History**. It's a 210-foot observation tower that gives you an absolutely spectacular view of the Soo Locks and the entire city. It was cool to look down and see all the places we'd been that day with just a turn of the head. If you get a chance, get up there.

Twilight Walking Tour
(906) 440-5910
www.twilightwalkingtour.com

We ended our day in Sault Ste. Marie with a **Twilight Walking Tour**. These are wonderful small-group tours that share the music, history and folklore of the area. Our tour guides were Jim Couling and his wife Mary. As we walked through the city park, they sang local folk songs and told fascinating stories about Sault Ste. Marie's past and present. It was an experience I won't soon forget.

If you're looking for a fun and fascinating U.P. adventure, get UP to Sault Ste. Marie soon.

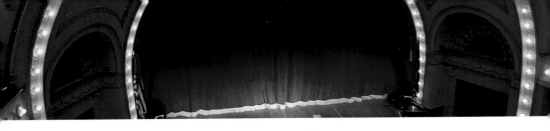

Cheboygan used to be one of the greatest logging towns of the Midwest. In 1900 over 46 million feet of Michigan lumber shipped out of the harbor there. But now it's become an awesome place for people who love to live and play by the water. The town is holding onto its history with cool new businesses opening every year. There are interesting shops, cool eateries and the whole atmosphere there really makes you relax.

Cheboygan Opera House
(231) 627-5841
403 N. Huron St., Cheboygan, MI 49721
www.theoperahouse.org

Whenever I go north in Michigan, people always ask if I've been to the **Cheboygan Opera House**, so I thought I'd see what everyone was talking about. I have to tell you: I've never seen another place like it. When you first see the building, you're surprised at how modern it is. But when you step into the actual theater, it's like stepping back in time.

The first two incarnations of the theater burned down in 1877 and 1903, so eventually, after a long period of being condemned, it was saved in the 70s by the Art Council and protected with a safer and more modern outer facade. The theater is classic, absolutely beautiful, and it's been meticulously restored by passionate people who understand its importance to the community.

According to many of the volunteers who care for this historic place, the Opera House is also haunted by a husband and wife team. Apparently these two are friendly ghosts who will only play the occasional practical joke on theater goers. While we were there, we heard a door slam in a part of the balcony where no living person was. I'll admit, I was a little spooked by the experience. Are there really ghosts there? I don't know. Is there a beautiful Opera House there you should see? Absolutely.

The Gildner Gallery
(231) 627-2761
216 S. Main St., Cheboygan, MI 49721
www.gildnerartgallery.com

Next we went to a very cool place called **The Gildner Gallery**. Downstairs it's a top-notch flower shop called The Coop that has everything you need for fine floral occasions. But upstairs is a whole different story.

Upstairs owner Ann Gildner has brought art to downtown Cheboygan. The gallery space up there is very organic and features works from tons of talented local artists. It also serves as an artist co-op and think tank. You'll find a great mixed bag of creative stuff, from classic oils to funky watercolors and mixed media masterpieces.

Ann is very passionate about the art she creates and the art community she's helped create in Cheboygan. If you like your art and friendly people all wrapped up in a groovy place, put this place on your Michigan bucket list.

Hack-Ma-Tack
(231) 625-2919
8131 Beebe Rd., Cheboygan, MI 49721
www.hackmatackinn.com

Our last stop in Cheboygan was kind of hard to say and a little hard to find, but once we found it, we knew we were in the right place. It's a real hidden treasure called **Hack-Ma-Tack**. Built almost 120 years ago, Hack-Ma-Tack was originally a hunting and fishing lodge, but now it's an incredible gourmet restaurant and inn. The four-story bell tower on the building was actually used back in the day to call hunters in for supper.

Believe me, this place is magical. It's an old-school, retro hunting lodge that feels right, and artists from around the country have contributed to the incredible atmosphere. It has an upscale hunting and fishing motif featuring everything from canoes suspended overhead to funky lamps and fascinating artifacts from historic hunts. The name Hack-Ma-Tack is actually a Native American word for the tamarack tree, which is the wood used in its construction.

The inn sits on the banks of the Cheboygan river and features five hundred feet of dock space where boaters float up, tie up and sit down to an outstanding meal. The food at Hack-Ma-Tack is a big part of why this place has become a family tradition. It's classic American fare done right. You'll find delectable dishes like Great Lakes whitefish almondine and their signature slow-roasted prime rib. Classic food in a classic setting. Hack-Ma-Tack is seasonal, so please call ahead or check their website.

Looking at some of the artifacts from years gone by made me wish I'd discovered Hack-Ma-Tack a lot sooner. But now that I know how to say it and where it is, I'll be back for sure. I'll also be back in Cheboygan real soon. It's the kind of town that makes you glad you live in the great state of Michigan.

Story behind the name:
Never Leave a Man Behind

There are things you're not supposed to do, like leave a member of the crew in Sault Ste. Marie. Sometimes things are out of our control. If you want to know the whole story and you see us in person, ask. We'll tell you what really happened. We just won't print it; we don't really want to embarrass anyone.

Chapter 7

Season 1, Episode 7

•Munising
•Ann Arbor

I've tried to explain to people who haven't been up to Michigan's Upper Peninsula that even though you're still technically in Michigan, it feels like a whole different world. I love it up there.

They call Munising the U.P.'s best kept secret. The town sits right on the southern shores of mighty Lake Superior and offers tons of great family-owned restaurants and coffee shops where you can relax and enjoy some of the bluest skies you'll ever see. It's the kind of place where you feel at home right away. Also, when you're in Munising, ask about all the waterfalls near town. There are so many to see, it's amazing!

Pictured Rocks
(906) 387-3700
Grand Marais, MI 49839
www.nps.gov/piro

Munising is also home to one of the most beautiful and incredible natural wonders of the world, the **Pictured Rocks National Lakeshore**. Over forty miles of two-hundred-foot sandstone cliffs, waterfalls and pristine beaches that meet crystal-clear, blue-green water. The colors you'll see and the rock formations are like nowhere else in the world. These cliffs are one of the most incredible things you'll see in Michigan, so if you get a chance, it's totally worth the drive.

Seaberg Pontoon Rentals
(906) 387-2685
1330 Commercial St., Munising, MI 49862
seabergpontoonrentals.tripod.com/seabergpontoonrental

There are great boat tours you can take of the Pictured Rocks, but if you want to get up close and personal and see the rocks your way, rent your own pontoon boat at **Seaberg Pontoon Rentals** just outside of town. Sherron Seaberg and her husband Jim have everything you need to have a great day on the water. This way you can spend the entire day exploring the area at your own pace. Just pull your pontoon boat up to a beach along the way and have a picnic lunch in one of the most incredible places on the planet. This would make a great Michigan memory.

Van Landschoot & Sons Fish House
(906) 387-3851
116 E. Varnum St., Munising, MI 49862

The U.P. is also known for serving some of the best food you'll find anywhere, so we went looking and found a place that makes something called whitefish sausage. If you want fresh fish, **Van Landschoot & Sons Fish House** is the place to go in Munising. Their boats go out daily and you can get your fish whole, filleted, smoked or, if you like something different, in a sausage.

At first the thought of a sausage being made of fish seemed unsavory, but at the Fish House it was fishy, sausagey and absolutely delicious. They make the sausage daily and if you like trying new things, this is a fish-alicious treat for your tummy. They have all kinds of fresh and smoked fish. If you go, tell 'em Tommy sent ya!

The Dogpatch Restaurant
(906) 387-9948
325 E. Superior St., Munising, MI 49862
www.dogpatchrestaurant.com

After a hearty fish sausage sampler, the crew was still hungry, so we had a quick bite at a place the locals enthusiastically recommended. **The Dogpatch Restaurant** is as much fun to be in as the food is to eat. Going to the Dogpatch is like getting swallowed up by a giant country bumpkin cartoon. If you like Lil Abner and you love big portions, get yourself to the Dogpatch and feast on their tasty vittles.

Afternoon Delight

W e can all agree that **Ann Arbor** is one of the coolest cities in Michigan. It's full of fascinating people, awesome edibles, cool shops and over 40,000 University of Michigan students. College towns are great places to live because of all the energy and ideas the universities bring to the community.

Ann Arbor is a very comfortable and intellectual place where people are passionate about learning and independent thought, and boy do they love good food. There is no shortage of absolutely awesome restaurants in Ann Arbor, some of which have become a way of life for many people.

Afternoon Delight
(734) 665-7513
251 E. Liberty St., Ann Arbor, MI 48104
www.afternoondelightcafe.com

Since 1978, this place has been one of the biggest institutions in Ann Arbor, and it's not even part of the university. It's actually a restaurant called **Afternoon Delight,** and people have been passionate about it for generations. When we were there we even talked to a woman who drove three hours just to have their corned beef hash.

No matter what the weather is like, every Saturday and Sunday morning, people stand in line (sometimes up to an hour and a half) just to have breakfast or lunch there. Why? Because owner Tom Hackett is totally committed to making everything at the restaurant fresh and real. If you don't believe me, just try the muffins. They're Tom's original recipe and they haven't changed in over three decades because they're simply perfect.

Back in the late 70s, Afternoon Delight was the first restaurant in Ann Arbor to offer what some people call "California fresh." They specialize in fresh salads, sandwiches and great breakfasts. If you're looking for a little afternoon delight, you'll be delighted with what you find.

Coach & Four Barbershop
(734) 668-8669
806 S. State St. Ann Arbor, MI 48104
www.coachand4.com

Let's face it: every Michigan city has its share of great businesses, cool experiences and fascinating characters. Well, where we went next, we found all three. The **Coach & Four Barbershop** is the place to go in Ann Arbor if you love sports, want to hear some great stories, get a good haircut and learn about the town.

Owner Jerry Erickson is what I like to call "the real deal." He's been manning the main chair there for forty years and is probably one of the greatest guys you'll ever have lower your ears. This is a good old fashioned men's barbershop that's filled with enough cool and colorful sports memorabilia to keep your eyes busy through your entire cut, and the conversation is always a blast from the past. Jerry's most famous regular customer was the legendary, late, great University of Michigan head football coach Bo Schembechler. How cool is that!

For what Jerry had to work with, he gave me a great cut and shared some fascinating stories. Next time you're in Ann Arbor and you need a haircut, stop by Coach & Four. They'll cut all of them for you. Ha!

Zingerman's Deli
(888) 636-8162
422 Detroit St., Ann Arbor 48104
www.zingermans.com

I had heard of **Zingerman's Deli**, and I had even heard of the guy who started it all, Ari Weinzweig, but until I met Ari I had no idea what a true food guru he was. Not only is Ari a pioneer in what he calls "real" food, his love of Ann Arbor and the passion for what he's doing are the real reasons for his great success. Ari has created a food philosophy and culture that's become almost a way of life for a lot of people.

If you've never been to Zingerman's before, you're missing a great food experience. Not only can you get an incredible deli sandwich there, you'll also find great artisanal, Michigan-made meats, cheeses, breads and desserts. It's a great place to meet, eat and rub elbows with local foodies.

Zingerman's also has their signature Roadhouse Restaurant, their own bake house where they make fresh bread and a creamery where they make incredible cheeses and gelato. If that's not enough, they also roast their own coffee, make awesome, healthy candy bars and even offer fascinating behind-the-scenes food tours. Ari has become so successful that people come from around the world to participate in his training seminars on business and leadership.

If you want to become a genuine foodie and you need a place to get started, get to Zingerman's Deli in Ann Arbor and start training those taste buds.

The Ann Arbor Hands On Museum
(734) 995-5439
220 E. Ann St., Ann Arbor, MI 48104
www.aahom.org

You know how when you take your kids out, you constantly have to tell them not to touch stuff? Well, there's a place in Ann Arbor where not only will they learn a lot, you can tell them to touch everything.

The Ann Arbor Hands On Museum is something you and your kids have to put your hands on to really appreciate. It's a place where all the basic principles of science come to life in hands-on exhibits you can see, touch and learn from. It's been proven that the best way to learn is to do. Well, there's so much to do at this place, it's amazing.

There are four floors and over 250 exhibits ranging from basic science and engineering to thoughtful cultural displays. This is a great place for kids of all ages and a fun way to learn how the world around us works. There's so much to do, see and learn at the Ann Arbor Hands on Museum that you and your kids could literally spend the entire day there. And the nice thing is, when you're done, your kids will sleep well and dream smart!

Ann Arbor is one of those cities I thought I knew a lot about, but what I didn't know is how much I don't know. But now that I know how much I don't know, I know one thing for sure. I know I'll be back. No doubt about it.

Story behind the name:
Good Enough for Bo

It's a known fact that Bo Shembechler didn't have a lot of hair to work with. Kind of like our fearless leader, Tom. When we stopped into Coach & Four barber shop in Ann Arbor, it was clear that if this barber shop was good enough for Bo's game-day hair cut, then it was certainly good enough for Tom's on-camera cut.

Chapter 8

Season 1, Episode 8

Here is a tale of two cities that, when combined, make a
great place to visit, stay and play. Tawas City and East Tawas
are both fun and sandy sunrise-side destinations. The two towns
are so close that folks who know and love the area just call it Tawas.
This whole community knows how to live right. There are great shops
and restaurants, and the people are really friendly. If that's not enough,
just across the street are the beautiful shores of Lake Huron.

Charity Island Tours
(989) 254-7710
P.O. Box 171, Au Gres, MI 48703
www.charityisland.com

It was my first time exploring the area, so I asked the locals what there was to do, and the response was overwhelming. One place a lot of people recommended was **Charity Island**. It's about an hour offshore and it sits smack dab in the middle of Saginaw Bay. There's a great sunset dinner cruise you can take to the island, but we opted for a morning trip just to have a look around. The trip out was awesome. The water was beautiful, the air was clean and we had a cool encounter with a thousand-foot Great Lakes super freighter. It was an awesome sight to see up close.

As soon as you get close to the island you realize just how big it is. It's a 222-acre island with three miles of shoreline. It's even got an eleven-acre inland lake. When you arrive, you start to feel totally removed from civilization. All you hear is the quiet of the island.

Whenever anyone visits, they are always greeted dockside by Karen and Bob Wiltse. They purchased the island in 1992 and are committed to preserving its illustrious history. Karen and Bob actually live in the Historic Charity Island Lighthouse and host the fantastic gourmet dinner. You get to dine and learn all about the island in one of Michigan's most beautiful spots. I'm definitely going back with my wife for the dinner cruise. Points for Tom!

Kiteman Jack's
(989) 362-4615
112 Newman St., East Tawas, MI 48730

If you're ever in East Tawas and someone tells you to go fly a kite, there's a place and a guy by the same name that's right on the beach. **Kiteman Jack's** is right by the dock at the marina, and it and he have been an institution of fun for more than twenty years. The best thing about Kiteman Jack is if you buy it, he might even help you fly it. Flying a kite at the beach is oh so easy. Just hook it up and let 'er go. I totally felt like a kid again. Buy it and try it for yourself.

Tawas Bay Beach Resort
(989) 362-8600
300 E. Bay St., East Tawas, MI 48730
www.tawasbaybeachresort.com

I've got a great trivia question for you. How many full-service resorts are there in Michigan on Lake Huron? The answer is one. **Tawas Bay Beach Resort** has a seven-hundred-foot beach on Tawas Bay, a restaurant, lounge with entertainment, a conference center and even a hip little beach bar called Bikinis. If you want a place where you walk to both the beach and town, the Tawas Bay Beach Resort might just be your spot to stop.

Klenow's Market
(989) 362-2341
201 Newman St. E., Tawas, MI 48730
www.klenowsmarket.com

Before we left East Tawas, a lot of folks told us we just had to stop by **Klenow's Market** right downtown. I guess they smoke more than just the fish and beef there. Apparently they also smoke the competition. They're a great little all-purpose market that has won some major awards for their smoked meats. They make incredible smoked salmon and even make their own smoked jerky and salami sticks. I had a salami stick with the jalapeno cheese inside… wow. Great folks carrying on a great, smoky tradition.

This tale of two cities has one clear message: Tawas City and East Tawas make up one great place to explore.

In all my travels across Michigan, **Monroe** was one of my biggest surprises. I only live about an hour and a half from there and I've always thought it was just a little industrial town with some factories and a couple strip malls. Oh my gosh, was I way wrong. Monroe is a beautiful city that's rich in both history and classic architecture. It's also a modern city with great new places to eat, stay and explore downtown. There's no shortage of creativity, determination or enthusiasm with the people of Monroe.

One of Monroe's most outspoken supporters is John Patterson. John heads up the Monroe County Tourism Bureau, and his love for this town knows no bounds. John told us about an amazing local artist named **Betzi Pipis**. Betzi grew up in Monroe, attended the College for Creative Studies in Detroit and is now making quite a mark for herself in the international art world. Her works are on display as far away as Madrid and London.

We met up with Betzi to experience some of her works. She colorfully combines the real with the surreal to create abstract portrait paintings that are turning the heads of art critics across the globe. Betzi is showing the world that there's a ton of talent in Monroe, Michigan.

The Hotel Sterling
(734) 242-6212
109 W. Front St., Monroe, MI 48161
www.thehotelsterling.com

Next, we stumbled onto probably our biggest surprise in Monroe. If you've ever been to the hip boutique hotels of New York or L.A., you'll feel right at home at **The Hotel Sterling**. Ken Wickenheiser put everything he learned from his travels around the world into this hotel, and it's honestly one of the coolest places I've stayed at in a long time. Every room is cool, elegantly funky and completely unique.

The hotel is made up of three 150-year-old buildings that were renovated, connected and modernized. They were updated but still have a hip, rough and rustic feel about them. Because of the differing layouts of the buildings, every room has its own shape, personality and individual atmosphere. The entire experience at the Sterling is very metropolitan and proves that you don't have to be in a big city to stay big city.

The River Raisin Jazz Festival
www.riverraisinjazzfestival.com

Now, let's talk jazz. **The River Raisin Jazz Festival** happens every summer right in downtown Monroe on the banks of the Historic River Raisin. It's one of the largest and best free jazz festivals in the entire country. The festival takes place at St. Mary's Park, and every year over fifty thousand people come to see some of the biggest names in jazz, including Kenny G, Chuck Mangione, David Sanborn, Bob James, Arturo Sandoval, Spyro Gyra, Earl Klugh, Chris Botti, Ray Parker Jr., Nelson Rangell, Larry Carlton, Rick Braun and many, many more.

This is a great four-day family friendly event that features great food, outstanding live performances and beautiful views of the river. It's a wonderful way to expand your musical horizons.

The Bolles Harbor Café
(734) 457-2233
13986 Laplaisance Rd., Monroe, MI 48161
www.bollesharborcafemonroe.com

The culinary arts are also a rich part of Monroe. If you're hungry, some really good food is never far away. John turned us on to an unassuming little place down by the marina called **The Bolles Harbor Café**. As soon as we walked in, we were met by Silverio Conte, a chef with a passion for both people and the food he prepares.

In the kitchen, Silverio is part prizefighter, part artist and one hundred percent Italian. As chefs go, he's what I like to call "a natural." His foods are simply and passionately prepared. And most importantly, he doesn't over complicate his dishes. He lets you taste the natural flavors of fresh, local foods.

When we were there, Silverio brought out some of his best for us to taste (love my job). We dined on pulled slow-roasted pork, handmade gnocchi, fresh Lake Erie walleye with white wine sauce and hand-tossed pizza. They were all family recipes and all simply delicious.

I'll never look at the Monroe exit sign on I-75 the same again, because now that I know what's there, I'll be back again, and again… and probably again!

Story behind the name:
A Tale of Two Tawas

Not sure why Dickens' A Tale of Two Cities made us think of Tawas. We didn't see any French peasants there. In hindsight, I admit it was a stretch.

Chapter 9

Season 1, Episode 9

• Rochester
• Boyne City

Whenever you hear me talking about Michigan cities that have a great sense of place, Rochester is one of those cities. It's what every hometown should be. It's beautiful, vibrant, welcoming, has great people and is creating new opportunities for people and businesses every day. Rochester is also very rich in history. In 1817 it was the first settlement in Oakland County, and a ton of the structures there remind you of the town's rich heritage.

If you're into biking and being healthy (I highly recommend being healthy; it's really good for you) the Paint Creek and Clinton River trails come right into town. They're a great way to explore Rochester and lower your carbon footprint by getting out of your car. Rochester is also a comfortable place to live. There are tons of beautiful homes within walking distance of town. Pick one out and move right in. Just make sure it's for sale first. As for the town, it's awesome. There are tons of great shops, restaurants and fun things to do, and something cool is always happening downtown.

Rochester Mills Beer Company
(248) 650-5080
400 Water St., Rochester, MI 48307
www.rochestermillsbeerco.com

In every town, there are those business people who just have a knack for making good things happen. One of those people in Rochester is Mike Pleaz. He's the owner of **Rochester Mills Beer Company**, and he's an innovator who's always looking to the future.

When Mike opened his doors in 1998, his brewery was one of the original six in the state. Now Rochester Mills is Michigan's largest brew pub and features 450 seats, a hip martini lounge, a full stage for live entertainment and a menu full of incredible edibles. All the beer they brew is awesome, but my favorite is Rochester Red. It's mmm, mmm, I'll have another please!

A cool thing about Rochester Mills is that it's located in the historic Western Knitting Mill building, and Mike went way out of his way to preserve its original character. He and his team refurbished the original hardwood floors, columns, beams and exposed brick walls. Great atmosphere for a brew.

Mike also believes in being green and sustainable and sourcing locally. Every year, he and his chefs go on a farm tour to find the cleanest and freshest local produce for his restaurant. If you're looking for an enlightened place to throw back a few Michigan-made brews, Rochester Mills is good company to keep.

South Street Skateshop
(248) 651-0555
410 S. Main St., Rochester, MI 48307
www.southstreetskateshop.com

If you've got kids around the house uttering phrases like, "I'm goofy footed" or "Watch this switch front feeble grind," you might want to know about this place, because it's totally rad, dude. I'm not sure what any of that means, but I know it's all good!

South Street Skateshop is a Mecca for skateboarders all across the Midwest. It's a world-class store that has everything a skateboarder needs to do their gnarly thing. They even have an incredibly knowledgeable and friendly staff of young experts who understand this strange new language and will help you look and board your best. I say "look" because not only does South Street have all things skateboarding, they also have an incredible selection of hip, cool and unconventional street wear that will help you make a definite statement.

In 1995, Linda and Von Gallaher (two of the nicest people you will ever meet, ever) opened their doors to a community that absolutely loved what they were doing. South Street really embodies the skateboarder's free spirit and artistic edge. It's also an incredibly colorful and wonderfully organized place. Even if you don't skateboard, I recommend checking out their clothing.

So, like, dudes. Get over to South Street and get your goofy foot in the door. You'll be a better boarder for it!

The Big Bright Light Show
www.downtownrochestermi.com/events/big-bright-light-show

Now for the main reason we went to check out Rochester. It's called **The Big Bright Light Show**, and it happens every year between Thanksgiving and New Year's. Back in 2006 the DDA's Executive Director Kristi Trevarrow had an idea, and that bright idea has helped put Rochester, Michigan on the map across the country. Now get this: they literally wrap almost the entire downtown with over 1.5 million brightly colored holiday lights. Each building has its own color and is covered with strands about every two inches. The entire town is wrapped in an explosion of color.

When you drive into Rochester, it's almost like you're driving right into a cartoon, and standing in the middle of town during the Big Bright Light Show is a surreal sensation that's nearly impossible to describe. The lights come on every night around sunset and stay on until the wee hours. It takes two months to put them up every year, but it's totally worth it. The show brings people into Rochester from across the country to eat, shop, take photos, get engaged—you name it. If you're looking for a unique holiday experience, you've got to experience the Big Bright Light Show.

And if you're looking for a great town to live, work or play in, Rochester has everything you need for a wonderful quality of life, Michigan style!

Having never been to **Boyne City** before, I have to say that the drive into town was beautiful. The homes along the lake are spectacular, and the town is clean and comfortable. It's a beautiful lake community I could easily live in. Boyne City is located at the far east end of one of the biggest and most spectacular lakes in northwest Lower Michigan, Lake Charlevoix. Just one drive through town tells you that this is a hip and very healthy community. There are tons of new and classic shops to choose from and some fantastic restaurants.

You can tell they really take a lot of pride in this town. It's also a great family community with beautiful spaces right on the water to enjoy. And if you're into boating, this is probably one of the best places in the entire Midwest to be. You're only twelve miles from the town of Charlevoix by water, and from there, you've got the entire Great Lakes to explore.

SOBO Arts District
www.boynecitymainstreet.com/visitor-pad/a-and-e/
sobo-arts-district

Until recently, there was a part of Boyne City that was all but forgotten, before a bunch of local artists and entrepreneurs got together and created what they call **SOBO**, and it totally changed the landscape. What used to be closed-up storefronts and abandoned buildings is now a thriving and very funky art district, and it's putting a national and very creative spotlight on Boyne City.

SOBO was inspired by the SOHO art district in lower Manhattan, New York City. In New York, SOHO stands for SOuth of HOuston Street, but in Boyne City it stands for SOuth BOyne. The idea all started with Liz Glass, who thought, "You know, giving this place an identity might help people notice what creative stuff we're doing here." And it sure did.

Lake Street Market
(231) 582-4450
306 S. Lake St., Boyne City, MI 49712
www.lakestreetmarket.com

Liz owns **Lake Street Market**, a cool and eclectic place in the SOBO district that's a combination gourmet market, deli, wine store, bakery, cheese shop and photography studio.

Thanks to Liz's vision, over one hundred Michigan artists now display their works there for all the world to appreciate. If you've got some art in your heart, visit Boyne City's SOBO District and celebrate its great food, friendly people and creative spirit.

One of the best things about living in Michigan is all the great hiking. Scott MacKenzie is a huge Boyne City supporter, and he took me on a great one. It's called Avalanche Point, and it's just outside of town. This hike is not only a great workout; once you get to the top, you've got incredible views of the town, Lake Charlevoix and the entire surrounding countryside. When you're up there, this is something you should really experience.

Van Dam Custom Boats
(231) 582-2323
970 E. Division St., Boyne City, MI 49712
www.vandamboats.com

Next we went to a place that will float your boat, literally. It's called **Van Dam Custom Boats**. Run by Steve Van Dam, they make incredible hand-crafted custom boats. After seeing their work, I'd say they actually build floating works of art that are shipped to clients around the world.

As a young man, Steve got bit by the elusive boat-builder's bug and spent years in Canada learning the craft. He then came back to "boaters' paradise," a.k.a. Boyne City, and is now known as one of the premier boat builders on the planet. At Van Dam they start with a pile of wood, do their own custom design work and turn out boats that literally turn heads. If you're ever in Boyne City, stop in at Van Dam Custom Boats and see what 'real' boats look like.

As we were about to leave town, I ran into a really good friend Jim Flynn who's been vacationing in Boyne City since he was a kid. He offered up a boat ride for me and the crew. I lost my hat on the wild ride, but we sure had a great time in Boyne City.

Story behind the name:
Light the Town!

The chant heard at every Rochester Big Bright Lights event. We lit the town... then Tom unplugged the lights for a nanosecond.

Chapter 10

Season 1, Episode 10

•Detroit
•Petoskey

I love going to Detroit because there's a true renaissance happening there. Inspired people are finding opportunities. New businesses are opening everywhere, and more and more people are venturing out to reconnect with the city.

Good Girls Go to Paris
(313) 664-0490
15 E. Kirby St., Detroit, MI 48202
www.goodgirlsgotopariscrepes.com

Our first stop in Detroit was in Midtown at a place called **Good Girls Go to Paris**, and if you like to eat, you're in for a real treat at this place. About four years ago, on a dream and a dollar, Torya Schoeniger opened the doors, and now Good Girls has become one of the coolest places to chow downtown. Her specialty is crepes and she has one for just about every appetite, from sweet to savory.

While we were there Torya tried to teach me how to make a crepe, and I have to tell you, it's nowhere near as easy as it looks. She has an amazing menu of crepes all named after close friends of hers. Even though Torya and I are now good friends, I don't think you'll see my mangled masterpiece on the menu anytime soon.

At Good Girls you'll see all kinds of people from all across Southeast Michigan enjoying crepes, each other's company and all the innovative new businesses that are springing up in the Midtown area. It's a great sight to see, and it's talented, positive and motivated people like Torya who are helping lead the Detroit renaissance. Her crepes alone are worth a trip to the Motor City.

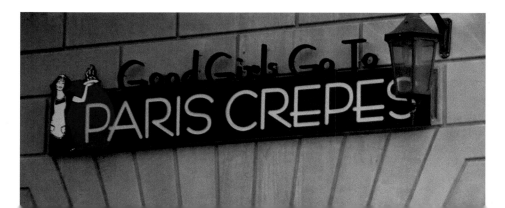

The Sphinx Organization
313-877-9100
400 Renaissance Center, Ste. 2550, Detroit, MI 48243
www.sphinxmusic.org

Next we got to meet a man who's literally changing the lives of children in Detroit and around the world. Aaron Dworkin is the founder and daily inspiration behind **The Sphinx Organization**. They're leading the charge to increase the participation of underserved Black and Latino youth in classical music. Sphinx is literally changing the face (and the faces) of the American symphony.

Less than four percent of all orchestras are Black and Latino combined, and through the Sphynx Organization's special programs and national competitions, more and more of these talented kids are setting out to participate in this amazing art form. They are getting involved both on stage and behind the scenes. Aaron and his team have spent over fifteen years now changing the racial landscape of this calling, and it's becoming as beautiful and diverse as the music itself. Thanks, Aaron!

Dabl's African Bead Museum
(313) 898-3007
6559 Grand River Ave., Detroit, MI 48208
www.mbad.org

Our last stop in Detroit was a cultural experience that expanded our horizons all the way to another continent. It's called **Dabl's African Bead Museum**, and just walking around the building is an awesome experience. The entire outside of the museum is an artistic expression of the man inside, and that man is Olayami Dabl. This place is an incredible collection of beautiful and sometimes rare beads, beadworks, textiles, sculptures and other cultural relics which exemplify the vastness of the African culture.

Dabl is a fascinating and artistically gifted character who's put his heart and soul into this place. Learning all about the history and culture that comes from these beads made for a fascinating afternoon. Dabl is an African historian who has lectured extensively on African Material Culture to international audiences for over thirty years. If you want to experience a new art form that's as old as time itself, check out Dabl's African Bead Museum.

As always, we had a great time in Detroit. There are so many interesting people to meet and new places to discover that we'll be back again and again.

There's no question that **Petoskey** is one of Michigan's crown jewels. It's a beautiful town filled with friendly people, great shops, restaurants, awesome bay views and tons of cool things to do. There's no wonder it's such a popular summer and winter vacation spot for so many families. We went in the winter, and if you're thinking they hibernate there, nothing could be further from the truth. Petoskey is wide awake in the winter. There are people out everywhere. Businesses are bustling, and despite the cold, you always get a warm welcome.

The Perry Hotel
(231) 347-4000
100 Lewis St., Petoskey, MI 49770
www.staffords.com/perry-hotel-4

During our stay, we were lucky enough to bed down at one of Petoskey's most notable landmarks, **The Perry Hotel**. The service and hospitality we got at this historic hotel were incredible and the food fantastic. If you want great accommodations mixed in with beautiful views and a ghost story or two, plan to stay at the Perry Hotel.

Symons General Store
(231) 347-2438
401 E. Lake St., Petoskey, MI 49770
www.lakeandhoward.com

After settling in, we headed to a place right in the heart of town. Actually it's two places. Up front it's **Symons General Store**, and in back it's an incredible gourmet restaurant and wine cellar called Chandler's.

Symons is the real deal. It's an authentic little general store that'll totally take you back to a time when people came to shops like this to get almost everything they needed. It also sits in one of the first brick buildings built in Petoskey. Symons fills its shelves with locally sourced foods, and the artisanal cheese selection is one of the best you'll find anywhere.

Chandler's Restaurant
(231) 347-2981
215 Howard St., Petoskey, MI 49770
www.lakeandhoward.com/SGS_INC/Chandlers.html

I met up with Tommy Kaszubowski, the talented young executive chef at **Chandler's Restaurant**, and after showing us Symons, he took us someplace special. Below Symons is an incredible wine cellar that also doubles as a dining room for Chandler's. So you can actually enjoy some of Tommy's signature dishes surrounded by wines of the world. We had a chance to have dinner down there that night, and it was an outstanding experience.

Tommy has a real "out of the box" approach to cooking. He likes to create unique dishes that blend different flavors from around the world, but he still keeps it close to home. Tommy has a passion for creating locally and seasonally, and his flavor profiles are mmm, mmm Michigan good. Symons and Chandler's are two great places in one.

Crooked Tree Art Center
(231) 347-4337
461 E. Mitchell, Petoskey, MI 49770
www.crookedtree.org

After breakfast the next morning, we walked to a place everyone in town was telling me I had to see. It's called **Crooked Tree Art Center**, and not only is the building unusually beautiful, what I saw inside was absolutely amazing. The art center, which is in a renovated formerly Methodist church originally constructed in 1890, brings thousands of visitors to the area every year.

Inside are thousands of incredible pieces of all kinds of art from some of Michigan's most talented artists. I honestly saw some of the most creative stuff I've seen in years.

Liz Ahrens is the executive director at Crooked Tree, and her endless energy and passion for art was completely contagious. She helps orchestrate everything from year-round art exhibits to performance theater and classes in music, pottery and dance and other educational programs.

Liz took us on a guided tour of the center. This is where I first discovered the U.P.'s incredibly talented found-object artist, Ritch Branstrom. His whimsical tin can fish were on display, and they were very creative and very cool.

The Crooked Tree Art Center really is one of those inspirational places that make you proud to be from Michigan. You might never think to visit a place like this when you're on vacation, but checking out local art can be a blast, and it really gives you a great community perspective.

Next we discovered a great Michigan success story. It's the story of two guys who took advantage of Michigan's tremendous resources and are now literally enjoying the fruits of their labor.

American Spoon
(231) 347-7004
413 E. Lake St., Petoskey, MI 49770
www.spoon.com

Justin Rashid and his business partner Larry Forgione started **American Spoon** back in 1981, and it's been a sweet ride ever since. Larry and Justin shared a dream to produce the finest fruit preserves in the world from Michigan fruit. Larry developed the original recipes, Justin selected varieties of Michigan fruit and as the French say, *viola*. American Spoon was born.

It all started when Justin (a wild-food forager) had a friend in New York (Larry) who was looking to become the great American chef. He wanted to use all American ingredients, so Justin started sending him morel mushrooms. When Larry asked, "What else do you have back there in Michigan?" Justin brought him to Michigan. Larry saw the tremendous agricultural resources, put down roots in Petoskey and the partnership was born. After deciding to concentrate on making jam, American Spoon came to be, and now they ship their incredible spreadables around the world.

The company credo is, "Make the best preserves in America using Michigan fruit," and that's exactly what they're doing. From humble beginnings to a fruitful enterprise, you'll taste a mouthful of Michigan with every American Spoon.

City Park Grill
(231) 347-0101
432 E. Lake St., Petoskey, MI 49770
www.cityparkgrill.com

On our way back to the Perry Hotel, the crew and I stopped for a bite to eat at one of Petoskey's most historic restaurants, **City Park Grill**. When you walk in, you're instantly transported back to the late 1800s. The bar is spectacular, the food is awesome and some pretty famous folks used to frequent this place. As a matter of fact, the second seat from the front of the original bar used to be Ernest Hemingway's favorite spot. So I sat down and enjoyed their signature Hemingway Martini, a great way to cap off our adventure in Petoskey.

Regardless of the season, there are tons of fun and interesting things to do in Petoskey. You really owe it to yourself to get up (or down) there, explore the town and have your own UTR adventure.

Story behind the name:
Farewell to Arms

When you sit at the same bar as Ernest Hemingway, you start to think you hear ghosts. You're occupying the same space in time as one of the greats. It's a weird feeling. And it was a great way to wrap up this show, with Papa's favorite martini in hand, sitting at his seat at the bar.

Chapter 11
Season 1, Episode 11

•Hamtramck
•Frankenmuth

Hamtramck is one of the most interesting, eclectic and diverse communities you'll find anywhere. Some people would say Hamtramck is going through a bit of an identity crisis right now, but the reality is, it's a place in transition that's presenting great opportunities for everyone and an open palette for urban expression. Hamtramck used to be a predominantly Polish community, but now it's home to all kinds of people and cultures who all have one thing in common: a genuine love for their city. All you have to do is turn around, and you'll find another cool place to explore.

Hamtramck Disneyland
Alley between Sobieski and Klinger Streets, Hamtramck, MI 48212

Speaking of cool places, here's a strange and wonderful place that should be one of the first places you stop when you're in Hamtramck. It's called **Hamtramck Disneyland**, and the man behind this bizarre backyard masterpiece is Dmytro Szylak. He came to Hamtramck from the Ukraine right after WWII, and after working for GM for thirty years, he retired in 1997 and spent two years putting together the most amazing carnival of Americana I've ever seen. If you've got an artistic sweet tooth, there's definitely enough eye candy there to give you a brain cavity. Everywhere you look you'll find familiar childhood memories exploding from his backyard.

Dmytro is in his 90s now, so he's just sitting back and enjoying the creative fruits of his labor. If you find his Hamtramck Disneyland and he's outside, make sure to shake the man's hand; he's a true Michigan treasure.

Detroit Threads
(313) 872-1777
10238 Joseph Campau St., Hamtramck, MI 48212
www.detroitthreadsstore.com

Hamtramck is a pretty hip place, and a lot of cool people hang out there. You know, people with "a look." Well, if you've seen our TV show, you know that I don't really have a look. As a matter of fact, I look like a guy who's looking for a look. So I looked for a place in Hamtramck where I could get a look and found a place that looked pretty good. It's called **Detroit Threads**. It's a retro resale shop and record store that's got everything vintage. The vinyl collection is incredible, and if you're in the market for something hip to wear, believe me, you'll find it.

Owner Mike Smith is one of the hippest cats you'll meet anywhere, and whether you're in need of some vintage threads or you're looking for some classic vinyl to groove to, he's your man. If Mike looks kinda familiar, it's because he looks like every rock star you've ever seen rolled up into one cool dude. He's real, a genuinely nice guy, and will have stuff you didn't even know you needed. He set me up with a total 70s look that got me tons of looks on the street. Sweet!

Maria's House Made Salsa
(313) 733-8406
www.mariashousemadesalsa.com

The next place we went to was Maria's Comida, a Mexican-Asian fusion restaurant in the heart of Hamtramck. It was owned and operated by the Pronko Family, the nicest people you will meet this side of the sun. They offered an unlikely culinary combination that was absolutely out-a-sight. The crew and I went back many, many times.

Shortly after we featured them on UTR, they started making their own line of fresh, homemade salsas that became so popular, the Pronkos eventually stopped restauranting and started bottling. It's called **Maria's House Made Salsa**, and when you taste it, you'll be in salsa heaven. Their salsas are now available at a number of retail chains, so keep an eye out for them. The restaurant is no more, but their salsa lives on so you can dip another day! And trust me, when you dip that chip, you'll taste the love they put into every jar.

Public Pool
(313) 405-POOL
3309 Caniff, Hamtramck, MI 48212
www.apublicpool.com

One of our Facebook friends told me about **Public Pool** in Hamtramck. So I thought, what better way to end our day than with a refreshing swim? Well, it didn't take me long to figure out I wouldn't need that new swim cap I bought. Turns out Public Pool is a massively hip place where local artists of all kinds can come and express themselves. You'll see everything from musical performances and the spoken word to experimental interactive art displays. It's a place that gives expression and creative energy to the community.

The evening we were there the exhibits were all about mankind's relationship with the automobile and its influence on the human condition. Nine local artists came together to express their interpretation of that relationship. The exhibits were fascinating, thought provoking and extremely creative.

Then, to drive the event home (pun intended), artist Chip Flynn put together a crazy demolition derby in the streets of Hamtramck, the likes of which I've never seen before. It was a wonderfully bizarre experience featuring robotic fiberglass cars and a wild and crazy robot. The crowd loved it.

If you get the chance, I highly recommend you immerse yourself in art at Public Pool. Just remember, you won't need that swim cap.

If you're looking for another great Michigan adventure, Hamtramck is definitely one of them. From the historic St. Florian Church that's been there since 1907 to the classic Polish bakeries and restaurants, it's a great place to be. And once you've been there, believe me, you're officially cool.

If you live in Michigan, there's a good chance you've made it to **Frankenmuth**, and if you've been there, you know how much fun it is. But, if you haven't been there, what the heck are you waiting for?

Frankenmuth was founded back in 1845 by some real Germans who came there from Franconia, Bavaria, and this town is as German now as it was then. Well, except for the fact that everyone speaks English now. That sure makes it a lot easier when you're shopping. Speaking of the shopping, it's incredible. There are so many cool stores and unusual things to buy that you may need to stay a night or two just to make up your mind. Don't worry, they have many awesome places that will put you up.

The first thing I did when we got to Frankenmuth was become German. I bought myself an authentic German hat, some lederhosen, some strudel and a Bavarian beer. I even learned how to count to ten in German, but I stopped at three because it's a family show.

Willi's Sausage Company
(989) 652-9041
316 S. Main, Frankenmuth, MI 48734
www.willissausages.com

Everybody knows that if you're German, sausage is two of your favorite food groups, so to make sure the transformation was complete, I stopped by **Willi's Sausage Company.** They make over one hundred different sausages right there on site. Now that's German!

Frankenmuth really is a one-of-a-kind destination. And whether you spend a day or a week there, you won't run out of chicken dinners to eat, beer to drink or great family fun stuff to do.

Snowfest
www.zehnders.com/zehnderssnowfest

Now I've been to Frankenmuth before, but what was totally under my radar is that they have a huge festival there every January that literally turns snow into a show. It's called Zehnder's **Snowfest**, and it's been going on for more than twenty years now. Boy, where have I been?

Everybody knows that if you want an authentic German-style chicken dinner, Frankenmuth is THE place in Michigan to go. What I didn't know was that teams from all over the world go there to compete in a massive snow-carving competition that you just have to see to believe.

Talented teams from the Netherlands, Mexico, Russia, China and even Morocco fly in to compete in this crazy, cool competition. You won't just see Frosty the Snowman at this event. These incredible artists carve full-size oxen, giant eagles and complete landscapes out of twenty-foot-high compressed blocks of snow. One inventive team actually carved an entire life-size rock band performing on stage. They carved the people, amplifiers, guitars, drums and even the guitar strings. Mind blowing!

Zehnder's Inn
(800) 863-7999
730 S. Main St., Frankenmuth, MI 48734
www.zehnders.com

The crew and I just had to top off our day in Frankenmuth with one of **Zehnder's Inn's** authentic chicken dinners. We ate, we laughed, we ate, we talked, we ate, we drank and well… we ate. By the time we were done, we were a lot more German than when we got there. About five pounds each more German.

Frankenmuth was totally worth the drive… and the five pounds!

Story behind the name:
Mike…You Still with Us?

There's something funny about dressing Tom up in funky clothing and doing a mini fashion show inside Detroit Threads in Hamtramck. Owner Mike was a great sport and we felt compelled to recycle his joke in the Frankenmuth segment.

We realize that what makes us laugh about certain segments might go over the heads of viewers, but it still makes us laugh.

Chapter 12

Season 1, Episode 12

·Houghton Lake
· U.P.

For over sixty years, the community of Houghton Lake, which by the way is on Houghton Lake, has been hosting a winter festival called Tip-Up Town USA. For ten days every January, Fishermen come from all over the Midwest to put up shanties, drill holes in the ice and catch fish. They catch walleye, pike, bluegill, perch and even a fish called a crappie. I'm not a fisherman, but I'd probably avoid that last one.

Tip-up Town
(800) 248-5253
1625 W. Houghton Lake Dr., Houghton Lake, MI 48629
www.houghtonlakechamber.net

Even though I've known about this event for a long time now, I really thought it was just about ice fishing. Boy, was I wrong. What was totally under my radar is that the vast majority of people who come to this festival don't fish at all. They come to have a blast at one of the biggest and best winter festivals you'll find anywhere. I was going to try ice fishing, but I figured I'd have better luck catching a corndog over at the fair.

When I got to the main festival, the scene was almost surreal. In the middle of winter, the lake often freezes to more than two feet thick and turns into a giant playground for literally thousands of snowmobilers. There were thousands of them for as far as the eye could see, and they even had helicopter rides taking off on the ice.

The main **Tip-up Town** carnival takes place right on the shores of Houghton Lake and has everything a family needs to have fun in, on and over the snow. There are rides, games, shows, great food, ice slides, play areas for the kids and a warm and family friendly atmosphere that makes you totally forget the cold.

If regular family fun isn't quite satisfying enough for you and you're feeling a little adventurous (even a little nutty in the head) you can also try the Polar Bear Dip. People actually line up for hours in the freezing cold just to say they were tough, brave and crazy enough to jump into the freezing water. Call me a coward, but this is one stunt I'll try in my next life... maybe.

Lyman's on the Lake Bait & Tackle
(989) 422-3231
6560 W. Houghton Lake Dr., Houghton Lake, MI 48629
www.houghtonlakefishing.com

If you're actually going to Tip-up Town to fish, **Lyman's on the Lake Bait & Tackle** has everything you need for a successful day on the ice. I spent some quality time learning the ins and outs of ice fishing with Lyman. He's the real deal. And even though he was polite, I think he knew right away that I wouldn't be pulling anything out of the ice that day. Except maybe a frosty cold adult malted beverage.

When all was said and done, not only did I have a totally different perception of what this event is really all about, the crew and I had a winter blast. Tip-up Town truly does have something for everyone, and that, by the way, includes you.

There's no other place like it on earth, and the great thing about it is, it's all ours. The incredible winter adventures you can have in Michigan's **Upper Peninsula** will create memories that will last a lifetime. As writer, thinker and Nobel laureate Sinclair Lewis once wrote, "Winter's not a season, it's an occupation," and in the U.P., it's a fulltime job. And it's a job I absolutely love. If you're going to have winter, you may as well do it up right, and in the U.P., they do it up right alright.

Top of the Lake Snowmobile Museum
(906) 477-6298
W11660 U.S. 2, Naubinway, MI 49762
www.snowmobilemuseum.com

On this trip, we turned left as soon as we crossed the Mackinac Bridge and drove one hour west on U.S. Route 2 to the little town of Naubinway. That's where we found one of the coolest places ever. It's the **Top of the Lake Snowmobile Museum** and it's run by Charlie Vallier and his wife Marilyn. When it comes to the history of this sport, I don't think anyone is nicer or knows more than these two. The museum just moved into a brand new facility that has tons more space, and they've got some of the wildest and rarest snowmobiles you find anywhere.

What really struck me about some of the vintage snowmobiles is the great sense of art and design that went into making them. They were almost more form than function, and I swear, if you look closely, some of them actually have a personality.

Honestly, even if you're not a snowmobiler, the Top of The Lake Snowmobile Museum in Naubinway is a fascinating way to spend the afternoon. Besides, then you get to say you've been to Naubinway in the U.P. How cool is that?

Stormy Kromer
(888) 455-2253
1238 Wall St., Ironwood, MI 49938
www.stormykromer.com

We left the museum and headed about as far west as you can go in the Upper Peninsula. We drove 264 miles to the town of Ironwood, right on the Wisconsin border. It's so far, they're even on central time there. We were in search of the iconic cap of the U.P., the Stormy Kromer, and at long last we found both the factory and the fellow who saved it.

Stormy Kromer is indeed the classic cap of the U.P. It's been around for over one hundred years and it's made right in Ironwood. A dozen years ago, Bob Jacquart was sitting in a coffee shop when he overheard someone say that because of tough economic times the Stormy Kromer Company might stop making this iconic cap. Well, the Stormy Kromer tradition was so strong in Bob's family that he figured out a way to buy and save the company.

George "Stormy" Kromer was a real guy. He was a semi-pro baseball player and railroad engineer back in the late 1800s. Problem was, Stormy kept losing his ball cap when he'd stick his head out the train window. In 1903, he asked his wife Ida to modify an old baseball cap to help keep it on in windy weather. She fashioned a hat that would not only stay on, but would pull down to cover his ears and keep him warm. Soon other railroad workers wanted a Stormy Kromer cap, and the business was born.

Now Bob, his wife Denise and their daughters Gina and Kari are keeping Stormy Kromer's legacy alive. They saved the company, are employing tons of townspeople and are carrying on an important part of the U.P.'s legacy. Next time you're up in the U.P., look around. Stormy Kromers abound.

Next, we traveled back to the Upper Peninsula's largest city, **Marquette**. It's located right in the middle of the U.P. on the shores of Lake Superior. We came to Marquette this past summer and fell in love with the place. This city has everything: great shops, cool restaurants and a great urban feel that's set in the middle of some of the most beautiful natural surroundings imaginable. It really is a great place to be.

U.P. 200
(906) 228-3072
P.O. Box 15, Marquette, MI 49855
www.UP200.org

This time we came to Marquette to see something I'd never seen before, a two-hundred mile dogsled race called the **U.P. 200**. It's an Iditarod qualifier that brings mushers and their teams in from all over the Midwest. The race actually starts off right in downtown Marquette. The morning of the race, they bring in heavy equipment, dump tons of snow and actually build a dogsled trail right through the middle of the city. This takes a lot of time and energy, but when you see the start of the race, it's extremely cool.

The morning of the race we got to experience what's called the vet check. This is where every single dog is thoroughly examined by a veterinarian to make sure they're healthy and ready to run. I have to be honest; I had my reservations about how dogs were treated in this sport until I saw how happy and healthy they all were. The relationship the dogs have with their owners is amazing. These dogs love two things: they love their owners and they love to run.

Putting on a race this size takes a ton of people who are dedicated to the sport. Students from Northern Michigan University even volunteer their time to help make the race happen. It's a total town effort that brings everyone together for fun and a ton of community spirit.

We had some time to kill before the race started, so we ran over to the NMU campus to see the Superior Dome. It's their stadium and field house, and it's one of the largest wooden dome structures in the world. Just walking into the dome is a real experience, but we got to do something really cool. We got to take the catwalk all the way to the top. It's amazing that something this mammoth can be built entirely out of wood.

When it gets close to the start of the race, downtown Marquette really comes alive. More than seven thousand people line the streets to cheer on the mushers and their canine companions. They say the older you get, the more often you should do something for the very first time. If you've never experienced The U.P. 200, it's time you did.

The great thing about this trip north wasn't just the cool people I met, the things I learned or the places I saw. It was also about the inspiration it gave me to come back and discover more.

Story behind the name:
One Block South of the Blinking Yellow Light

When you hit the U.P., it's completely different. For instance, there are less traffic lights. So in Naubinway, they can use the one blinking yellow stop light in town as a landmark on how to find the Top of the Lake Snowmobile Museum. It didn't stop us from blowing past it the first time and having to double back.

Chapter 13

Season 1, Episode 13

Lansing, Michigan attracts people for a lot of different reasons. It's the capital city, so a lot of people go there to help move Michigan forward. It's also a beautiful city that does a great job of mixing modern urban living with great natural places. We went to the Lansing area to discover three great Michigan stories and to find out why Lansing is continually voted not only one of the best places to start a new business, but also one of the best places for young people looking for opportunity.

Sweetie-licious Bakery Café
(517) 669-9300
108 N. Bridge St., DeWitt, MI 48820
www.sweetie-licious.com

Our adventure started in the little town of DeWitt, just north of Lansing at a place I thought I'd never find. Ever! It's called **Sweetie-licious Bakery Café**, and just stepping inside takes you back to a time when simple pleasures were a lot simpler. When you meet Linda Hundt you find out right away that she's as sweet as the pies she makes. You won't meet a more sincere or motivated person anywhere, and she's put her genuine love for people into the incredible pies she makes. Believe me, you can taste it. Linda's pies have become a national sensation. She's won over a dozen first place awards and even appeared on The Food Network. Linda's staff is a blast and they go out of their way to source fruit from local farmers.

Linda invited me to make a pie with her, so we each made her famous pie that holds two titles: First Place, Crisco National Pie Championship and Best of Show, Food Network. It's called Tom's Cheery Cherry Cherry Berry Pie, and it is named after her late brother-in-law Tom. Mine tasted really good, but Linda's actually looked like a pie.

The reason I said I never thought I'd find a place like this is because a number of years ago, my wife Cathy started baking homemade pies. Her pies were (and are) so good that I completely stopped eating store-bought pies. They just didn't even compare, until I tried Sweetie-licious. Sorry, Honey!

It's passionate, talented and motivated people like Linda Hundt at Sweetie-licious who are reminding the world why Michigan truly is a great place to be.

Lansing's historic Old Town area is a thriving collection of new, innovative and creative restaurants and businesses. Young people have reclaimed the area and turned it into one of the most fun and interesting places to go in Michigan. One of these people is Chad Jordan. He's smart, focused and motivated. Now combine all that with a good idea, and you've got a recipe for success.

Cravings Gourmet Popcorn
(517) 485-3404
1220 Turner St., Lansing, MI 48906
www.cravingspopcorn.com

Chad's business is called **Cravings Gourmet Popcorn**, and it's gathering more devoted patrons every day. Their mantra is, "Pure Popcorn Addiction," and I have to tell you, after trying Chad's incredible flavor mixes, my whole family and I were hooked. Chad actually takes advice and suggestions from his loyal customers and comes up with some unusual and awesome popcorn concoctions. The flavors are always changing, but you'll find savory flavors like White Cheddar BBQ, Spicy Chipotle, Bacon Cheddar and Spicy Dill and Garlic. His Premium Signature Gold Caramel Corn is also an outstanding sweet and salty snack.

Chad's love for having a good time inspired him to create these wonderfully addicting popcorn snacks. His fond memories of watching Big Time Wrestling and eating popcorn with his grandfather were his inspiration, and the love he gets from his loyal fans and the community keeps him going. At Cravings they pop and mix fresh every day and use only premium Michigan corn, butter and oils. You'll find about twenty flavors there at any given time, and they will also custom blend flavors for you.

Chad's enthusiasm is contagious, his popcorn is addicting and his story is inspirational. Just add salt and you've got another Michigan success story!

Scientific research has proven that the urge for a good cup of coffee is so powerful in the human brain, that if you don't get it, you could quite possibly go insane. Actually, I made that up, but if you love good coffee like I do, it's not far from the truth.

Biggby Coffee
See website for locations
www.biggby.com

Bob Fish (aka Biggby Bob) is the founder and CEO of the Lansing-based **Biggby Coffee** chain. He took his love of coffee and combined it with his love for Michigan to create one of the fastest-growing and most successful businesses in the Midwest. Bob got his appreciation for a good cup of coffee in Europe. When he came back to the states, he saw that the American mindset was trending toward quality, not quantity and decided to introduce them to a great cup of coffee. Thanks to pioneers like Biggby Bob, a lot of food producers are returning to traditional methods, which is why things like bread, beer, wine and now coffee are so much better than they used to be.

Bob fell in love with Michigan while attending Michigan State University. As he put it, Michigan is earnest, honest, hardworking and an absolutely beautiful place to live. The corporate culture at Biggby Coffee is also outstanding. Everyone, including Bob, takes a turn working the phones at the front desk. It's a great way to get personally connected to your customers. Bob is also an avid social networker. You won't find a more fun and engaging website or Facebook presence than Biggby Coffee.

Bob is also known to occasionally show up at Biggby locations to sip some joe with the locals, so next time you stop by a Biggby Coffee for a fresh warm cup, keep an eye out for Bob. You won't meet a nicer guy anywhere.

W yandotte is one of the oldest cities in Michigan, so it's rich in both history and tradition. It's also become one of the most modern and forward thinking communities in the entire Midwest. Wyandotte is known as "The heart of Downriver," and I can see why. Everyone I talked to had a lot of heart and a ton of love for this place.

The River's Edge Gallery
(734) 246-9880
3024 Biddle Ave., Wyandotte, MI 48192
www.artattheedge.com

If you're looking for a cool and eclectic gallery where you can see and even purchase art from some of Michigan's most talented and progressive artists, you're looking for **The River's Edge Gallery**. There's an incredibly active and passionate art community in Wyandotte, and River's Edge is proof positive how much creative energy we have here in Michigan.

I had no idea Wyandotte was such an epicenter for Michigan art, and everything in this gallery is home grown. You'll find everything from classic oils to sculptures and even found-object art. From the sublime to the wonderfully bizarre, this place is chock full of interesting eye candy. Check their website for upcoming shows featuring some of Michigan's most renowned artists.

The first floor features house artists. The second floor has circulating shows, and the third floor has three studio spaces as well as more house artists. The gallery is also the headquarters for Patt Slack Designs, which has been serving the Metro Detroit area for thirty-five years. Patt spent some time with us the day we were there, and she truly personifies the passion for art in Wyandotte.

Joe's Hamburgers
(734) 285-0420
3041 Biddle Ave., Wyandotte, MI 48192
www.joeshamburgers.net

Now here's a culinary concoction that's so uniquely American, they don't even try to make it in other parts of the world. On the surface of the grill, it seems pretty simple, but if you really do it right, it's an art form, and in Wyandotte, I think I found a masterpiece. I'm of course talking about sliders, and at **Joe's Hamburgers**, owner Jeremy Sladovnik practices the fine art of preparing this true American delicacy.

Jeremy went to Motz Hamburgers in Detroit, had a slider, fell in love, asked the owner Bob Milosavljevski (don't say it out loud; you'll hurt yourself) how he did it, got a quick lesson and decided to fire up a grill and throw down downriver. He opened his own place, named it after his super cool Grandpa Joe and has been grilling ever since.

The burgers at Joe's Hamburgers aren't just good. They're %#$%^% great! He's taken the slider joint to a whole new level with savory selections like the spicy Jalapeno Joe and a huge burger simply called The Chubby. He even serves deep fried pickles and Twinkies, and get this: when Jeremy was in Canada playing junior hockey, he learned to make the brown gravy-covered French delicacy, poutine. Sounds weird, looks messy, tastes incredible.

Jeremy is really making a name for himself in the burger world, and it couldn't happen to a nicer person. Ten minutes with this guy and you're best buddies. He's genuine, sincere, an amazingly funny person and has a heart of gold. If you're looking for a messy, mouthwatering meal at a great Michigan place, check out Joe's Hamburgers.

If you're looking for a new community to explore, Wyandotte has fun, interesting and your name written all over it.

Story behind the name:
Swamp Rabbit

Ahhh. Swamp Rabbit. Sometimes you know exactly what you're in for with a segment. Then there's the infamous muskrat segment in Wyandotte. You just never know. We're glad we did it. We're glad we don't have to do the same segment over and over. We ate it. It was good, but not, "I'm craving me a swamp rabbit" kind of good. You know?

If you're not sure what I'm referring to, go to our website and watch episode thirteen of season one.

Chapter 14

Season 2, Episode 1

• Ann Arbor
• Dearborn

When I think of Dearborn, the first thing that comes to mind is just how many things come to mind! It's a great Michigan city with deep automotive roots. It's also a welcoming city that's embraced cultural diversity with its beautiful historic neighborhoods and great sense of community. Oh, and did I mention? It's a heck of a lot of fun, too!

Dearborn Music
(313) 561-1000
22501 Michigan Ave., Dearborn, MI 48124
www.dearbornmusic.com

If you go to Dearborn (which we did) and you love music (which we do) **Dearborn Music** has been an institution there for more than fifty years. Rick LeAnnais and his family bring mounds of music to the Michigan masses. Even the music you don't know you like yet is there.

Sure, you can get your music off the Internet, but for genuine music lovers, this is an incredibly deep place where you can come, look, touch, explore, listen and get lost in a three-dimensional world of music. From classic vinyl to the latest releases, it's all there, and Dearborn Music also has genuine music heads on staff who will help you find almost anything you're looking for. And, speaking of classic vinyl, I even found a "Domino" album. It's a band I was in back in the late 80s, and it was only a buck… bonus!

Rick makes sure this place is constantly evolving with the music industry and modern technology, so something tells me it'll be there in another hundred years. If you love music, you'll love Dearborn music.

While we were at Dearborn Music we were lucky enough to run into one of Dearborn's most prominent citizens and supporters, Ismael Ahmed. Not only is Ismael a University of Michigan-Dearborn associate provost, he also hosts a hip and progressive world music program on Detroit's public radio station WDET.

This Island Earth with Ismael Ahmed
WDET 101.9FM Detroit, Saturdays 5p.m.-7p.m.
www.facebook.com/ThisIslandEarth

Ismael is a social activist, a humanitarian, an intellectual and just happened to be starved like us, so he agreed to take us to one of his favorite places to eat.

M&M Café
(313) 581-5775
13714 Michigan Ave., Dearborn, MI 48126

Elaine and Maurice Lteif own a cool and eclectic eatery called **M&M Café**, and their awesome blend of Mediterranean and American food is just part of the reason this place is so popular. The other reason is just about everyone who comes in the door gets a hug from Elaine. For thirty years they've been putting a lot of love into the food, and word of mouth alone has made this place a true Dearborn gem. Back in the kitchen, Chef Maurice has mastered the art of putting the word "home" in home cooking, and Elaine has managed to make this entire community their extended family.

Whether Maurice is cooking American or Lebanese, he's completely comfortable on both continents. From the burgers, salads and incredible sandwiches, to grilled kafta, hummus and laban, everything is fresh and creatively prepared and presented. All the Middle Eastern dishes are carefully explained on the menu. If you want to feel the love for M&M Café, just read the reviews. Then go there, try the food and write one for yourself.

Arab American National Museum
(313) 582-2266
13624 Michigan Ave., Dearborn, MI 48126
www.arabamericanmuseum.org

Next, Ismael took us to a place that's near and dear to his heart, the **Arab American National Museum**. Inside we met up with Devon Akmon. He's the deputy director at the museum, and believe me, he knows all things Arab America. This museum is the first and only one of its kind in the nation, and the displays they have there are both inspirational and eye opening.

I had no idea how many important and influential Arab Americans there were or how many important contributions they've made to this country and to the American way of life. From political activist Ralph Nader to Christa McAuliffe, the New Hampshire school teacher who gave her life in the Challenger Space Shuttle disaster, the museum is fascinating, interactive and offers up a ton of surprises. Surprises like the fact that the official White House Santa Claus for over fifty years and through seven presidents was also an Arab American.

If you celebrate diversity and would like to experience the real Arab American story, spend some time at the Arab American National Museum. We had a blast, learned a lot and left enlightened.

Green Brain Comics
(313) 582-9444
13936 Michigan Ave., Dearborn, MI 48126
www.greenbrain.biz

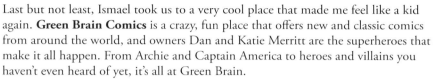

Last but not least, Ismael took us to a very cool place that made me feel like a kid again. **Green Brain Comics** is a crazy, fun place that offers new and classic comics from around the world, and owners Dan and Katie Merritt are the superheroes that make it all happen. From Archie and Captain America to heroes and villains you haven't even heard of yet, it's all at Green Brain.

Comic books have never gone away because of their unique ability to tell a quick, colorful and dynamic story that visually involves the reader. They're good for young minds and old. And speaking of young minds, comics are also a great way to get kids excited about and engaged in the process of reading. Thanks to Superman, Spiderman and the Fantastic Four, I'm a proficient reader today.

Dan and Katie explained that they continue to love this medium because of the fantasy, literacy and emotional connectivity it gives the reader. It's a great and healthy way to escape and dream, if only for a few minutes.

If you're looking for a super fun adventure that's inexpensive and that you can put in a bag and take home with you, I highly recommend a visit to Green Brain Comics.

Also, if you're looking for a great place to live, eat, stay or play, stop by Dearborn. It's a place where they love life and all kinds of people.

Like so many cities in Michigan, **Ann Arbor** is such a cool place, we couldn't wait to get back. The city is literally wrapped around the University of Michigan, and the energy that comes from this combination makes Ann Arbor one of the most stimulating and interesting places to live anywhere.

Kerrytown Market
(734) 662-5008
407 N. Fifth Ave., Ann Arbor, MI 48104
www.kerrytown.com

When we were in Ann Arbor last time, Ari Weinzweig over at Zingerman's told us about a place we really needed to check out. **Kerrytown Market** is a collection of historic buildings that have been renovated, connected and turned into a great place to shop, eat or just spend the afternoon.

Kerrytown is a great gathering place for the entire community. It creates a genuine sense of place for the people who live in this area. It's also a great place to shop for fresh produce, meet for coffee or lunch, or even shop for clothing and specialty items.

The atmosphere is inviting and the layout is perfect for wandering and wondering.

Now, this is really cool. At the top of the familiar bell-tower at Kerrytown sits a very special seven-ton musical instrument! It's a chime made up of seventeen bells. Ten of the bells were originally cast in the 1920s for a church in Massachusetts. But the other seven bells were specially made in the Netherlands for Kerrytown back in 1997. But that's not the really cool part. What's cool is that on certain days, they actually let you play the bells. I did it. Just don't ask me how it sounded.

The Spice Merchants
(734) 332-5500
Kerrytown Mall, 407 N. 5th Ave., Ann Arbor, MI 48104
www.spicemerchants.biz

The market has so many unusual places to explore, but the intoxicating aromas we encountered made our next discovery easy to find, but even harder to leave. Lisa Freeman owns **The Spice Merchants** shop at Kerrytown, and she puts more spice into her life than most people do in a lifetime. I had no idea how many spices there were. From common spices like cinnamon and cumin to more exotic ones like cardamom and saffron, this place will totally spice up your life. The Spice Merchant is like a three dimensional spice rack with all the flavors of the world at your fingertips. Lisa took a personal passion and turned it into a thriving Michigan business. She really is the original spice girl. Your nose will tell you where her shop is when you walk by it, and your taste buds will thank you later.

Monahan's Seafood Market
(734) 662-5118
407 N. 5th Ave., Ann Arbor, MI 48104
www.monahansseafood.com

Lunchtime at Kerrytown offers a number of really good options, but the one that hooked me and the crew was **Monahan's Seafood Market**. For more than thirty years now, Mike and Lisa Monahan have been selling and preparing fresh seafood for all of Ann Arbor to enjoy… and now, for the UTR film crew. You can buy fresh fish to go, get a quick carryout meal or sit, relax and enjoy any one of their aquatic entrees.

Their philosophy at Monahan's is pretty simple: fresh, fresh, fresh. They don't bring in pre-cut filets; they buy whole fish, cut them up fresh and prepare their seafood dishes the old fashioned way. I had a Vietnamese bluefish sandwich for lunch and the flavors were incredible.

Ann Arbor is the perfect place for Mike and Lisa to be doing their thing. The food scene there is way ahead of the curve. It's truly a foodie's paradise. I was trying to think of a clever way to say it, but I'll just say it. If you love fresh seafood that's expertly and creatively prepared, Monahan's Seafood Market is worth the drive to Ann Arbor and a trip to Kerrytown Market. If you already live in Ann Arbor… bonus!

Michigan Theater
(734) 668-8463
603 E. Liberty St., Ann Arbor, MI 48104
www.michtheater.org

There are a lot of things that give a city a sense of culture and community, and for Ann Arbor, the **Michigan Theater** is one of those unique places. It's where the performing arts, music and movies meet the masses. It's kinda like a culture sandwich. The Michigan Theater has been the creative heart and soul of Ann Arbor for almost a century now, and it's one of those places that, if you've got it, you take good care of it.

When we were there, I spent some quality time with Russ Collins. Russ has been the theater's executive director for over thirty years, and his continuous efforts have kept this historic American theater alive. The theater was built in 1928, the same year as Detroit's Fox Theater, and is one of a dying number of classic movie palaces built at that time. Thanks to a community that rallied to save it, the Michigan Theater is now a complete multimedia entertainment venue where you can enjoy everything from local and touring stage plays and symphony performances to movies and modern music concerts.

Just going to this great theater is an experience in and of itself. From the incredible, classic architecture to the original pipe organ that is still in use, it's a rich and cultural experience you're just not going to get down at the mega mall movie-plex. My hope is that in one hundred years, people will still be going to the Michigan Theater. It's where the arts belong, and luckily, it belongs to all of us right here in Michigan!

As for Ann Arbor, let me know when you're gonna go, and I'll meet you at Kerrytown.

Story behind the name:
We Made it to season two!

Crazy how fast a season goes and then we're onto season two. We are the luckiest guys in the room.

Chapter 15

Season 2, Episode 2

•Harbor Country
•Kalamazoo

Harbor Country is a collection of eight small towns located along the shores of Lake Michigan in extreme southwest lower Michigan. From north to south, they are: Sawyer, Harbert, Lakeside, Union Pier, bustling New Buffalo, Grand Beach, Michiana, and a little farther inland, Three Oaks. Just don't ask me to name the Seven Dwarfs!

Harbor Country is virtually unknown to most people in Michigan, which is why vacationers from other states spend so much time there. They even play a game there called, "Find the Michigan license plate." It's true; even though you're in Michigan, you see plates from every other state but ours. The area was even voted one of the best weekend getaways in the Midwest and has also been called the Riviera of Lake Michigan.

Warren Dunes State Park
(269) 426-4013
12032 Red Arrow Hwy., Sawyer, MI 49125

Our first stop in Harbor country was **Warren Dunes State Park** on Lake Michigan. If you're looking for a beautiful Florida beach, don't go to Florida (wrong peninsula), go to Warren Dunes. The beach is huge, the sand is incredible and it has something a Florida beach won't have: the beach backs up to some gigantic sand dunes. This is a great park and beach for families and, yes, even camera crews.

When you're exploring Harbor Country, the main road you drive is the historic **Red Arrow Highway**. It was named after some brave men from this area who fought in WWI. The Red Arrow runs north and south and takes you past beautiful scenery, funky little art shops and of course (you know us) some great restaurants. Yes!

Mesa Luna
(269) 426-4878
12868 Red Arrow Hwy., Sawyer, MI 49125

Speaking of restaurants, the next part of our trip took us south to the town of Sawyer and an awesome little restaurant called **Mesa Luna (formerly The Soe Café)**. The mantra at Mesa Luna is, "Local people, using local produce, to make honest food."

When we ate there Executive Chef Chad Miller was the heart and soul of this great place, and he worked continually to craft a great seasonal menu featuring the best Michigan has to offer. The restaurant works directly with local brewers, wine producers, farmers and artisan food producers to make the experience there exceptional.

There's an old saying that "what grows together, goes together," and it rings true every day at Mesa Luna. Watching Chef Chad and his crew make food magic in the kitchen left no doubt why this is a local favorite. Make sure to call ahead before visiting Mesa Luna. Depending on the season, their hours of operation can be quite abbreviated.

After dinner we continued south on the Red Arrow Highway to the town of Lakeside, and by the time we got there, the shadows were getting long and our collective attention span was getting pretty short. So we found an exceptional place to stay.

The Lakeside Inn
(269) 469-0600
15251 Lakeshore Rd., Lakeside, MI 49116
www.lakesideinns.com

The Lakeside Inn was an incredible find. It's a beautiful, rustic inn that's been there since the 1880s, and it's an absolute landmark in this area. The interior is classic hunting lodge, with great spaces to catch up on your reading or just take a nap. You can even rock your cares away out on their classic, one-hundred-foot-long front porch.

Another great thing about the Lakeside Inn is right across the street they have a beautiful path through the woods that takes you down to a secluded, private beach on Lake Michigan. The beach really made me feel like I was someplace special. Oh, that's right, I am. I'm in Michigan!

The next morning, we woke rested, refreshed and ready for another action-packed day of exploring Michigan's Harbor Country. But first, we needed a good, hearty breakfast. So, you know us. We went for ice cream.

Oinks Ice Cream
(269) 469-3535
227 W. Buffalo, New Buffalo, MI 49117
www.oinksicecream.blogspot.com

Oinks is an ice cream parlor in New Buffalo you simply have to see to believe. It's all things pig. The place is filled with thousands of funny, weird, classic and crazy pig things that all have one thing in common: they're there to make you happy.

Twenty-five years ago, Carey Vink's father created Oinks and started collecting cool and unusual pig stuff. Now Carey continues the tradition that so many people come back to enjoy every summer. At Oinks Ice Cream Parlor you can enjoy dozens of flavors of Michigan ice cream. We tried so many, we all suffered with a pretty good case of brain freeze.

If you're looking for a fun and healthy way to start your day, do what we do on the UTR crew. Pig out at Oinks!

Third Coast Surf Shop
(269) 932-4575
22 S. Smith St., New Buffalo, MI 49117
www.thirdcoastsurfshop.com

Third Coast Surf Shop is a cool and funky sports store in New Buffalo where, believe it or not, they surf on Lake Michigan. That's right, I said surf, and if there's any other water sport that involves a paddle or a board, they'll teach you how to do that too.

Ryan Gerard is one of the owners at Third Coast, and he's a true wizard of the water. When the conditions are right, he and his friends actually hang ten along Lake Michigan's southern shores. Even though surfing in Michigan is a bit under the radar, it's been going on there since the late 1950s. Winds coming across the lake can sometimes create swells as high as twenty-six feet and surfable waves up to ten feet high. Ryan's been riding Michigan's wide surf for over fifteen years.

Since the surf wasn't up that day, Ryan took me to a nearby river and showed me the fastest-growing water sport in the world: paddle boarding. You actually stand on what looks like an oversized surfboard with a two-ended paddle and propel yourself along the river. I honestly thought I was doomed to dunk, but it turns out paddle boarding was an absolute blast. It's almost like I was walking over the water. It was very different, and very cool!

If (or should I say WHEN) you come to Harbor Country, stop by the Third Coast Surf shop. If it involves water, they'll make sure you have fun with it.

We had a great time on Michigan's Harbor Country. You should definitely go, so you'll be one of the few Michigan people who know about it.

447
W. South Street

The
Kalamazoo
House
Bed & Breakfast
circa 1878

Kalamazoo is another college town that's alive with renewal, progress and a ton of great reasons to go there. Between Kalamazoo College and Western Michigan University, over 25,000 young people totally energize this community. And the city's mix of modern and classic is perfect. Every time I go to Kalamazoo, I'm reminded how comfortable, cool and eclectic the city is.

Kalamazoo House Bed & Breakfast
(866) 310-0880
447 W. South St., Kalamazoo, MI 49007
www.thekalamazoohouse.com

If you like staying right in town, but you don't like giving up all the comforts of home, do what the UTR crew does: just drop your bags off at the **Kalamazoo House Bed & Breakfast**. It's a fully restored Victorian home, built in 1878, that has incredible hospitality, and every room is completely unique. It was one of the nicest places we've stayed in a long time. Come to think of it, this place has a lot more comforts than my home. I gotta work on that!

Owners Terry and Laurel Parrott have made this place a destination for people who want outstanding accommodations, and they are two of the nicest and sincerest people you will ever meet. Their knowledge of the home's history is incredible and the food they serve is outstanding. A good measure of how nice a place is, is by how many people you tell about it. I have to say that everyone I know now knows about the Kalamazoo House.

Water Street Coffee Joint
(269) 373-2840
315 E. Water St., Kalamazoo, MI 49007
www.waterstreetcoffeejoint.com

I've always considered myself to be a bit of a coffee connoisseur, but when I realized I don't really know a darn thing about the stuff, I stopped by **Water Street Coffee Joint**. They're what you'd call a micro-roaster, and they've perfected both the science and the art of what makes a great cup of coffee. They've got a number of cool and funky coffee cafés across Kalamazoo that offer local art, gourmet edibles, a great cup of local brew and loads of locals loving their coffee.

Willard Street Roasting House
(269) 488-2802
610 W. Willard St., Kalamazoo, MI 49007
www.waterstreetcoffeeroaster.com

To expand my coffee consciousness, I made a visit to Water Street's historic **Willard Street Roasting House** where they actually store, roast and distribute their incredible coffee. My caffeinated sensei for the day was Ben Angelo. He's an actual roast master. It's like being a kung fu master. Only, I guess he's more of a kung fu roaster. Ben was great.

He took me through the entire process, from fair trade sourcing of the beans, right up to and through the roasting process. The Willard Street Roasting House is not a retail location, but it is open to the public, so you might want to stop by, up your knowledge and go to coffee college like I did.

Can-Do Kitchen
(269) 492-1270
511 Harrison St., Kalamazoo, MI 49007
www.fairfoodmatters.org/candokitchenInfo.php

You've heard the old expression, "Too many cooks in the kitchen…" Well, in Kalamazoo, we found a kitchen that wants all the cooks it can get! It's called the **Can-Do Kitchen** and it's a food business incubator. What they're doing is awesome. They help folks with great food ideas get off the ground, in the kitchen and into their own business by giving them a place to create and test their potential products. This helps future food inventors and restaurateurs develop their plans and products before taking the risk of investing in a brick and mortar location. It also gives them a better chance for success. Fair Food Matters and The Can-Do Kitchen also offer cooking classes as well as connections to food licensing and business workshops.

Happy Mouth Vegan Treats
(269) 364-1350
507 Harrison, Kalamazoo, MI 49007
www.happymouthvegantreats.com

Just one of the small businesses Can-Do Kitchen was helping when we were there was **Happy Mouth Vegan Treats**. It's the brainchild of Tamara Harris and DiAdrian Washington, and they hope to someday bring their meat-free treats to the streets for all of us to, well, eats. They were working on developing their line of vegan doughnuts that day, and I'll be honest, when I first heard the words vegan and doughnut together I figured I'd smile, take one bite and just be polite, but they were delicious. If all goes well, thanks to the Can-Do Kitchen, you'll see Happy Mouth Vegan Treats in stores near you soon.

If you get a chance, come explore the rest of Kalamazoo. Sure there's coffee and donuts there, but there's also a whole lot more to explore.

Story behind the name:
Donuts and Coffee

Vegan donuts and locally roasted coffee.
Sometimes it's that simple.

Chapter 16

Season 2, Episode 3

Detroit
Traverse City

Detroit is such an incredible place that we went back again.
There's so much growth and energy happening there right now
that it's overwhelming. I even came up with a great theme for this
new Detroit segment that's called "Detroit: earth, wind and fire."
But for some reason it turned out to be wine, cheese and fire. I'm
not sure how it happened, but I'm guessing it was the wine. Yeah,
it was the wine.

Motor City Wine
(313) 483-7283
1949 Michigan Ave., Detroit, MI 48216
www.motorcitywine.com

Most people don't think of Detroit as a wine destination. But because of the renaissance happening there, Detroit is becoming the place to be for a lot of great reasons. So, why not wine? Remember, there are only two kinds of wine in the world. The kind you like and the kind you don't like. Well, we found a place where they have great wine at great prices. In other words, they have the kind of wine I like!

Motor City Wine combines local art, live music and a great selection of affordable wines you can taste, and if you like, even take home. David Armin-Parcells and Mark Szymanski created what they like to call a "value boutique," and the wine tasting you can do there is far from stuffy. It's amazing how much fun you can have while you're learning about wine. There's a hip urban intimacy about this place that's attracting wine lovers from far and wide. You'll rub elbows and taste great wines in a space that's cool, casual, sophisticated and a lot of fun.

So if you're looking for a place where you can enjoy local music, buy local art, meet cool people and taste some really good wines, Motor City Wine is that kind of place. I think you'll like dig it the most!

For thousands of years mankind has marveled at the mysteries and folklore behind the mystical art of fine cheese making. I just made that up, but actually, have you ever wondered how the stuff is really made? And did you know that some of the best cheese in the world is made right in Detroit?

Traffic Jam & Snug
(313) 831-9470
511 W. Canfield, Detroit, MI 48202
www.trafficjamdetroit.com

Traffic Jam & Snug is a landmark restaurant and pub in Detroit, and if you're in the know, you know it's a lot more than that. It's also a bakery where they make incredible breads, a microbrewery that was Michigan's very first brew pub, and last but not least, a dairy where they make award winning artisanal cheeses.

When we were there, we met up with Chris Reilly. Not only is Chris the brew master at The Traffic Jam, he's also the resident cheese master! When Chris isn't making award winning beer, he's making some of the best cheese you'll find anywhere. And if you're a foodie, they periodically offer classes where you can learn how to make your own cheese right at home.

This really is a fun and educational experience. Chris took us through the entire hands-on process of making cheese and explained both the history and science behind it. From mold spores and coagulants to fat globules and protein matrices, we learned it all and made a beautiful batch of asiago blue cheese.

If you like making things and you like cheese, check in with the folks at Traffic Jam & Snug. While you're there, you might want to stick around for some great food and a few brews. It really is a one-of-a-kind kind of place.

Have you ever thought about what fire is? I did, so I looked it up. It's actually a chemical reaction that happens when oxygen in the air and a fuel source are heated to a certain point. When that happens, there's a chemical reaction and boom, you've got fire. The real trick is to get the fire to entertain and amaze you. For that, you'll need to add one more thing into the mix.

The Detroit Fire Guild
(313) 444-BURN
www.detroitfireguild.com

The Detroit Fire Guild is a group of fire and circus performers who've combined their talents to create one of the hottest and most fascinating shows around. They do both public and private performances, and the things they do with fire will absolutely amaze you.

When I spent some time with the performers, I got the distinct feeling that they were more than just a group. They're really more like a family, and they have this incredible support system for each other that really emphasizes creativity and individuality.

We were treated to our own personal show at the Russell Industrial Center. It was a perfectly surreal setting for a perfectly surreal experience. You can't help but be in awe of what it is the Fire Guild does.

As they demonstrated some of the techniques they use, I thought about the amount of practice that must go into an art form like this. When you're playing with fire, there's really not much room for error. They were breathing fire, twirling fire batons and dancing with rings of fire. It really was spectacular. If you're interested in learning this art form or would like to check out one of their performances, look them up and check them out. It'll be an evening you'll never forget.

With this segment we tried to wine, cheese and fire you up about exploring and rediscovering Detroit. Why do you think we're there so much? Because there's so much there!

When people tell me they love **Traverse City** because it's got everything, I can't really argue with that. It's a great city that's set in one of the most beautiful parts of Michigan. There's enough to explore there to keep you busy for a lifetime. And if you're a foodie, it truly is one of the best places for your palate.

Tall Ship Manitou
(231) 941-2000
13390 SW Bay Shore Dr., Traverse City, MI 49684
www.tallshipsailing.com

All my life I've wondered what it would be like to sail on one of those giant sailing schooners from the 1800s. Little did I know that in Traverse City, they have the **Tall Ship Manitou.** It's a 114-foot, double-masted ship that offers sailing adventures from two hours up to four days. They even conduct educational school programs onboard. Finally, a chance for me to get my sea legs and actually learn something.

Our captain, Dave McGinnis, knew these waters, knew his ship and probably knew right away that I knew absolutely nothing about sailing. In one word, Dave was great. He taught us a ton and even let me help out a bit. Imagine yours truly hoisting the main and trimming the jib. At least that's what I think I did.

I'd never been on a ship this size before, so I was also surprised to see that the galley was bigger than my kitchen at home. Nicer, too. I couldn't help but think how cool a four-day bed and breakfast sail on this ship would be. They also do shorter sunset cruises with gourmet edibles on board. Nice!

We had a great afternoon sailing Grand Traverse Bay aboard the Tall Ship Manitou, and it was another one of those experiences that reminded me how lucky we Michigan folk are. If you're looking for another outstanding adventure, whether it's just you, you and the wife or the whole family, set sail on the Manitou. And now that I'm an old salt, you can even tell 'em Tom sent ya. I promise they won't make you walk the plank!

On UTR we're always looking for cool or unusual places to stay, even if it means driving a few extra miles. So we headed seventeen miles straight north out of Traverse City, up the Old Mission Peninsula through some of Michigan's most beautiful wine country. Why did we drive so far? I'll tell you why: to stay at the oldest continually operating inn in northern Michigan.

The Old Mission Inn
(231) 223-7770
18599 Mission Rd., Traverse City, MI 49686
www.oldmissioninn.com

The Old Mission Inn was built in 1869, and their motto is, "Come as strangers, leave as friends." Angie Jensen and her husband Bruce own and operate the inn, and they've gone to great lengths to preserve the inn's incredible history. The grounds are breathtaking and the inside of the inn is an incredible walk back through time. Believe it or not, Angie and Bruce are only the fourth owners of the inn. The first owner had it thirty-three years, the second forty-three and the third fifty-three. They've only owned it fifteen, so they have a lot more history yet to help create at the inn.

The Old Mission Inn is a place where you can relax, regroup, and at the same time, learn a tremendous amount about northern Michigan's illustrious past. It's a place whose former guest list not only spans the globe but includes the likes of Joe Louis and even Babe Ruth.

The Old Mission Inn really completed our trip and gave us a true appreciation for Michigan's rich history. As for Traverse City, it doesn't have everything; it has everything, and then some.

Story behind the name:
That's a Really Big Tree

There are trees. Then, there are really big trees. Tom's son thought that this tree we found up north was a real big tree.

Chapter 17

Season 2, Episode 4

•Muskegon
•Flint

The city of Muskegon sits on a natural harbor that makes it one of the best places to live in Michigan if you love the water. People there call it "the lake effect," and it's easy to see why. They have miles of shoreline with beautiful sand beaches and places to live right near the water, and if you're into any kind of boating, it truly is the place to be. As for the city, it's got a great downtown that's full of history, and the classic architecture alone makes Muskegon worth the trip. There are also places to stay right in town, some where you can even boat right up to your hotel. And if that's not cool, I don't know what is!

Mia & Grace
(231) 725-9500
1133 3rd St., Muskegon, MI 49441
www.miaandgrace.com

Mia & Grace is a restaurant that's really turning culinary heads in western Michigan. It's owned and operated by Jeremy and Jamie Paquin (along with help from their little daughter Mia) and when it comes to food, I promise you won't find anyone more passionate than these two.

It's a relatively new restaurant where they do things the old fashioned way. Everything that comes out of their amazing kitchen is made from scratch. I mean everything. They literally hand make everything you eat, from the catsup, mustard and soda pop to the bread, pastas, sausages, pickles and cheese. They even grow a ton of their own spices. Good thing they live right above the restaurant, because these two food gurus put in an incredible amount of hours. But to them it's a genuine labor of love.

Jeremy and Jamie are also on a first-name basis with over a dozen local farmers. Everything is local, fresh and full of flavor, and they really like to surprise you with the menu. They creatively combine familiar foods with unexpected and even exotic ingredients for a dining experience you'll be telling your friends about. From the BBQ duck crepes and their signature homemade hotdog (incredible), to their blue cheese stuffed dates and the bacon melt with fried oysters, everything will surprise and delight you. All in a place that's comfortable, casual and totally unpretentious.

If you're looking for someone who absolutely personifies today's food movement, Jeremy and Jamie are just that. If you're a genuine foodie, you know what to do next. :-)

USS Silversides
(231) 755-1230
1346 Bluff St., Muskegon, MI 49441
www.silversidesmuseum.org

Next, we visited something I had no idea was even in Michigan, let alone Muskegon. It's the **USS Silversides,** an authentic World War II submarine that's permanently docked at the Great Lakes Naval Memorial and Museum. It's a great piece of history you can explore on your own, take a guided tour of or if you call ahead, even arrange to spend the night on. How cool is that!

It's amazing to me that over ninety men lived, worked, ate and slept in such a confined space. After seeing submarines in movies all my life, it was so fascinating to actually be inside one. It really gives you a true appreciation of the men who served on these submarines during World War II.

If you're looking for something different, cool, fun and educational to do, the USS Silversides is right in Muskegon. It's an experience I guarantee you won't forget.

The next day I did two things I've never done before. One was to get up at four o'clock in the morning. I didn't know that time even existed. The other was to go charter fishing. And if you saw our Houghton Lake episode, you know that the only fish I ever caught came out of a bait tank.

Margie J. Sport Fishing Charter
(231) 799-2229
Great Lakes Marina, 1920 Lake Shore Dr., Slip B-2, Muskegon, MI 49441
www.fishmuskegon.com

When we showed up at the dock in the dark, all I kept thinking was, "Is this something you have to be a real fisherman to enjoy? I don't know the first, second or even the third thing about fishing." Well, as soon as I met Captain Drew Morris and his son Chris, I knew we were in good hands. They run the **Margie J. Sport Fishing Charter** in Muskegon, and they know everything you need to know, so you don't need to know anything. Which was good, because that early in the morning, I barely know how to tie my own shoes!

Right after Captain Drew confiscated our bananas (I guess they're bad luck on fishing boats), we set out for his favorite hot spot. Here's where I have to say that you really don't need to know anything at all about fishing to have a great time on a charter like this. Drew and his son Chris were a boatload of fun. They had everything we needed for fishing, and they taught us everything we needed to know (not to mention they did ninety percent of the work for us). I did, however, burn my biceps a bit by proudly reeling in a fourteen-pound king salmon. During the thrilling man vs. fish fight, we affectionately named the fish Steve. Don't ask.

Dockers Fish House
(231) 755-0400
3505 Marina View Point, Muskegon, MI 49441
www.dockersfishhouse.com

The day was a blast, and the entire crew got to reel in a fish, including my son Anthony. We caught three huge king salmon and two magnificent steelhead. The coolest surprise of the day was that Captain Drew has a special arrangement with a great restaurant right on the water called **Dockers Fish House**. So we docked, gave the chef two of our catch and he prepared a gourmet meal that totally blew us away. Actually, when we were done, a hurricane couldn't have blown us away; we were so full. But having your own catch prepared and served like that really brought the whole trip full circle and made it an exceptional Michigan experience.

As for Muskegon, now I can say I've been there, and that I'll be back again and again!

I'm a big believer in trusting how a city feels, and Flint feels good. I love the way the downtown is laid out. It's that perfect size I keep talking about. Big enough to have a great urban feel, but small enough to be completely walkable. There's modern and affordable urban living right downtown, and UM-Flint gives the city creative life and energy. I like it! Like a lot of Michigan cities, Flint is going through an exciting renaissance, and right now is a great time to live, visit or even invest there.

The Durant Hotel
(810) 900-4000
607 E. 2nd Ave., Flint, MI 48502
www.thedurant.com

From 1920 until 1973, **The Durant Hotel** was one of Michigan's premier hotels. Named after GM Founder and Flint Native William C. Durant, the hotel became a symbol of Flint's prominence and success. People from around the world came to Flint to do business, vacation and just be seen there. The Durant was a true Michigan icon but after hard economic times sat in ruin for years. Thanks to developers Richard Karp and Kevin Prater, this important part of Flint's heritage is back in business.

The building is now contemporary urban loft apartments and retail space, and it's thriving. What they've done with the Durant is nothing short of spectacular. It's been restored to its original grandeur and sits again as a cornerstone of progress and renewal in Flint. If you want to see an important part of Flint's past and future, check out the Durant.

Hoffman's Deco Deli & Café
(810) 238-0074
503 Garland St., Flint, MI 48503
www.hoffmansdecodeli.com

You know, some things just naturally go together, like peanut butter and jelly and liver and onions. Oh, and those little fish shaped crackers with that yellow cheese that comes out of a can. Mmmmmm... But when we were in Flint, we found a place that blew our minds. How about this combination: antiques and deli food. I know; it hurts just thinking about it. But at **Hoffman's Deco Deli & Café**... it hurts real good!

Hoffman's is the creative conglomeration of Mark Hoffman, his brother Heath and their father Nick. Upfront, it's a first-class, funky art deco deli that serves awesome sandwiches, salads and wraps. And in the back is an explosion of antiques the likes of which I've never seen before. It's crazy. It's wonderfully weird... and it totally works!

I have to say that this really is one of the funkiest, coolest places I've ever been to. And Nick, Mark and Heath are three of the coolest dudes you'll ever meet. Hoffman's has become the place for Flint's urbanites to eat, kick back and connect. The day we were there they even had an "Under the Radar" wrap on the menu. Nice!

As for Nick's Antique Emporium in the back, my wife Cathy is an antique aficionado and a classic clothing connoisseur. I took her to Hoffman's and her exact words were, "This place is to die for." The collection of collectables there is first class.

This is two generations working hard and thinking outside the box to make Flint a better place for the next generation. If you like good people, positive energy, great food and awesome antiques all smershed together, there's only one place I know of: Hoffmann's Deco Deli & Café.

Next we went to another place in Flint that completely blew our collective minds. If you like culture, science, music, art and history, it turns out Flint is a world-class destination.

Flint Institute of Arts
(810) 234-1695
1120 E. Kearsley St., Flint, MI 48503
www.FlintArts.org

Just east of downtown we discovered the **Flint Cultural Center**. In ten different institutions on one thirty-three-acre campus, Flint has everything you need to enrich your life and expand your horizons. From the Sloan Museum, which chronicles Flint's automotive history, to the beautiful Whiting Auditorium where they have incredible shows, to the world class Flint Institute of Arts, the Flint Institute of Music, the Flint Youth Theatre and Michigan's second largest planetarium, this place has something for everyone.

Take my word for it. Take some time, do some research and take the whole family there. The Flint Cultural Center is a beautiful, fun and amazing place for your mind. We had a blast!

As for Flint, the only way to know it is to see it for yourself! And if you haven't seen it in a while, you're gonna like what you see.

Story behind the name:
Fishon!

Charter fishing should really be called "Reeling in a Fish." FishON! is what the cap'n yells just before you reel until your forearm is screaming. Then you reel for another twenty minutes.

Chapter 18

Season 2, Episode 5

Charlevoix
Detroit

Charlevoix really is one of the most beautiful towns in Michigan. On one side you've got Round Lake and passage to Lake Charlevoix and on the other side is Lake Michigan. So if you're into boating or the beach life, it's absolute heaven. Charlevoix also offers great places to live and vacation, and the town has this comfortable sophistication about it that says, "Hey, I'm in the right place." It's a small yet iconic Michigan vacation town that really leaves you with a big impression.

Charlevoix was just recently named one of the prettiest towns in America by Forbes, and there's one man who's done a lot to make that happen. Now, I'd heard of Mister Rogers, Mr. Ed and even Mister Potato Head. But Mr. Petunia?

Meet Dale Boss (aka **Mr. Petunia**). He's lived there for all of his eighty-plus years, and he's a man with a single mission: to make Charlevoix Beautiful. Thirty years ago, he launched an effort to plant five miles of petunias through the heart of the city. The program took root, and every summer for the past three decades, Mr. Petunia has headed out at four o'clock in the morning seven days a week to water his beloved flowers. He's put more than forty million gallons of water on almost two million petunias.

The early years were tough, but now thanks to help from the community, he drives around a mechanical watering truck that gets the job done in much less time. This really is a community effort. Every spring a thousand local residents grab thousands of flats of flowers and plant the entire five mile stretch (both sides of the street) in an hour and a half. Incredible. Then they all head down to the town park for a big picnic.

Mr. Petunia is so dedicated to this task it's inspiring. In the thirty plus years he's been doing it, he's never missed a day. And the only days he gets off are when it rains. Thank you Mother Nature. Quite honestly, if there were more people like Dale Boss in the world, it would be a much better place. Even without a cape, he's a true super hero. Lucky for us, we've got Mr. Petunia right where he belongs, and right here in Michigan.

After we parted ways with Mr. Petunia, we thought we were having problems with one of the microphones. Turns out it was actually my stomach growling, so we set out to find some substantial sustenance.

Roquette Burger Bistro
(231) 237-9016
103 Park Ave., Charlevoix, MI 49720

We heard that the chef over at **Roquette Burger Bistro** was a real nice guy and that he was making incredible, fresh, local foods. So we set out to find him. It was easy. He's right downtown.

Paul Ramey has created a sophisticated little place that takes the term burger joint to a whole new level. It's actually a gourmet, locally sourced burger bistro with a creative flare and flavors that will bring you back for more, more and more. Paul is an admitted food geek and his passion for food totally shows. He came from the iconic Michigan preserves producer American Spoon. There he learned that simple ingredients treated properly make the best food.

Paul started growing a leafy salad green called arugula (roquette is French for arugula), craved a good burger one day, took a leap of faith and is now serving so much more than these marvelous meat sandwiches. He visits local farms almost every day, finds fresh ingredients and is making some sensational dishes in a kitchen so small, everything (including his homemade catsup) is literally within arm's reach.

Paul is fascinating to talk to, a blast to watch create in the kitchen and has made such a great impression in Charlevoix that people are coming from near and far to sample his high-brow chow. We had a great time at Roquette Burger Bistro and some awesome food. This new foodie movement sure has made producing this show a fulfilling experience, with the emphasis on both full and filling.

Authors Note: Last we heard, Roquette Burger Bistro was changing its focus to a gourmet BBQ joint. The new name will be "SOW - Smoke On The Water" and they will still serve the Bacon Jam Burger, Wild Mushroom Burger and Truffle Fries. The restaurant will continue to source locally and serve incredible edibles. They'll just be doing it barbecue style!

Mushroom Houses
Charlevoix Historical Society
(231) 547-0373
103 State St., Charlevoix, MI 49720
www.chxhistory.com

If you've ever wondered where hobbits and the Vernors Gnome go when they leave the shire and go on vacation, I'm pretty sure I found their summer homes in Charlevoix. Some people call them the **Mushroom Houses**, and some people say actual munchkins live there. All I know is the only place you'll see them is Charlevoix. And they're all the work of one man… Earl Young.

From 1918 through the 50s, Earl designed and built thirty homes in Charlevoix, and they range from the whimsical to the bizarre to the spectacular. All this from a guy who dropped out of architecture school. These homes are unique because their designs are extremely organic. Some of the roofs appear to be melting, and they're made completely from all natural materials and locally sourced stone.

Marsha Braun from the **Charlevoix Historical Society** took us on a driving tour of these beautiful homes, and we were amazed. They're all privately owned, so you can't go inside or on the property, but just driving by these unusual houses is totally worth it. From his famous "Half House" (which looks like Frank Lloyd Wright meets Fred Flintstone) to the magnificent "Boulder Manor," his work is original, natural and definitely one of a kind. The homes are mostly southwest of town. The locals will help you find your way.

Earl Young may not be with us anymore, but the way he built these homes, they'll be there for a long time for all of us to see. If you get a chance, take a tour of these gnome homes.

And if you get a chance, check out a sunset or two in Charlevoix. By the time you leave, I guarantee you won't want to.

There's so much developing and happening in Detroit right now that every time you turn around there's another reason to go there. You can feel the change in attitude and energy. So if you've got a spirit for adventure and discovery, right now the Motor City is a great place to be.

D:hive
(313) 962-4590
1253 Woodward Ave., Detroit, MI 48226
www.dhivedetroit.org

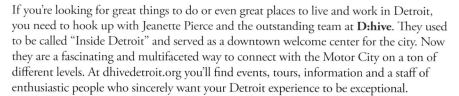

If you're looking for great things to do or even great places to live and work in Detroit, you need to hook up with Jeanette Pierce and the outstanding team at **D:hive**. They used to be called "Inside Detroit" and served as a downtown welcome center for the city. Now they are a fascinating and multifaceted way to connect with the Motor City on a ton of different levels. At dhivedetroit.org you'll find events, tours, information and a staff of enthusiastic people who sincerely want your Detroit experience to be exceptional.

Whether you're just visiting, you're moving there or even if you already live in Detroit, D:hive will make a personal connection with you and get you what you need. If you want to live, work, engage or even start a project or business in Detroit, they can totally get you going in the right direction.

Jeannette hooked the crew and me up with a historic Segway tour of the city that was educational, inspirational and a whole lot of fun. The tour started at Campus Martius Park, which was recently named one of the most transformative parks in America, and ended up traveling along Detroit's beautiful new river walk. It was an awesome, one-of-a-kind experience.

If you want to learn about the real Detroit, connect with the folks at D:hive. They'll check you out, hook you up, plug you in and get you buzzing around town in no time.

As you probably know, I've got quite a reputation for being a trouble shooter, danger seeker and a pretty good third-rate investigative reporter. So when I heard there were supposedly no grocery stores in Detroit, I decided to do some digging. After thoroughly interrogating Jim and Eric (they're genuine foodies) I discovered a place in Southwest Detroit that I fell in love with in three… two… one… guacamole!

Honeybee Market
(313) 237-0295
2443 Bagley, Detroit, MI 48216
www.honeybeemkt.com

Honeybee Market is by far the cleanest, most organized and well stocked specialty grocery store I have ever been in. It's lovingly owned and operated by Tammy and Ken Koehler, and they have about as much pride in this place as they do great foods.

The first thing I noticed when I walked in the front door was, that's right, free homemade guacamole and chips. I love guacamole. To me, it's its own food group, so I unapologetically partook.

Well, about ten minutes and four light green stains on my shirt later, I waddled into the store and instantly noticed how incredibly clean and well organized it was. A place for everything, and everything in its place. And if something is removed for purchase, it's immediately replaced before you can even say, "Holy guacamole." The selection there is also truly international. From the normal every day to the exotic hard-to-find items and fresh produce, it's all there.

Tammy and Ken are genuine and real people who love where they live and love connecting with this community through food. With passion, pride and plenty of elbow grease, they've turned this market into a food destination for people who love quality and variety. They treat you and feed you like family, and that kind of care is priceless. It you want a full and filling reason to come to Southwest Detroit, come to Honey Bee Market. If you can get past the guacamole at the front door, you'll do fine.

Detroit Film Theater at the DIA
(313) 833-3237
5200 Woodward Ave., Detroit, MI 48202
www.dia.org/dft/index.asp

The name **Detroit Film Theater** is one of those names that in one way says exactly what it is… "It's a theater that shows films in Detroit." But at the same time, the name doesn't even begin to tell you what the DFT is really all about and what it means to the City of Detroit.

If you're looking for a classic film experience that goes way beyond the mega mall movie madness, just go to the east entrance of the Detroit Institute of Arts, and there you'll find the Detroit Film Theater.

To find out more about this incredible place, the first thing we did was find Elliot Wilhelm. Not only is he the host of "Friday Night Film Festival" on Detroit Public Television, he's the film curator and founder of the Detroit Film Theater. Elliot has spent his entire life watching, learning and loving movies. And his passion for the fine art of filmmaking is why the Detroit Film Theater is alive and well today.

We're all so used to watching classic cinema on our TVs now that we're missing out on how these movie gems were meant to be seen: on the big screen. And to see them on a big screen in the historic theater they have at the DIA is what this experience is all about. If you want to add a little richness, variety and culture to your next movie night out, try doing more than just driving to the massive mall megaplex. Yes, the Detroit Film Theater is a theater that shows films in Detroit. But once you see a movie there, I guarantee you'll need a lot of words to tell your friends about it.

You'll also need a lot of words to tell your friends about all the cool stuff happening in Detroit right now. Because there's so much going on there that… well, I just don't have enough words.

Story behind the name:
He's Regular Size

A common joke when Tom is telling a story. For example:
"Eric's a HUGE fan of corn nuts. Actually he's regular size."
We groan and laugh and slap our foreheads.

Chapter 19

Season 2, Episode 6

•Ludington
•Rogers City

Ludington is another one of those Michigan cities that has everything you need for great living. For starters, the state park there is one of the best anywhere. It's got miles of beautiful sand beaches, huge sand dunes to explore and tons of hiking trails. As for the city, you couldn't ask for a better setting. Ludington Avenue takes you right down to the shores of Lake Michigan, and all along the way you've got great shops, cool restaurants and some pretty unique art galleries. There are also great neighborhoods just steps from downtown.

S.S. Badger
(800) 841-4243
701 Maritime Dr., Ludington, MI 49431
www.ssbadger.com

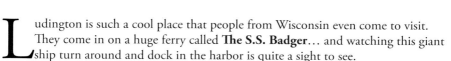

L udington is such a cool place that people from Wisconsin even come to visit. They come in on a huge ferry called **The S.S. Badger**… and watching this giant ship turn around and dock in the harbor is quite a sight to see.

The Blu Moon Bistro-Café
(231) 843-2001
125 S. James St., Ludington, MI 49431
www.theblumoon.net

We rolled into town about lunch time, and boy were we hungry. But when aren't we hungry on UTR? It wasn't long before we found our foodie fun-house for the day. You've heard the old expression, "Once in a blue moon." Well, from what we heard on the streets of Ludington, people eat at this place a lot more than that. If you read the reviews, **The Blu Moon Bistro-Café** is the best food for miles around, and Marilyn Cunic and her husband Randy are just the kind of people you'd expect to have a place this cool. Marilyn has a wonderful, bigger-than-life personality and Randy is the coolest dude around.

The Blu Moon Bistro is a true family business. Daughters Jordan and Lille (and now little Domonic) help make the place click, and son-in-law Jason is a very talented French-trained chef who also successfully serves an array of worldly delights including succulent, savory sushi. They moved back to Michigan from Colorado and North Carolina to open their dream restaurant, and now they've won the hearts (and stomachs) of the locals. The "Over the Moon" rooftop dining there is a very cool place to eat, and the full bar makes it all magical.

From the amazing food that comes out of their kitchen to the artistic and welcoming atmosphere, it's no wonder the Cunics have found success and happiness in Ludington.

After lunch we were lucky enough to run into tennis legend and TV celebrity **Murphy Jensen**. Murph and his brother Luke were the 1993 French Open Doubles champs.

Ludington is his hometown and the Blu Moon is his favorite place to chow. After talking about how much we both love that part of Michigan, Murph said it best when he said, "Most people call Ludington paradise, but I get to call it home." If you ever see Murphy Jensen on the streets of Ludington, after you've had one of the mostest funnest conversations of your life, make sure to tell him the UTR boys said hi.

A.M. Galleries
(231) 845-6648
115 W. Ludington Ave., Ludington, MI 49431
www.amgalleries.com

One thing I've discovered doing this show is that Michigan is all about art, and local artist **Andy Thomas** is all about Ludington. He owns **A.M. Galleries** in town, and he gives local artists everything they need to succeed. I always said that if you want to know more about the pulse and personality of a community, talk to some of the local artists. Andy has helped create and accelerate the growing art culture in Ludington. It's become a movement that's moving artists to Ludington and turning this area into the art Mecca for Michigan's middle mitten.

Creative, motivated people like Andy Thomas made us glad we came to Ludington… and even gladder he's doing his thing right here in Michigan. If you want to see some incredible art and hang out with some of the talented people who create it, check out A.M. Galleries.

The Mitten Bar
(231) 843-7616
109 W. Ludington Ave., Ludington, MI 49431
www.mittenbar.com

Next, we ran into a brand new watering hole in Ludington that features all drinks Michigan. That's right, if it's made in the Great Lake State and makes you feel funny, it's probably there. It's called **The Mitten Bar**, and on the sign outside you'll see the words, "A Michigan Ideology." That's because owners Megan Payment and Brian Josefowicz focus on buying from local breweries, wineries and distilleries only. They firmly believe that the way to a strong Michigan is through supporting and buying from the people that surround you. So they tirelessly searched near and not too far to bring you the best adult beverages Michigan has to offer.

Megan and Brian created a destination for people who love local libations. They've also gone beyond that by featuring live music and special events every week. It's a great place to go and learn more about all the incredible potables our state has to offer. It's really nice to see young people living their dreams right here in Michigan, especially when a frosty cold adult malted beverage is involved… bonus!

Ludington truly is one of Michigan's west coast jewels. We came, we saw, we ate, we drank, we laughed, and if we play our cards right, we'll be back to do it all over again.

When we heard that **Rogers City** had the only stop light in Presque Isle County, we didn't really know what to expect, but I'll be honest: this town was one of the nicest surprises we've run into yet on UTR. The town is spacious, classic Americana, and it's spotless, with street after street of well-kept homes and beautifully landscaped yards. It's the kind of town you roll into and say, "I could totally live here." Rogers City is also a harbor town with a great nautical history and very cool places to live and play right on Lake Huron.

Tour America Bike Shop
(989) 734-3946
268 N. 2nd St., Rogers City, MI 49779

After a quick tour of town (aka, we got lost) we saw a place that looked so crazy cool, we just had to stop. It's called **Tour America Bike Shop** and when you walk into this place, you will be amazed and pleasantly overwhelmed. If Pee Wee Herman didn't buy his bike here, he sure should have.

This crazy bike shop is part funhouse, part racing museum, part antique store, part flea market and the complete brainchild of Marcus Opie, the mastermind behind the mayhem. But don't be fooled. Even in the midst of this eclectic conglomeration is a serious bike shop that can provide you with everything you need, no matter what kind of biking you do.

After giving up race car driving in his earlier years, Marcus went to Greenfield Village in Dearborn, saw the Wright Brothers' original workshop, got inspired, got up to Rogers City and opened for business. Oh, and in the meantime, he collected about eleven billion cool and unusual things to display around his shop.

Marcus is a fascinating character, and almost everything in his place has a story. If you're looking for some new trees to pass and squirrels to dodge, come see Marcus at Tour America in Rogers City. He'll get you what you need and even tell you about some beautiful new places to ride. P.S. Marcus goes south every winter, so make sure to call ahead.

Domaci Art Gallery
(989) 734-3035
169 N. 3rd St., Rogers City, MI 49779
www.domaciartgallery.com

They say art imitates life. So if you're looking for a creative reflection of the community, do what we always do on UTR: talk to an artist. Mary and Tim Pritchard are the proud proprietors of **Domaci Art Gallery**. It's a hip, new place in Rogers City that features some very innovative Michigan artists. You'll find everything from modern wall art to Mary's creative ceramic jewelry and even cool funky things like boxes made out of hundred-year-old reclaimed wooden ship beams. When you walk into this place, you think you're walking into a gallery in New York City, and as many as sixty Michigan artists will be on display at any given time. Absolutely worth a stop.

While we were there I also got to meet and spend time with young Rogers City artist **Bailey Budnik**. Bailey is extremely smart, amazingly creative and way beyond his years. I was mowing lawns at thirteen. Bailey is making almost life-sized abstract robots and other really cool stuff with his found-object art. Very progressive and very cool. Keep your eye on this young man.

Truth is… we had so much fun at Domaci that the entire crew was invited to a home cooked, gourmet dinner at the Budniks. The food and hospitality they served up totally made us feel like family. They even put us up for the night. I don't think we've ever met better people in a better town. Thanks, Budnik Family!

Plath's Meats
(989) 734-2232
116 S. 3rd St., Rogers City, MI 49779
www.plathsmeats.com

Rogers City really is a beautiful city and a great place to meet people. Speaking of meat people, if you're driving through town and you spot a giant statue of a smiling hotdog on the road, there's a good chance you've found **Plath's Meats**. Since 1913 they've been proving positive that tradition is a great recipe for success. John Plath and his brothers are the third generation of meat men behind an age-old family philosophy.

What meats do they specialize in? They hand craft homemade pork products like smoked bacon, ham and a variety of sausages. They also have an incredible smoked pork loin that is known internationally, because they ship their Michigan-made specialty meats around the world. They use the best ingredients and produce all their products with great care and pride. Their bacon is so good, it's actually its own food group. You can taste the tradition because they still do things the old fashioned way. If you like savory smoked meats, you've got to meet the meat men at Plath's.

Knaebe's Mmmunchy Krunchy Apple Farm and Cider Mill
(989) 734-2567
2622 Karsten Rd., Rogers City, MI 49779
www.mmmunchykrunchyapplefarm.com

Have you ever heard of an apple farm and cider mill that grows thirty different kinds of dwarf trees or that has a donut-making robot? Neither had I, until we discovered **Knaebe's Mmmunchy Krunchy Apple Farm and Cider Mill**. It's a wonderfully wacky place that's run by two of the most sincere, delightful and crazy people you'll ever meet… Ma and Pa Knaebe.

Now, the fact that we were coming must have leaked out, because the reception we got was a production to say the least. There was singing, hugging, a big sign, general craziness and before I knew what was happening, I was in the kitchen with a donut-making robot they lovingly refer to as Bob. I think I ate as many as I made. Bob didn't seem to mind.

This place is simply amazing. It's so cool inside that it looks like it was art directed for a Hollywood movie. Planes hanging from the ceiling, trains running around the walls and colorful displays of funky stuff Ma and Pa have collected over the years. But not only does Knaebe's offer all kinds of eye candy, they also make and bake incredible pies, cookies, doughnuts and cakes. There's cool gift stuff for the folks and even train rides for the kids.

Now, I know I say a lot of things are amazing, but I've been to a gazillion cider mills in my life, and this place is amazing. So, if you want friendly, cool, crazy and tasty, check out Knaebe's Mmmunchy Crunchy. And, if you want another great Michigan place to explore, try Rogers City. We did. And we will again. If we don't get lost.

Story behind the name:
I Have the Feeling
I'm Being Watched...
You ever get that feeling?

You ever get that feeling when a three-foot-tall eye is on the wall behind you?

Chapter 20

Season 2, Episode 7

• Ypsilanti
• Leland

Ypsilanti is one of those Michigan cities that may be hard
to spell, but it's real easy to like. It's urban, it's walkable and
it's got a great, earthy energy to it. The city is filled with historic
places, some pretty unique shopping and beautiful neighborhoods
that surround the downtown. And being attached to Eastern Michigan
University keeps the city wired, inspired and far from tired. It definitely
keeps this city moving forward.

Ypsilanti is also one of those Michigan cities that if you've ever met someone who's spent any time there, they have a real passion for it. **Amy Probst** is one of those people. Amy is an accomplished writer and actor who loves Ypsi so much, she offered to be our guide for the day. Good thing, because she kept us laughing and learning about this great place the entire time we were there.

We met up with Amy on something the locals call "The Tridge." It's a really cool three-way bridge that connects Ypsilanti's hip, historic Depot Town with Riverside Park and Frog Island. If you're looking for a beautiful place to spend an afternoon, this is definitely it.

Before we ventured off, Amy told me that her favorite thing about Ypsi is its overwhelming sense of community. No matter who you are, what you do, what you look like or where you live, everyone connects and cares for each other. A wonderful social amenity indeed!

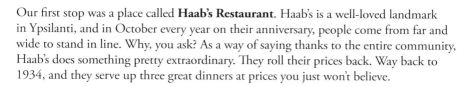

Haab's Restaurant
(734) 483-8200
18 W. Michigan Ave., Ypsilanti, MI 48197
www.haabsrestaurant.com

Our first stop was a place called **Haab's Restaurant**. Haab's is a well-loved landmark in Ypsilanti, and in October every year on their anniversary, people come from far and wide to stand in line. Why, you ask? As a way of saying thanks to the entire community, Haab's does something pretty extraordinary. They roll their prices back. Way back to 1934, and they serve up three great dinners at prices you just won't believe.

On that special day, owner Mike Kabat always shows up in full top hat and tails. He started this tradition back in 1981, and he's keeping it alive for all the right reasons. Back then, as a way of saying thanks to its loyal customers for supporting Haab's during tough economic times, Mike decided to give back. So he rolled the prices back to when the original Otto Haab opened the doors there in 1934. Get this: the chicken dinner basket was fifty cents, the spaghetti dinner only forty cents and the barbeque sandwich a measly twenty cents.

Well, it wasn't long before the aroma of the food got to us (like we need an excuse to eat) so I sat down with the crew and enjoyed a complete chicken dinner for only forty cents. The real shocker came when they brought the bill. Our table of four ate for $2.12. Incredible.

You've heard the old expression, "You are what you eat." Well, at Haab's Restaurant, they are what they serve, and that's a ton of community spirit. Every town should have a restaurant with a heart as big as Haab's. As for the prices, thank goodness they don't keep them that low year round, or I'd be a Tom and a half.

Enjoying a sense of place in a community is so much easier and fun when you live right in the middle of it, so if you're looking to connect with a great town, check out Ypsilanti. A lot of the great old buildings are being brought back to life and converted into some very cool downtown loft spaces. Amy lived right downtown for years and loved it.

The Tap Room
(734) 482-5320
201 W. Michigan Ave., Ypsilanti, MI 48197
www.taproomypsi.com

Ypsi has great food downtown and great places to live in town. But how 'bout a unique place to tip back a few frosty cold adult malted beverages with some friendly conversation? No problem. If you're looking for a cool place to rub elbows with some real characters, **The Tap Room** spells character with a capital C. The history, the stories and the people make for a very earthy and entertaining evening.

The first thing you'll notice when you get there is that the door handle is not much higher than your knees. Legend has it that during World War II, little people worked in the airplane wings at the Willow Run Bomber Plant nearby. The original owner accommodated these pint-sized patriots by installing a lower handle on the front door. There's even a portion of the bar inside that was made shorter so they could reach their drinks. A very cool thing to do.

Brian and Lisa Brickley are continuing the Tap Room's great tradition with good food, great live music and an atmosphere that makes anyone fit in instantly. This place is so interesting and unpredictable, the night we were there, we ran into the international dreidel spinning champion Alan Black. I challenged him. He won.

Amy was right; the people of Ypsi have a genuine love for the Tap Room. It's a great place to let your hair down, let it all out and have a good time. It's real, it's fun and full of interesting people. Just like Ypsilanti and Michigan.

After a great adventure in Ypsilanti, we headed five hours northwest to one of my very favorite places, the beautiful little resort town of **Leland**. It's located right on the shores of Lake Michigan in one of the most beautiful parts of the Lower Peninsula. If you're looking for a classic Michigan vacation experience, Leland is that place.

Just south of town we made one very important stop at a place that was so much fun to say, we stayed a while.

Baabaazuzu
(231) 256-7176
1006 S. Sawmill Rd., Lake Leelanau, MI 49653
www.baabaazuzu.com

Baabaazuzu is another great innovative Michigan success story. They make one-of-a-kind fashion creations out of castaway wool sweaters that are destined for a landfill. It may sound simple at first, but a lot of Michigan creativity and ingenuity goes into the process. Sue and Kevin Burns created Baabaazuzu and are now exporting their crazy creations around the world.

It all started with a laundry error at home when Kevin accidentally dried a whole load of wool sweaters. (Been there. Done that.) Sue got creative when she decided to make lemonade out of lemons by cutting up and making matching hats and mittens out of the shrunken sweaters for their little girls. That's when the proverbial light bulb went on over her head, and now she and her incredible staff are turning yesterday's wool garments into today's high fashion.

Everything they make is cut, sewn and assembled by human hands right at Baabaazuzu. It's so amazing to think that every single piece of clothing they make is a completely unique, one-of-a-kind reclaimed creation. No two things are alike and they make all kinds of women's and men's clothing and accessories.

At Baabaazuzu, they like to say that when you wear their apparel, you'll never, ever pass yourself on the street. I'm not even sure that's possible anyway, but I do know one thing for sure. This stuff is funky, cool, colorful and it's made right here in Michigan.

Riverside Inn and Restaurant
(231) 256-9971
302 E. River St., Leland, MI 49654
www.theriverside-inn.com

This was my crew's first trip to Leland, so we needed a nice place to stay, a great place to eat and we also wanted to learn a little history about the area. So on a tip from our new friends at Baabaazuzu, we discovered the historic **Riverside Inn**. It's a 110-year-old inn and gourmet restaurant that's located right on the Leland River, just a block west of town. People say it's one of the most romantic places you can visit in Michigan. After seeing it, I agree.

Owner and innkeeper Kate Vilter made us feel right at home. The Riverside Inn is a perfect fit for Leland, and Kate and her mom Barb have done an outstanding job of retaining its original beauty. The setting is absolutely beautiful and the dining experience is most certainly worth a stop there. The food truly is gourmet, with an emphasis on sourcing fresh and local. The menu is varied and very, very good. Their bar is also something you should check out. It's classic and extremely cool.

If you're planning a special weekend, a romantic getaway or if you just want to go someplace really nice, the Riverside Inn in Leland sure is a swell place.

Fish Town
(231) 256-8878
203 E. Cedar St., P.O. Box 721, Leland, MI 49654
www.FishtownMI.org

In Leland, right down by the docks is an awesome place called **Fish Town**. It's an authentic old fishing village with cool shops and great places to eat. This has always been one of my family's favorite places to spend an afternoon. You can get everything from Michigan-made wines and cheeses to candy and clothing. But the coolest thing about Fish Town is that it's not one of those fabricated, recreated tourist traps; it's an authentic old fishing village that's got enough history and atmosphere to take you way back into Michigan's past. It's a very unique place that attracts people from across the country.

Carlson's Fish
(231) 256-9801
205 W. River, P.O. Box 406, Leland, MI 49654
www.carlsonsfish.com

Something a lot of people don't know is that Fish Town is also still a real working fishing village. All kinds of Great Lakes fish are caught, cleaned and sold right there on the docks, and if you're looking for fresh fish, **Carlson's** of Fish Town is the place to get it. We caught the folks at Carlson's in the middle of processing the day's catch. Their family has been fishing these waters for six generations now. Great people. Great fresh fish.

Manitou Island Transit
(231) 256-9061
P.O. Box 1157, Leland, MI 49654
www.manitoutransit.com

Now, here's the under the radar part about Leland. Every year tons of people come to Fish Town. But most people don't know that if you get on a big boat at the end of the dock, you're only an hour and a half away from one of the best Michigan adventures you'll ever have. Since 1917 the Manitou Island Transit Company has been taking people out to explore both **North and South Manitou Island**. These two beautiful and rugged islands are about fifteen miles off shore and are part of the Sleeping Bear Dunes National Lakeshore.

The seas were high the day we went, so the ride out was an absolute blast. Holding onto the person next to you really is a great way to meet new people. We took the trip out to South Manitou Island. The island is only about three miles across but actually feels much bigger. No one really lives on the island anymore, but it's become an incredible place to camp or just explore for the day.

When we arrived we met up with Mike Grosvenor. His family has been there for generations, and he knows everything there is to know about these islands. Mike owns the Manitou Island Transit Company and they offer fun and educational tours of the entire island.

There were two things I'd heard about on the island that I really wanted to see. The first one was the **shipwreck of the Francisco Morazan**. It's a Liberian freighter that ran aground off the south end on the island back in 1960. It's unbelievably close to shore, and the huge ship is only partially submerged. It's quite a sight to see.

Next we went to explore what they call **The Valley of Giants**. It's a forest deep in the island's interior filled with mammoth and ancient cedar trees that date back to the time of Columbus. They're only in this one spot on the island. Unfortunately, new giant cedars aren't replacing these, and the Valley of Giants will one day disappear, so you really should put this on your Michigan bucket list and come see these trees.

The trip out to South Manitou Island was a great Michigan adventure. If you're going there for the very first time, I highly recommend you take the guided tour. It's a great way to see everything and learn all about the island.

As for Leland, if you're going there for the first time, I highly recommend you sit back, relax and enjoy it, because you'll never find another place like it.

Story behind the name:
Look Kids, Fish!

Mom always said, "Don't stand close to the fish when it's being unloaded from the truck." She was right. Tom took a mouthful of fish juice just as a whitefish hit the pile. Yum.

Chapter 21

Season 2, Episode 8

Detroit
Saugatuck

Every week thousands of people enjoy Detroit's Eastern Market, one of the most authentic urban adventures in the entire United States. This six-block public market is alive with great places to eat, cool places to shop and more than 250 vendors and merchants processing, wholesaling and retailing food, glorious food. You'll see people from all walks in search of fruits, vegetables, flowers, homemade jams, maple syrups, locally produced specialty food products and gourmet meats. It's a fascinating conglomeration of character, characters and crates and crates of fresh edibles.

Eastern Market
(313) 833-9300
2934 Russell, Detroit, MI 48207
www.detroiteasternmarket.com

The great thing about this urban melting pot is that it gives you fresh things to melt in your pot when you get home. **Eastern Market** is also becoming a Mecca for Michigan-made products. It's far from just being a market. It's also becoming a destination for people looking for a unique urban village where they can live, start a business… or both.

FD Lofts
(313) 832-3000
3434 Russell St. #108, Detroit, MI 48207
www.urbanlifedevelopment.com

One of the very cool and unique live/work places there is called the **FD Lofts**. Bob Heide of Urban Life Development is a progressive thinker who took this fascinating piece of history and turned it into a model of transformation and renewal in Detroit. This 1917 building was once the Detroit Fire Department's repair facility, where they would fix broken fire trucks. Originally, the site was used as the fire department's horse hospital and training track, where horses would learn to pull the pump wagons.

Now this beautifully restored building offers unique business space, live/work space and a variety of really cool lofts to live in. Even though the interior of the FD Lofts has all the modern amenities, a lot of the original design elements were left to give it a historical and industrial feel. It's very cool. The people who live and work there are looking for a true urban experience, and with Eastern Market right next door, they get that and more.

Detroit Manufacturing
(313) 529-2988
P.O. Box 07070, Detroit, MI 48207
www.detroitmfg.com

The FD Lofts are definitely a cool place to call home and a great place to set up shop. Robert Stanzler is one guy who's done just that. His company, **Detroit Manufacturing**, is just one of the cool businesses housed there, and his designs have turned Detroit pride into a fashion statement. He's a unique and talented artist whose hats, t-shirts, jackets and hoodies have been on the pages of GQ and Rolling Stone and worn by celebrities like Eminem, Aerosmith, U2 and the Foo Fighters, just to name a few. Robert's company is all about putting Detroit on your sleeve and supporting the city he loves.

No matter what your personal style is, Detroit Manufacturing is sure to have something to fit it. All their wearables are designed and made in the Motor City, so when you wear them, you know that you're supporting a Detroit company that's supporting Detroit. Robert is another great Michigan success story who was born, raised and stayed right in Detroit.

The Eastern Market has an urban authenticity unrivaled in North America that's steeped in tradition and fascinating stories. Thanks to dedicated supporters like Robert Stanzler, Bob Heide, Dan Carmody and all of the great people we met down there, I'm pretty sure this great market will be around for generations to come.

Saugatuck and its neighbor **Douglas** are two towns that really function as one incredible place to experience Michigan. I wouldn't really call them resort towns; they're more like resort communities. When you're there, you can really feel that it's more than just a great place to play; it's also a wonderful place to live and work. There's something for everybody, and everybody loves it there.

Both these port communities are on Kalamazoo Lake. Saugatuck is to the north and Douglas is to the south, and they're both just a stone's throw away from Lake Michigan over some beautiful tree-covered dune hills. And if you're into anything that floats, this place is heaven on earth. It really is a boater's paradise!

Sea Suites
(269) 426-0381
P.O. Box 1020, Saugatuck MI 49453
www.seasuites.com

With all the things to see and do, you're definitely going to want to spend a couple days there, and if you're looking for a place to stay, we found a pretty unique one. **Sea Suites** is an actual floating "boat and breakfast" docked right there in the harbor, and it's the only one of its kind in Michigan. Whether or not you feel at home on the water, innkeepers Sally Coder and Pete Morrison will definitely make sure you feel at home with them.

In 1998 Sally and Pete decided to move up north. When they couldn't decide whether to buy a cottage or a boat, they did both. This incredible floating Boat and Breakfast was specially designed and built for them, and it's got all the luxuries of a fine bed and breakfast. The rooms are super cool, the breakfasts super yummy and you couldn't ask for better company than Sally and Pete. They're genuinely special people who will help arrange all your fun or just let you relax and unwind.

So if you're there, check out the Sea Suites. Or should I say check in, because when it comes to making sure you have a good time and a comfortable stay, this place will definitely float your boat!

Now, one of my favorite things about Saugatuck is the climb up **Mount Baldhead** (for obvious reasons) and the best way to get there is the **Chain Ferry** that runs from downtown, right across the channel to the trailhead. This is the only remaining chain-driven ferry in the entire U.S., and it's been in use since 1838. The driver actually hand cranks the ferry across the channel to the other side, and that's where you'll find the stairway to baldness.

The climb up Mount Baldy is an invigorating 282 steps, so make sure you're hydrated and in pretty good shape. Or just take your sweet time like I did. The view from the top of downtown Saugatuck is incredible, and there's a dune climb on the other side that takes you all the way down to **Oval Beach** on Lake Michigan. Oval Beach is another Michigan gem that's been rated among the twenty-five best shorelines in the world by Conde Nast's Traveler, and if you spend a day there, you'll know why. It's beautiful.

Hungry Village Tours
(269) 857-1700
400 Culver St., Saugatuck, MI 49453
www.hungryvillagetours.com

Next, we were in for a real treat. We went on a relatively new tour you can take that shows you all the behind-the-scenes stuff that makes this area such a great food destination. It's called **Hungry Village Tours,** and if you're a foodie, David Geen will totally make you wish you lived there.

This is a small-group, guided tour that takes you from place to place where you get to meet the people at the forefront of the food movement there. We had fascinating and in-depth conversations with everyone from coffee roasters and artisan cheese makers to chefs and organic farmers. If you're into knowing the who, what, when, where, why and how of what I like to call real food, this is something you need to experience. After hopping in their official van, our tour included the following fascinating food stops:

- Uncommon Grounds Coffee Roasters
  www.uncommongroundscafe.com

- A goat cheese farm called Evergreen Lane Creamery
  www.evergreenlanefarm.com

- Fenn Valley Vineyards
  www.fennvalley.com

- An organic blueberry farm called Pleasant Hill Farm
  www.pleasanthillblueberryfarm.com

- Lunch at Salt of the Earth, a rustic American eatery and bakery
  www.saltoftheearthfennville.com

- Khnemu Studio and Fernwood Farm
  www.fernwoodfarmestate.com
  www.khnemustudio.com

- Summertime Market
  www.summertimemarket.com

It was a great day and our expert guide David Geen kept us tasting, laughing and learning the entire time. If you're looking for a totally unique and enlightening Michigan foodie experience, I highly recommend Hungry Village Tours.

The Red Dock Café
(269) 857-2185
219 Union St., Douglas, MI 49406

Our last discovery in Saugatuck might be a bit hard to find, but when you do find it, you'll swear someone put you into a Star Trek teleporter machine and sent you straight to the tropics. It's called **The Red Dock Café**, and it's actually way out on the end of a dock on Kalamazoo Lake. It's the same dock where you'll find the Sea Suites. This crazy place is a little bit Jamaican, a little Key West and a whole lotta fun. The atmosphere is relaxed, casual, tropical and the people are super friendly. The food and drinks are phenomenal, too. Just being there made even me feel kinda cool. To get there you can just walk to the end of the dock or do what the local boaters do… float in, tie up and get down.

The man with the plan is Chef Tony Amato, and the Red Dock is a total reflection of his personality and lifestyle. His background was in fine dining, but he woke up one morning and said to his wife, "I want to open a hotdog stand and play music real loud." They moved to Saugatuck, opened the Red Dock and never looked back. I've been going to this area for twenty-five years and never knew the Red Dock existed until now. It's a well kept secret in these parts and the magic of this place is all word of mouth. And if you're looking for live original music, it happens there every Sunday from four o'clock until eight o'clock in the evening.

Three things to keep in mind about The Red Dock: they're only open during the summer (which totally makes sense), they close every night at sundown and the place is cash only. So bring some green.

The three things you need to keep in mind about Saugatuck and Douglas are: come hungry, stay for a while and leave happy. That's what we did, and we had an awesome time.

Story behind the name:
Pop Pop Americano

Some songs get stuck in your head… then there's this little gem. If you know it, I'm sorry. If you don't, please don't go looking for it. It'll never leave your cranium.

When we were in Saugatuck we were trying to film an opening segment on water. There was a boat with a speaker system on board that The Who would find too loud. They kept blasting this song.

The horror.

Chapter 22

Season 2, Episode 9

• Grand Rapids
• Mt. Pleasant

Grand Rapids is a city that's full of innovation, forward motion and great energy. Everywhere you look, great things are happening. It's a metropolitan city with great restaurants, culture, history, beauty and tons of business opportunities. If you're looking for a place to live, work or play anywhere in the world, I'd put GR on your list.

Art Prize
41 Sheldon Blvd. SE, Grand Rapids, MI 49503
www.artprize.org

You know what I always say: if you don't know what to call something, just call it what it is. And that's exactly what **Art Prize** is: a huge art competition every fall in Grand Rapids where you get prizes if you win.

Actually, Art Prize is a lot more than that. It's become an art phenomenon, with nineteen days, three square miles, almost two hundred different venues and over 1,700 artists from around the world competing for almost a half million dollars in prize money. Everywhere you look in downtown GR you'll find some of the most amazing, creative and overwhelming art you'll see anywhere.

Grand Rapids has a great collaborative spirit, and the entire city embraces this colossal event. The entire downtown turns into a giant gallery with art literally everywhere. You'll see everything from colossal displays in public spaces to showcases in stores, lobbies and even on the sides of buildings. From giant sculptures and even mechanical contraptions to classic, modern and the abstract, every creative kind of art in every medium is represented. It's eye candy for the human spirit.

The real prize in Art Prize is what it does for the human condition. After experiencing it, you feel alive and proud to be a creature from Planet Earth. And even prouder to be from Michigan.

Next time you're looking for something cool to look at in a cool city with tons of cool people and cool things to do, check out Art Prize. It's one of the coolest things you'll ever do.

Ritch Branstrom
(906) 399-1572
www.adhocworkshop.com

One of the artists we followed through Art Prize was **Ritch Branstrom**. He's an amazing found-object artist who shared an incredible story with us. For years he concentrated solely on his art and went without a television. One day he decided to reconnect with the broadcast world and went out to buy a TV. He returned home, turned it on and the very first thing he saw was Under the Radar Michigan featuring some of his art at the Crooked Tree Art Center in Petoskey. Imagine not watching a TV for years, and the first thing you see when you turn one on is some weird guy with a hat and mustache jumping up and down about how great your tin can fish art is. Wonderfully weird, and so UTR! If you get a chance, look up Ritch's work. Incredible.

Slingshot Bikes
(888) 530-5556
342 Market St. SW, Grand Rapids, MI 49503
www.slingshotbikes.com

If you want to lessen your carbon footprint on the planet (I know I've got one) there are three things you need to do. First, lose two of your tires. Then go see the guys at Slingshot Bikes in Grand Rapids. **Slingshot** is a bicycle company that's committed to Michigan and keeping their products local. If you're looking for a high performance custom bike to ride, Slingshot will show you the way. Slingshot could go anywhere in the world to produce their bikes, but they stay in Michigan because of the tremendous talent pool here. From welders and powder coaters to engineers, the people, pride and resources are all right here.

Singshot also has something really cool called "Sling Power Technology." It's an amazing power transfer design that uses a coil spring to turn the dead portion of your pedal stroke into an additional power source. It sounds complicated, but it's beautifully simple and absolutely brilliant. You really need to see it to fully understand it. I got to ride one of their amazing bikes through downtown Grand Rapids, and it was a blast.

At Slingshot they are crazy about riding, and they have a singular focus: to help you have the ultimate riding experience. So next time you're looking for a bike, look at Slingshot. They're great bikes that are great for Michigan.

Yesterdog
(616) 336-0746
1505 Wealthy St., Grand Rapids, MI 49506
www.yesterdog.com

For years people have been trying to invent a better hotdog. Well, at **Yesterdog**, they don't have to, because they already did. And, they did it over thirty-five years ago.

Yesterdog is a crazy, fun, eclectic place that has a cult following so big, you'd almost call them a small nation. It's located in the East Town area of Grand Rapids and has been serving up delectable dogs for generations.

This is an old-school hotdog diner where you make your order, toss your tip into a bucket on the wall behind the counter and dig into your dogs. Not only do they have the classic Yesterdog with chili, onion, mustard, pickle and ketchup, they also have the Ultradog, Cheddardog, Krautdog, Killerdog and even a Veggiedog.

Owner Bill Lewis claims he started Yesterdog back in 1976 because he wanted to do something where he couldn't get fired. It worked. People love this place so much, he probably couldn't close even if he wanted to. Yesterdog is so popular we even ran into the former mayor of Grand Rapids there. The walls are covered with Grand Rapids history, and when you're done your shirt will probably be covered in chili.

I'll be honest with you, for a boy who grew up on Detroit Coney Island hotdogs, these Yesterdogs were pretty darn good. Of course, to make sure, I had to sample three or four. Pure research. Boy, the things I have to do on UTR to maintain our integrity. Yesterdog totally lived up to its reputation as a fun and crazy place to get an outstanding hotdog.

And, as always, Grand Rapids lived up to its reputation as one of the greatest places in the world to live, work or play on the planet. Disclaimer: I don't know about the other planets. I've only been to this one.

Next we went to beautiful **Mt. Pleasant**, smack dab in the middle of Michigan's mitten, and "pleasant" is the perfect word for this town. It's the kind of place that when you get there, you instantly feel like it's your hometown. Mt. Pleasant continues to move into a positive future for a ton of reasons, but the biggest one is Central Michigan University. It's the home of the Chippewa and more than 20,000 students expanding both their minds and Michigan's future.

Well, you know us at UTR, we weren't in town ten minutes before we decided to find some great places to eat. Turns out we found three without hardly trying.

The Brass Café
(989) 772-0864
128 S. Main, Mount Pleasant, MI 48858
www.thebrasscafe.com

The first one we tried was **The Brass Café**. Emma Currie and Susan Paton are the proud proprietors of this fine establishment, and you'll never find two people more passionate about what they serve or where they live. Emma came all the way from Scotland to study at CMU. Soon after that she met Susan, fell in love with Michigan and decided to find the American dream. And as far as I'm concerned, they both found it with this place.

The food at the café is exceptional. Emma and Susan have gone out of their way to develop relationships with local farmers, bakers and suppliers, so almost everything you eat is sourced locally. Just down the street from the restaurant, they even opened the Market on Main, which is a great little specialty grocery store, deli and bakery. It's just another sign of their continued commitment to downtown Mount Pleasant.

I ate a specialty hamburger they serve called "The Big Brassy." It's handmade with locally grown organic ground beef and stuffed with gorgonzola, mascarpone and fresh mozzarella on a paprika-oil-brushed local bakery bun with baby arugula, pancetta, house-smoked grilled onions, their patented A-128 sauce and a fried Amish egg on top, with hand-cut Kennebec fries and mayo. Need I say more?

At the Brass Café it went way beyond their food. We really enjoyed the honest approach they take toward everything they do. We had a great time. Made some new friends, and as always, ate way too much, But, hey… we take our job seriously.

There's a revolution going on in Mt. Pleasant right now, but there's no need to be alarmed, and no need to stay in your homes, because this revolution is all about flour power… solid!

The Flour Uprising
(989) 779-8000
112 N. Main, Mount Pleasant, MI 48858
www.theflouruprising.com

The Flour Uprising is a funky little bakery with a big heart and tons of stuff to make you feel good inside. The difference is they use locally grown, all organic ingredients. So bye, bye guilt… and hello happiness.

Annette Pratt blends happy with healthy every single day. I asked her how she came up with the name, and she told me that her mission was to start a bakery that was different, better, healthier and action oriented. She's done just that by offering a wide selection of organic, whole wheat and gluten free fun things to eat. She's got something great there for everyone.

Annette is perhaps most famous for making something that has become the official sweet comfort food of Mt. Pleasant. It's called a "Whoopie Pie," and it's kind of like a cross between a sandwich cookie and a cupcake. It's two small cakes with the creamy filling in the middle instead of on top. I actually made some with her and made a huge mess, but man were they good. Now I know why everyone in Mt. Pleasant loves these wonderful little things.

If you've got a sweet tooth, bring it and the rest of your teeth to the Flour Uprising. I've said it before, and I'll say it again. It don't get none, not, no better. It's a triple negative… it works.

Camille's on the River
(989) 773-0259
506 W. Broadway St., Mount Pleasant, MI 48858
www.camillesontheriver.com

Our last fabulous food find of the day was a restaurant called **Camille's on the River** that's attached to another great restaurant and microbrewery called Mountain Town Station. It sounds complicated, but it's really not. Camille's on the River is a new gourmet restaurant in Mt. Pleasant that's not only turning heads, it also turned one young chef's future into a great Michigan success story.

Owner Jim Holton made this new dining destination possible. He attended CMU twenty-five years ago, fell in love with the town, decided it was a great place to raise a family and eventually opened a restaurant. Now he employs hundreds and feeds thousands.

Chef Brent Peterson started his illustrious culinary career in the back of the kitchen at Mountain Town Station in a place he affectionately calls "Dish Town." Brent went on to study the culinary arts in Chicago, where he could have taken his talents anywhere in the world. Instead he came back home to make his future in Mt. Pleasant.

Brent's philosophy in the kitchen is simple: use fresh, local ingredients and respect those ingredients. Combine that with Jim Holton's drive for supreme customer service, and you've got an exceptional dining experience. At Camille's on the River we found great Michigan stories and superb Michigan foods.

As for Mt. Pleasant, be forewarned: you won't find an actual mountain there. What you will find is a very cool city with a real sense of place and community. Oh, and some pretty darn good food!

Story behind the name:
Go Fetch, Rusty

Ritch Branstrom created the best found-object dog ever, Rusty, who is made of car parts, tree trunks and other stuff. Rusty was a good dog. Awful at playing ball, but he was a good dog.

Chapter 23

Season 2, Episode 10

• Lexington
• Bay City

For a lot of reasons, Lexington is becoming one of Michigan's favorite staycation destinations. If you're looking for a great little harbor town to spend a weekend, a week or the rest of your life in, Lexington is the perfect place. It has that classic resort town atmosphere, with everything from traditional businesses to some pretty funky, cool places to check out. And it's got some beautiful places to enjoy the water.

L exington actually has a special place in my heart because I spent a lot of my childhood vacationing in that area. When we arrived, I discovered the same beautiful little place I remembered. After a quick, nostalgic trip through town, we headed up the road a piece to visit a place I could totally enjoy, now that I'm an adult that is.

Blue Water Winery and Vineyards
(810) 622-0328
7131 Holverson Rd., Carsonville, MI 48419
www.bluewaterwinery.com

I'm talking about **Blue Water Winery and Vineyards**. It's a classic, award-winning vineyard that's doing it right, right here in Michigan. Connie Currie and her husband Steve Velloff came to Lexington over a decade ago and discovered both a community and a microclimate that loved what they wanted to do. What they've created there is a beautiful vineyard with all the trappings of Napa including great wines, beautiful scenery, a quaint outdoor tasting area and even some resident alpacas.

You don't usually think of this part of Michigan as a wine region, but Connie and Steve decided to give it a go. With a healthy dose of intuition, a bit of number crunching and a microclimate that seemed to like grapes, the first seeds were planted. Now more than twelve thousand vines and many awards later, they're bottling their dream. There's so much love for this winery that tons of people show up every year at harvest time to help pick the grapes. If that doesn't say community, I don't know what does.

Make no mistake; this wine is good. Recently, Blue Water Winery and Vineyards received two gold medals from the 2013 San Francisco International Wine Competition for their Cab Franc and Norton. They have also received a Silver Medal from the 2014 San Francisco Chronicle Wine Competition for their 2011 Pinot Noir. Proof positive that Michigan Thumb wines rock.

In town Connie and Steve even opened a great place where you can taste, talk and buy great wines and now beers. It's called **The Lexington Brewing Company & Wine House** and it's located in a historic landmark building that actually used to be the old town hall. That's right, Connie and Steve are now also brewing great hand-crafted Michigan beers for all to enjoy. On Friday and Saturday nights you can even dance and groove to some of Michigan's best bands while enjoying your home grown beer and wine.

After spending an afternoon at the Blue Water Winery and Vineyard, I realized that you don't need to go all the way to California to have a great wine adventure like this. So don't be a wine snob. Try some of the traditional and fruit wines produced right in Michigan's thumb region. They're great wines, and they have the same net effect as those other wines—bonus!

Thumbfest
www.thumbfest.org

This is an actual true story. When we put Lexington on our production calendar and called to start scheduling things, we didn't know **Thumbfest** was happening or even what it was. But thank goodness we stumbled on it, because it was extremely cool.

Thumbfest is a folk music festival that's been happening in Lexington every summer for over a decade now. On the Saturday before Labor Day, musicians from all over the country come to perform on one of almost a dozen stages spread throughout town. From New Orleans brass to classic Americana, if it's acoustic, it's here.

Over five thousand music lovers come to this festival every year to relax, shop, eat and even stay the night. If you're looking for great weekend getaway with a catchy melody, check out Thumbfest. If I had brought my guitar with me, I would have totally performed that day. But then again, I'm trying to bring people to Lexington, not scare them away.

When it comes to being a Michigan resort destination, Lexington really moved up a weight class in recent years, and the man behind a lot of its development is **Adam Buschbacher**. This amazingly motivated entrepreneur almost single-handedly built what was called the Smackwater Block, a collection of upscale shops, eateries and even a beautiful, first-class live entertainment theater. Adam's moved on to develop other parts of the state now, but expect good things from this block. At the time this book was published, rumor had it that the great eateries, shops and theater will continue under the name of "Sweetwater." Whatever the name ends up being, this is a great block for all things fun and tasty. Totally worth exploring.

If you haven't been to Lexington recently (or at all for that matter) you really owe it to yourself to check this place out. We at UTR give Lexington a hearty two thumbs up.

Bay City was another big surprise to all of us on the UTR crew. Everywhere we looked there was cool, classic architecture that took you back to a time when buildings actually had personality. Back to when structures were as much artistic form as they were function. Every time we turned around, you could hear someone on the crew say, "Wow, that's a cool building." Another really great thing going on in Bay City right now is all the new development. A lot of very cool living spaces are coming into downtown, creating jobs, new energy and a great sense of place. Like in so many other Michigan cities, people are reconnecting with their downtowns to improve their quality of life.

Not only did we fall in love with the classic buildings downtown, some of the homes and neighborhoods surrounding Bay City will blow you away. Thanks to the lumber barons of the late 1800s, **Center Avenue Historic District** has some of the most beautiful, spectacular and enormous homes you'll see anywhere. Some of them are even bed and breakfasts now, so check that out too.

You don't have to go to Europe to see incredible churches. Besides, it's far away, it's expensive and they talk funny over there. Here in Bay City the churches are spectacular. **The First Presbyterian Church** there dates all the way back to 1883. And everywhere you look around town, you see majestic steeples accenting the skyline.

Another incredible structure is the **City Hall**. It was completed in the late 1800s and has a bell tower that rises 185 feet above the city. This place is totally worth checking out.

The Bay City Motor Company
(989) 891-0900
1124 N. Water St., Bay City, MI 48708
www.TheBayCityMotorCompany.com

One place we heard about in town was **The Bay City Motor Company**. When it comes to classic and collectable cars, these guys are the real deal. David Cotton's family has been part of the Michigan automotive scene for well over a century. Walking into Bay City Motors is like taking a step back in time. Their showroom resembles a mini museum of American motor history.

Bay City Motors is a candy store for car lovers. It's a used car store for classic and high-end automobiles. Twenty-one thousand people come through the doors there every year. Some to buy, and some just to appreciate these great collectibles. The day we were there I got to sit and visit with David in a 1932 Ford Model B Cabriolet... outstanding.

As David so eloquently put it, Bay City Motors is nostalgia, enjoyment, design, creativity and performance. If you're into classic cars, get in your car and go see these cars.

The Bay Antique Center
(989) 894-0400
1010 N. Water St., Bay City, MI 48706
www.bayantiquectr.com

If you're an antique lover, Bay City is the absolute epicenter of antiquing in the Midwest, and **The Bay Antique Center** has about eleven billion square feet of all things old. Michelle Judd and her family own, arrange, operate and orchestrate this huge conglomeration of cool stuff, and it all started with her grandpa. He loved to find antique treasures so much, he used to send them home when he was stationed over in Germany during the war.

I wasn't into antiquing until I walked into this place. There's over sixty-thousand square feet of everything old you can imagine. From classic clothing to furniture, gas pumps, signs, jewelry, art—you name it. It's wonderfully overwhelming. The Bay City Antique Center is so big, people have even been known to get lost in there. I'm not naming any names, because I don't want to embarrass myself.

Try this test. Go there and wander around for a while. If you don't leave with something you love, I guarantee you'll still have fun just looking. Oh, and if you see me there, remember, I'm not lost. I'm just having a little trouble finding my way out. There's a difference. I think.

The Old City Hall Restaurant
(989) 892-4140
814 Saginaw St., Bay City, MI 48708
www.oldcityhallrestaurant.com

Here's a quick UTR "Hunger Note." You know us, we like to eat. So, we checked out **The Old City Hall Restaurant** right downtown. Now, there are two great things about this place… 1. The food is awesome… and 2. Back in the late 1890s, this place was the actual city hall. So if you're looking for great food, great service and a really cool atmosphere, check out the Old Town Hall Restaurant. Tell 'em UTR sent 'cha!

The State Theater
(989) 892-2660
913 Washington Ave., Bay City, MI 48708
www.statetheatrebaycity.com

Our last stop turned out to be probably the biggest surprise of the day. **The State Theater** in downtown Bay City is a crazy, wild explosion of art deco colors, all wrapped up in an incredible ancient Mayan temple theme. When you enter the front doors, it's like you were just swallowed by an ancient Mayan birthday cake. The eye candy there is amazing and the atmosphere is awesome. We didn't even stay for a movie and we still had a blast just looking around.

This incredible theater was designed in the 1930s by none other than C. Howard Crane, the very same man who designed Detroit's famous and fabulous Fox Theater. It's one of three Mayan Temples in the entire U.S. The State Theater is also one of those special places that anchors the arts to the community there, and that, my friends, is a priceless thing.

If you're looking for a theater that's as much fun as the movie you're about to see, see the State Theater. And if you're looking for a Michigan city with a brilliant past and a bright future, check out Bay City.

Story behind the name:
I'm All Thumbs

When you're in the thumb of Michigan,
you're hyper aware of your thumb.

Chapter 24

Season 2, Episode 11

• Lansing
• Ishpeming

Lansing continues to move Michigan forward, but not just through the efforts of our state government. There's also a lot of stuff happening on the ground there to help revitalize our economy. Everywhere you look, Lansing is alive with new business, cool spaces, great places and young faces bringing energy to downtown.

Accident Fund Building
(517) 367-8448
200 N. Grand Ave., Lansing, MI 48933

Our first stop was an iconic structure that's been part of Lansing's landscape for a long, long time. It sat empty for years, but now it's one of Lansing's economic cornerstones. Today it stands proudly as Headquarters to Accident Fund Holdings, who, along with parent company Blue Cross/Blue Shield of Michigan, partnered with Christman Development to bring this iconic building back to life. In doing so they've created a shining symbol of re-use, renewal and reinvestment in downtown Lansing. This reborn building is now bringing hundreds of people to downtown Lansing every day. But that's not what this incredible place used to be.

This classic art-deco-style building was originally the Ottawa Street Power Station and supplied Lansing with power and steam from 1938 until the late 1980s. When the plant became obsolete, it turned into an abandoned brownfield and sadly sat in the center of the city for years. One of the really unique original features of the building is the graduated coloring of the brick, which was designed to emulate the burning of coal. It's a beautiful building that any city would be proud to have.

Preserving history and taking a city into the future all at the same time is an incredible thing to accomplish. Not only has the **Accident Fund Building** fundamentally changed downtown Lansing, this renovation project won the prestigious Governor's Award for Historic Preservation. And it was all done with local talent and resources.

After a complete tour of the building, I realized what an incredible place this is. Hands down, it's one of the coolest buildings in Michigan. If you want to look into Michigan's past and future, all at the same time, next time you're in Lansing, just look for the Accident Fund Building. Believe me, it was no accident!

Lansing City Market
(517) 483-7460
325 City Market Dr., Lansing, MI 48912
www.lansingcitymarket.com

On our program you hear me talk a lot about how communities and neighborhoods have a great sense of place. Sometimes it's tough to explain exactly what that is. So in order to feel it for myself, I went to the **Lansing City Market** where all kinds of people come to gather, connect, shop and share. If you're looking for local Lansing, look no further. This market really does have everything. It's got great prepared foods, a cool bar to hang out at, live music to enjoy, tons of Michigan specialty products and plenty of fresh local produce.

Markets like this really are an important place to build community. In the old days, we used to sit out on our front porches and greet each other, but we don't do that so much anymore. At the Lansing City market, you get to rub elbows with fellow Lansing locals and actually meet the people who grow and make your food. The montage of people and personalities at the market totally makes this trip worth taking.

The sights and sounds of the market were intoxicating, so the guys and I wandered off to take it all in. We ended up at a place called **Sarge's Soups and Sandwiches** for a pulled pork sandwich. Sarge was a blast and his sandwiches were so good, I almost dropped and gave him twenty.

So if you're scratching your head, trying to figure out what the phrase "sense of place" means, the place to go that will put you in the know is the Lansing City Market. If Lansing is a little too far, try your own city market if you've got one. If you don't have one, start one and give me a call when it's done.

Next, we headed up to **Ishpeming** in Michigan's beautiful Upper Peninsula. A lot of people don't go to the U.P. because they say it's too far. To that I simply say, nothing is too far, if you're having fun in the car, and if you've seen our show, you know that UTR is just another way to spell FUN.

In the blink of an eye and about eleventy billion laughs later, we pulled into Ishpeming. The town is filled with great history, hearty people and tons of natural beauty. Ishpeming is also the birthplace of organized skiing in the United States, so when you're there, be sure to visit the **U.S. Ski and Snowboard Hall of Fame and Museum**. If you're wondering what the word Ishpeming means, it's a Native American word meaning "high place" or "heaven," and this place really is heaven for people who love the great outdoors.

We met up with **Elizabeth Peterson**, the executive director of the Ishpeming Chamber of Commerce, and after giving us the lay of the land, she took us tubing down a huge hill and onto Teal Lake. We had a blast, but it was then that I realized I wasn't properly equipped or adorned to survive a U.P. winter, so I had to get me some supplies.

Wilderness Sports
(906) 485-4565
107 E. Division St., Ishpeming, MI 49849
www.wildernesssportsinc.com

Elizabeth sent us straight to a place right in downtown Ishpeming called **Wilderness Sports.** Being a down-state flatlander, I needed some help, and they hooked me up with everything I needed to become a genuine Yooper. Sandee Sundquist took me through the store personally and set me up with choppers (a.k.a. mittens), socks, two pairs of long johns (I have skinny legs) and even a pair of snowshoes. Becoming a Yooper with Sandee was a blast and she was a real good sport, which totally makes sense, because that's exactly what they do at Wilderness Sports.

Now that I was a full-fledged Yooper, I needed to know where to go to stay warm during the long cold U.P. evenings, so I met up with Randy and Kevin Kluck, a father and son team who had exactly what I needed.

Most fathers and their sons get together to bowl, golf or watch the big game, but these two joined forces to write what they call "perhaps the most important travel guide ever published." The book is simply titled **"Yooper Bars,"** and it features just about every cool, crazy, unique and historic watering hole in the entire Upper Peninsula. Dad and son spent an entire summer traveling, tasting and typing. Now their entire adventure can be yours. Just look at them as the Lewis and Clark of U.P. libations.

To illustrate how cool this is, we met up at one of the very pubs featured in their book. It's called Jack's Tee Pee Bar in downtown Ishpeming, and in 1959 scenes from the Hollywood thriller "Anatomy of a Murder" were actually shot there. Imagine Jimmy Stewart and Lee Remick sitting in the same booth we were in. Very cool.

If you're looking for fun and interesting places to enjoy adult beverages while visiting the U.P., you should get your hands on a copy of this important publication.

We laughed and had a couple adult malted beverages, but I still wasn't quite warm enough yet, so Rusty and Kevin walked me down the block to a place called Hickey's Bar to meet one of the U.P.'s most colorful characters. If you're from the U.P., you've most likely heard of this fine and funny gentleman. His name is Al **'Goofus'** Ammesmaki, and he's known for singing any number of U.P. anthems and performing them along with his wonderfully bizarre self-made creation: the polka-cello.

What exactly is a polka-cello? It's hard to describe. It's a combination of cymbals, horns, tambourines and drums all mounted to a single stick. Goofus holds it with one hand, operates all the aforementioned musical contraptions with the other, and turns a one-man band into about three with his boisterous voice and enthusiasm. In short, it's something you really have to experience to appreciate.

Goofus is part clown, part cheerleader, a local legend and all heart when it comes to loving this great Upper Peninsula. He performs at any function you have in mind, as long as you're interested in spreading positive energy and good cheer. Goofus warmed up his polka-cello, and after a few warming renditions, we were sufficiently warm in the U.P. It may not be easy to do, but it sure is fun.

Congress Pizza
(906) 486-4233
106 N. Main St., Ishpeming, MI 49849

Another way to stay warm during the long, cold U.P. winters is to put on a few extra pounds, and you know me, I discovered a great way to do that, too. I stopped by **Congress Pizza** for a quick conversation with Paul Bonetti about a food that apparently everybody in the U.P. knows about but me. It's a spicy, mostly pork sausage originally from northern Italy called **cudighi**, and it came to Michigan's U.P. over one hundred years ago along with Italian immigrants looking for work in the mines. The sausage was originally served with mustard and raw onions on a roll, which is exactly how we had it that day, and it was good-ighi. I may be only half Italian, but I ate the whole thing.

The Midtown Bakery & Café
(906) 475-0064
317 Iron St., Negaunee, MI 49866

Right next to Ishpeming in the town of Negaunee is one place that serves over 150 different flavors of cheese cake. I call that heaven. **The Midtown Bakery & Café** is a funky, cool gourmet bakery and sandwich shop that'll tempt you with just about everything they serve there. Marybeth Kurtz is the pleasant proprietor who makes it all happen every single day.

If you ever get the chance, this is one wonderful, colorful little place. It's a combination restaurant, bakery, coffee shop and quaint café, and all the food is fresh and lovingly prepared. Heck, we liked it so much, we went back three times before we headed home.

Marybeth opened her doors sixteen years ago, started experimenting with cheesecakes and is now the undisputed queen of this tasty treat. If you love cheesecake, you've got well over one hundred flavors to try there. We tried a variety, and those extra pounds I was talking about earlier to stay warm? I'm pretty sure I added a bit more insulation before we left.

A sandwich is just a sandwich, and a cheese cake is just a cheese cake until you come to the Midtown Bakery & Café in Negaunee.

Ishpeming Ski Club
P.O. Box 127, Ishpeming, MI 49849
www.ishskiclub.com

Now, onto what brought us to Ishpeming in the first place. It's the longest continually running ski club in the entire U.S. They call the **Ishpeming Ski Club** the birthplace of organized skiing in America, and there they have a monster ski jump affectionately called Suicide Hill. Since 1887, skiers and ski jumpers have been going there to compete and learn to fly on skis.

When we were there, I was so very fortunate to spend some quality time with the late, great Coy Hill. Not only was Coy one of the club's most decorated jumpers, he personified this club's long and illustrious history. Coy was one of the precious old-timers who, back in the day (when it wasn't so easy), helped build this club and the giant ski jump. He was a true gentleman and a wonderful character whose enthusiasm and passion for this sport helped send some of our very finest to the Olympics. Coy passed away while the program featuring him was in the process of being edited. We feel lucky to have known him. He will be sorely missed.

If you can, you should come see this jump and witness what these incredibly brave and talented young men and women do. In my humble opinion, these ski jumpers are the rock stars of the ski world. With giant skis on their backs, they climb hundreds of stairs and fly hundreds of feet through the air.

On the show, we suited me up and made it look as though I made one of these magnificent jumps. I acquired my genuine appreciation for these athletes when I carried those giant skis to the top of the jump and got a true perspective on the enormity of this feat. It looked like I did it, but I was really so scared up there. I respect those guys tremendously. Like I said, rock stars.

The competition we came to see that day celebrated the club's 125th anniversary, and ski jumpers from all over the world were there to compete. I've been watching ski jumping on TV all my life, but until I saw it in person, I didn't realize what an incredible sport it is. If you get the chance, get to the U.P. and attend one of these awesome competitions. It's something I guarantee you'll never forget.

And remember, Michigan's Upper Peninsula isn't far if you're having fun in the car. So, grab your imagination and your sense of humor. Get in the car and get up there. Before you know it, you'll be a Yooper too.

Story behind the name:
You're Too Old

When Coy Hill tells you you're too old, you'd better listen. Tom didn't. Coy was a good man and a great interview. One of our favorites.

Chapter 25

Season 2, Episode 12

• Ferndale
• Grand Rapids

The City of Ferndale has won all kinds of awards for their
public spaces, business development and downtown. It truly is
an enlightened city with a big heart and a lot of personality. Tons of
progressive people live, work and go there every day to enjoy one of
the coolest places to eat, shop and play in Michigan. If you're looking
for a sense of place, this is a great place to get it.

As you know, Under the Radar is a TV show about Michigan, and we have a lot of fans in Michigan. But we have a lot of fans in Canada, too. So Canadians, this is for you.

The Detroit Curling Club
(248) 544-0635
1615 E. Lewiston, Ferndale, MI 48220
www.detroitcurlingclub.com

The Detroit Curling Club is in Ferndale, Michigan, and that's where we found tons of Americans playing this traditional Canadian sport. The club has been in existence for over 125 years, and believe it or not, the first record of people curling in the United States was on Orchard Lake in Southeast Michigan way back in 1832. So Canadian or not, some Americans have been enjoying this sport for a long time.

Half the fun of belonging to any club is the people, and the folks at the Detroit Curling Club are fun, friendly and full of passion for this game. Curling is kind of like the Italian game bocce ball, only on ice and with a whole different set of funny words. It's pretty simple. You grab your broom, step on the slider, position your foot on the hack and deliver the stone. The object is to get the stone past both hog lines and closest to the button. See, funny words, and it's a ton of fun.

They say once you try curling, you're hooked. So if you've got an addictive personality and you like to try new things, stop by the Detroit Curling Club. It really is a great sport that everyone should try at least once in their life, and I can't tell you how much fun the crew and I had that day. But I won't lie: the mostest bestest part of the entire experience was having a beer with all my new curling friends after the game. I got to hear some great stories about curling, and I got to hear them all right here in Michigan. That, my friends, is what we're all about.

The Fly Trap
(248) 399-5150
22950 Woodward Ave., Ferndale, MI 48220
www.theflytrapferndale.com

If you want to catch flies, you use a fly trap. But if you want to catch a creative meal in Ferndale, you use **The Fly Trap**. Gavin McMillian and Kara and Sean McClanaghan own and operate this eclectic little diner, and from the crazy décor to the creative cuisine, these three came up with a winning recipe. Everywhere you look is something that will make you either scratch your head or make you smile. There's cool art, an array of wacky salt and pepper shakers and a real attention to all the details that make this place a finer diner.

As for the food, you couldn't get more creative than these folks. The proof is usually in the pudding, but at The Fly Trap, it was in the patrons. Everyone we talked to was beyond passionate for what they serve there. From breakfasts like Green Eggs and Ham and The Cowboy Curtis to dinners like Sean's Mushroom Fettuccini Bomb and the Fire-Breathing Dragon with grilled chicken, sweet basil and sambal peanut sauce, this casual place is crazy creative. And, for good measure, they even make their own artisan jams, jellies and hot sauces.

Next time you're in Ferndale... oh heck, if you're ever anywhere in Michigan, check out The Fly Trap. You'll get stuck on their food for sure. Get it, stuck? Oh boy.

B. Nektar Meadery
(313) 744-6323
1505 Jarvis, Ste. B, Ferndale, MI 48220
www.bnektar.com

Speaking of things that are sticky, at our last stop in Ferndale, we discovered you can do a lot more with honey than just spread it on toast. Brad and Kerri Dahlhofer own the **B. Nektar Meadery**, and they're making mead where no mead has been made before.

If you need a refresher course on what exactly mead is, it's an ancient alcoholic drink made from fermented honey, and it's thought to be one of the oldest adult beverages known to man. It's considered by many to be the ancestor of all fermented drinks.

Brad started off brewing his own beer as a hobby, which turned into a calling. He happened upon a chapter on mead in the back of a beer book, and the wheels were set in motion. His meads started getting so good that with his wife Kerri's encouragement, they took a drink of mead, a leap of faith and turned this part-time pastime into a fulltime Michigan success story.

What do B. Nektar meads taste like? Well, these aren't your great-great-great-great-great grandfather's meads. Yes, they do make traditional meads like Orange Blossom and Wildflower, but with other honey beverages like Zombie Killer, Funky Monky and Dwarf Invasion, you can bet your taste buds will be shocked and thrilled. At B. Nektar they make a whole variety of honey beverages with tastes as different as people. Some sweet, some dry, but all out of this world.

It's no wonder B. Nectar Mead is spreading from Michigan around the world. Everyone who tastes Brad's mead becomes mead-merized. For an absolutely unique and awesome taste experience, B. Nectar should definitely "B" on your A list.

Grand Rapids continues to be a driving innovative, creative and economic force in Michigan. In fact, there's so much happening that you'd almost have to live there to keep up. Not a bad idea! This modern city continues to be one of the best places to be in the U.S. There's a great energy and attitude that's bringing in new business, great spaces where you can connect with your fellow urbanites and really cool places to live right downtown.

Founders Brewing Company
(616) 776-2182
235 Grandville Ave. SW, Grand Rapids, MI 49503
www.FoundersBrewing.com

Every time we come to Grand Rapids, the crew and I always end up spending at least one evening enjoying frosty cold adult malted beverages at **Founders Brewing Company**. It's a brewery and restaurant that's literally become a destination for beer lovers who love food, and food lovers who love beer. That's called a win-win!

If you're serious about your beer, this place should be at the top of your shortest "short" list, and after winning second best brewery in the entire world, the recognition they're getting is well deserved.

Like a lot of people in Michigan, Mike Stevens and Dave Engbers were two hobby home brewers who decided to retool their careers and chase their dream. So they quit their jobs, took out huge loans and started Founders.

After spending some time making well-balanced but unremarkable beers, they nearly went bankrupt. They were trying to make beer that would appeal to a wide audience, and it wasn't working. So they decided that if they were going to go down trying, they may as well make the kind of beer they liked to drink. That simple decision was their stairway to beer heaven. With names like "Dirty Bastard," "Curmudgeon Old Ale" and "Devil Dancer," you can pretty much guess the kinds of beers Mike and Dave like.

Founders brews big-body, aromatic, in-your-face ales with tons of character and flavor, just what the true craft beer enthusiast ordered. Their philosophy is simple: "We don't brew beer for the masses. Instead, our beers are crafted for a chosen few, a small cadre of renegades and rebels who enjoy a beer that pushes the limits of what is commonly accepted as taste. In short, we make beer for people like us."

It's working. Founders Brewing Co. has evolved into one of the highest recognized breweries in the United States. They've been ranked in the top four breweries in the world and have a lot of their beers listed in the top one hundred beers. They've won more medals for their big, bold brews than you can shake a pretzel stick at.

Founders also is a great place to tuck a napkin into your shirt, rub elbows with all types and get a great bite to eat. Their sandwiches are outstanding and their specials sensational.

Next time you're in Grand Rapids, do what we do on the UTR crew: stop at Founders for a pint or two, then you'll see what I'm telling you is absolutely true. Wow, poetry!

Meijer Innovation Center and Test Kitchen
(616) 458-6050
70 Ionia Ave. SW, Grand Rapids, MI 49503
www.grid70.com

They say producing and preparing good food is an art form. Well, at the **Meijer Innovation Center and Test Kitchen**, it's also a science. Chef Ray Sierengowski is an actual food scientist who spends his days there making sure our food is healthier, safer and tastier too.

Meijer's Innovation Center is located in the Grid 70 building with other iconic Michigan companies like Amway, Steel Case and Wolverine World Wide. GRID stands for "Grand Rapids Innovation Design" and it's a creative hub where companies share ideas, resources and their desire to strengthen Michigan's economy.

Chef Ray shared a lot of what he does to help make Michigan's mega food chain Meijer respond to its customers' needs and wants. He is the heart and soul of Meijer's food product development, and his job is an absolute blast. He helps keep foods safe and savory with the use of just about every kitchen gizmo and gadget imaginable. Together we tested foods' viscosity, texture, temperature and, of course, taste. Chef Ray also helps Meijer stay greener and source locally.

Chef Ray is an amazingly knowledgeable and energetic food scientist who, quite frankly, could take his talents anywhere in the world, but lucky for us, he picked Grand Rapids. If you ever get the opportunity to visit the Meijer Innovation Center and Test Kitchen, you'll be amazed just how much research, preparation and care goes into everything they make available.

When it comes to having a real sense of place, where you live and work means everything. Next, we met a guy who used both his art and his heart to actually help create a neighborhood.

Sanctuary Folk Art
(616) 454-0401
140 S. Division Ave., Grand Rapids, MI 49503
www.sanctuaryfolkart.com

In the 1990s a four-block area right near downtown was nothing but boarded up buildings and blight. It was a part of Grand Rapids the economy left behind. But in 1999, artist and urban pioneer Reb Roberts started a personal crusade to change all that. On an empty street he and his wife Carmella opened his **Sanctuary Folk Art** store. Once their gallery was established, they went on to work closely with other local entrepreneurs and church groups to help turn the area into the thriving neighborhood known as Heartside.

Thanks to Reb and Carmella's collaboration with a variety of local artists, Heartside now features a variety of brilliant and inspiring murals. The power of urban art is amazing. It captures the community's attention and eventually attracts residents and businesses. With the help of other urban planners, visionaries and developers, Heartside is now making a strong comeback.

If you get a chance to visit Heartside, please do. The street art will amaze you, and Reb and Carmella will welcome you with open arms. Their Sanctuary Folk Art store has a groovy piece of art for everyone. The store features an incredible array of all kinds of folk art from western Michigan artists. These artists are, for the most part, not formally trained but are teeming with talent. It's a great place to visit.

Speaking of great places to visit, if you get a chance, spend some time in Grand Rapids. Like I said before, you just might end up living there. Oh, and if you do, be sure to stop by Founders, because that's probably where we'll be.

Story behind the name:
Chewy-ness-ness-ocity?

When the Meijer food scientists tell you that they have an instrument that measures the chewiness of food, you'd better believe that they have the coolest kitchen in Michigan.

Chapter 26

Season 2, Episode 13

Michigan Festivals Special

There are so many great festivals happening throughout Michigan at any given time, we'd almost have to devote an entire episode just to scratch the surface. So that's exactly what we did, and boy, did we have fun.

Ypsilanti Summer Beer Festival
www.michiganbrewersguild.org

What would a Michigan festival special be without a good old fashioned beer festival? So we went to the **14th Annual Summer Beer Festival at Riverside Park** in beautiful Ypsilanti, Michigan. It's the oldest and largest beer festival in the state. Thousands of beer lovers converged to taste over three hundred different beers from more than fifty different Michigan breweries.

If you're into beer, this is definitely the festival to be at. People come from far and wide to sample every Michigan brew imaginable. I honestly don't know what's more fun, the great beer or the colorful characters you run into. Everyone else was wearing pretzel necklaces, so I made my own custom pretzel hat. Easy to make, and it tasted great.

Whether you go for a good time with friends, to learn how to brew or to just drink great beer, Michigan's largest beer festival will not disappoint. The passion for this growing artisan activity is astounding, and you won't find a friendlier bunch of enthusiasts anywhere. They love their beer and love to share it with others. And keep in mind, not only does the beer make you feel good, helping the Michigan economy by drinking local brews makes you feel even better.

To make sure people drank responsibly and got home safe, the festival even had a "Blow Station" where you could check your consumption of beer. And if you had too much, they made sure you got home safe to enjoy more beer next year. A designated driver is always the best idea!

If a frosty cold adult malted brew is your beverage, put the Michigan Brewers Guild Summer Beer Festival in Ypsilanti on your bucket of beer list. Oh, and you might wanna bring a bucket of pretzels, too.

Bologna Festival
www.yalechamber.com/page-bologna.html

All my life people have been telling me I'm full of bologna. Finally, I found a place where I totally fit in. It was at the fantastically fun **Bologna Festival** in Yale, Michigan. For three days every July, this small town of two thousand turns into twenty thousand bologna-loving party-goers. If you're wondering why they have a bologna festival there, they've been making bologna in Yale since 1906, so it's a big part of the town's identity. They love their bologna and the humor that comes along with it.

Yale, we discovered, is a great Michigan town. Like all festivals, behind all the formalities and festivities, it's really all about community, and in Yale we met some of the nicest and most genuine people we've ever encountered.

Even though I'm full of bologna, my tank was getting low, so we headed over to the official bologna tent for a quick fill-up. They had bologna fried, in sandwiches and on a stick, just to name a few. You name it, and there was bologna in, on or around it. I probably don't have to tell you that the bologna there was second to none, and that when we were finished, that's exactly how much was left. None.

Like any good festival that goes back decades, there's always a lot of tradition. At the Yale Bologna Festival they have a bologna toss, a bologna parade, they crown a bologna king and queen and they even presented me with the official ring of bologna to the city. But the one tradition I loved most of all had everyone running for the bathroom. Actually, they were running with the bathroom.

That's right, as part of the Bologna festival, they actually race handmade, old fashioned outhouses right through the middle of town. It's crazy, it's weird and it's an absolute blast. Teams are made up from the local high school, and the competition gets pretty fierce. They even let me ride in one, and even though I got a couple splinters where the Michigan sun don't shine, riding in one of these outhouses was an insane blast. You won't see a funnier or more exciting race anywhere.

We had a tremendous time at the bologna festival. The people were wonderful. The town was beautiful, and once I was full of bologna, I felt like my old self again.

Bike Time
www.muskegonbiketime.com

If you like wind in your hair and bugs in your teeth, this festival is every two-wheeler's ultimate weekend. It's called **Bike Time**. It's in Muskegon, and even though it's only a few years old, it's now the fastest-growing motorcycle festival in the country. Every July, thirty-five thousand bikes from thirty-eight states (and over ninety thousand people total) converge on Muskegon for one thing and one thing only: the love of motorcycles.

This event truly is massive. It spans the entire downtown and has everything you need for a great time. There's good food, cool special events and more motorcycles than you'll probably ever see in one place. You'll see new bikes, colorful bikes, vintage bikes, incredible choppers and even some that look like they're from another planet.

One of the coolest things we saw at Bike Time was GR's Finest Street Bike Team Stunt Show. Those guys and girls were insane, and insanely talented. Some of the balancing and one-wheel tricks they did absolutely defied the laws of physics. But who cares? They were fun to watch and I had a corn dog in my hand.

The great thing about Bike Time is you see all types: families, couples, weekend riders and serious motorcycle dudes. They all come together for one simple reason... the love of motorcycles. I may not have one, but I still had a great time at Bike Time!

Cheeseburger in Caseville Festival
www.cheeseburgerincasevillefest.com

In 1999, the **Cheeseburger in Caseville Festival** started with a handful of people who loved Jimmy Buffett's tropical tendency to kick back and relax with a great cheeseburger. Now for ten days every August, Caseville becomes "Key North," and this beautiful little town of eight hundred hosts almost a quarter million people from around the world who love Buffett, burgers and crazy beachwear.

The day they invited us up to film at the festival was the same day they do the Parade of Fools. A coincidence? I don't think so. There was something like fifty thousand people in town for the parade that day, and I can see why. The floats were incredibly creative, and everyone had a great party spirit. The entire town turns into one huge good-natured celebration that's part Margaritaville, part Mardi Gras and all about having fun.

You'll find live music everywhere and plenty of great food to eat. I even entered a cheeseburger eating contest. I'm not sure what happened, though. By the time I got my condiments just right, somebody yelled, "I win!" Oh well, the cheeseburger was good.

There's plenty to see and do during the Cheeseburger Festival, and because it lasts ten days, you've got plenty of chances to partake. The Cheeseburger in Caseville Festival is so much fun, a vegetarian would even have fun there. So get the catsup, mustard and a map out, and make plans to be there next time. And don't worry; if you lose your shaker of salt, they have plenty.

The Red Flannel Festival
www.redflannelfestival.org

Every October in Cedar Springs, Michigan they have **The Red Flannel Festival** where the entire town shows up sporting their very best red flannel. It can be a hat, shirt, pants, socks, jacket or whatever, as long as it's red. It really is an amazing sight to see. A sea of red everything flowing up and down Main Street. People decorate themselves, their homes, even their dogs. And if you like colorful characters, you find plenty there. But you can bet that every one of them will be red.

Not only is this one of Michigan's oldest festivals, it also has a very unique story. Back in 1936 the winter was unusually cold and the nation was in the grips of a deep freeze. A newspaper writer in New York decried that you couldn't find red flannel underwear anywhere in the nation.

Well, when the local paper The Cedar Springs Clipper got wind of this, they wanted to set this gentleman straight. At the time the Clipper was owned by Nina Babcock and Grace Hamilton, who called themselves "The Clipper Gals." They answered the New York writer with a RED HOT editorial stating, "Just because Sak's Fifth Avenue doesn't carry red flannels, it doesn't follow that no one in the country does. CEDAR SPRINGS' merchants have red flannels!" The rebuttal was picked up by the Associated Press, word spread across the nation, the orders started pouring in and the rest, as they say, is history.

This festival really is classic Americana with all the trimmings. They crown a red flannel king and queen, there is great food to enjoy and plenty of fun games and special events happening the entire time. The day we were there thousands of people lined the streets for the big parade. And even though we weren't actually from Cedar Springs, you couldn't help but feel the genuine hometown pride. It's something every town should have.

Everywhere you look people in red having as much fun as you can possibly have: it's the kind of event you really wish was in your home town. No wonder people come from all over for this festival. So if you like classic American festivals and you just happen to have some red flannel in the closet, you know what to do.

Blowout
www.blowout.metrotimes.com

If you're looking for the largest local music festival in all of North America, there's only one place to go, and that's Hamtramck, Michigan. The festival is officially known as "**Blowout**" and is put on by one of the country's hippest alternative newspapers, the Detroit Metro Times. Blowout is also one of the longest-running music festivals of its kind in the United States. The festival supports the regional music scene by showcasing the very best local talent. Thousands of music lovers come from far and wide to catch up-and-comers and maybe even discover their new favorite band. There's something for almost everyone at Blowout!

The cool thing about Blowout is that it doesn't happen in one place, or on one day. The festival happens over many days and in over a dozen bars and nightclubs across the city. Hop in your car or take one of the official Blowout busses from bar to bar and get your next music fix. It's a ton of fun and you meet so many cool and fascinating people who are so very passionate about the music. The diversity of the music is incredible. There's jazz, pop, rock, soul, country, folk and rap. If you can't find something you like at Blowout, perhaps you're not from this planet.

The night we went, we hopped on the Blowout Bus and hit about eight different venues. The people are passionate, the bands are nonstop, the crowds are electric and we experienced some of the best music and live performances we've ever seen. If you're looking for four days of concentrated local music, Blowout will definitely blow your mind and rock your socks off.

If you're looking for great festivals, Michigan has one for everybody. So, just get on that there Internet. Find one you like, and knock yourself out UTR style.

Story behind the name:
Fasten Your Seatbelts...
Let's Get 'er Done

So many cool festivals all across Michigan. We jumped in the car and hit six of them.

Chapter 27

Season 3, Episode 1

•Lansing
•Marine City

Lansing is the birthplace of Michigan's sense of place. It's a city that by example continues to show the whole world why Michigan is a great place to be. There are probably 1,001 reasons to live, work and play there. And we've got three more great ones for you.

Michigan State Capitol
(517) 373-2348
It's the giant "Capitol Looking" building on the corner of Capitol Ave and Ottawa in downtown Lansing
www.council.legislature.mi.gov/lcfa/capitol-tours.html

Now, tell me honestly. When was the last time you were at our **state capitol**? Yeah, me too. Well, shame on both of us. This incredible structure is so full of history, culture and great stories that one hundred visits would only scratch the surface. It really is one of our state's crowning jewels, and all of us should see it.

You can tour the capitol all on your own, but I did a smart thing (I know, surprising for me). I hooked up with Valerie Marvin, and she knows more about this place than I probably know about myself.

There are so many incredibly fascinating things about our capitol that most people just don't know. For instance, did you know that the dome you see on the outside is actually one hundred feet higher than what you see on the inside? Also, ours is the only state capitol in the nation to have a rotunda floor you can walk on that's made entirely out of glass.

We all hear, read and talk about laws, policies and politics almost every day, but to actually stand in some of the rooms where it all takes place is a pretty cool experience. I didn't know that when the House of Representative is in session, anyone can sit in the public gallery high above and watch the entire process. I also didn't know that if things are running behind, the Speaker of the House actually has the power to stop time (with a hidden switch that turns off the wall clock) so they can get things done on time. Interesting. Wish I could do that!

The biggest thrill for me was getting to see the heart of it all, the Governor's office. This is where the Governor sits, thinks, signs and makes decisions that move Michigan forward. You can actually feel the power and tremendous history in the room. I didn't stay long, though. I was afraid I might move something backwards.

You know you're impressed when your first thought when leaving a place is, boy, I have to bring my family back there. And guess what? I totally did!

Fork in the Road
(517) 580-3556
2010 W. Saginaw St., Lansing, MI 48915
www.forkintheroaddiner.com

All that touring the capitol made us hungry, so we found a place at the fork in the road that's called, well, **Fork in the Road**. This place is much more than just a restaurant; it's where farm meets fork and the community meets to share a common philosophy about food.

The guys responsible for all this enthusiasm and adulation are Jesse Hahn and Benny Blanco Ackerman. These two young guys turned humble beginnings into one of Lansing's most talked about eateries. The cult following of healthy and tasty food lovers they've assembled is extraordinary.

It all started with a traveling food trailer they would tow to key locations around town, park and serve their fresh fare. What did they name it? "Trailer Park" of course. Now they've got Fork in the Road, a full brick and mortar monument to food sourced locally and served in cool and creative ways I wish I'd thought of.

Jesse and Benny cook what they like to call "slow food." Everything is from scratch, and these guys are on a first name basis with the growers who supply them. The menu is fun, funny and full of fantastic food.

If you're tired of the same old, same old, take a trip to Fork in the Road and see what a real commitment to real food tastes like. We tasted it… a lot… and we liked it… a lot!

The Lansing Lugnuts
(517) 485-4500
505 E. Michigan Ave., Lansing, MI 48912
www.lansinglugnuts.com

If we haven't given you enough reasons to come to Lansing, here's one more. And it's more fun than a barrel of monkeys. I should know; the UTR crew is one. I'm talking about **The Lansing Lugnuts**, a minor league baseball team that plays at Cooley Law School Stadium, right in the heart of downtown Lansing. Just walk into the stadium and you're instantly impressed. Thousands of loyal fans and first timers go there all summer long to yell, "Go, Nuts!"

The stadium is a beautiful state-of-the-art facility, and there's not one bad seat in the house. Not only is the baseball great there, they really go out of their way to make this a truly entertaining experience. With everything from great family contests and events between innings to specials like ladies night, they make it baseball and a whole lot more.

The day we were at the park, management actually let me throw out the first pitch, and like any finely tuned athlete, I took some time to stretch with the team on the field. Who knows, there might have been a scout at the park. After burning one in at a whopping forty-three MPH, I decided not to quit my UTR day job.

There's so much going on, on and off the field, that you can't help but have a great time. Now I know why people have been telling me to go to a Lansing Lugnuts game for so long. And now I'm telling you. I don't think you'll have more fun at a ballpark anywhere. This place is a definite home run… get it? Oh, boy.

Marine City is a great little maritime community that's located on the St. Clair River, halfway between Detroit and Port Huron. If you drive along Water Street, it does just that: takes you along the river. The street is dotted with beautiful little parks where you can sit, relax and watch the giant freighters pass by. There are also tons of interesting shops and great restaurants to discover. Also, if you're into antiquing, Marine City has great treasures for you to discover.

We get emails all the time from people who want us to come visit their city, and that's awesome. But when it came to Marine City, I think we got an email from every single person in town. One of the eleventy billion emails we got came from Scott Anderson. He wanted us to come to his town so bad, he offered to be our Sherpa guide for the day and show us around. Scott knew a great deal about Marine City and made sure we had a great time.

The Little Bar
(810) 765-8084
321 Chartier, Marine City, MI 48039
www.thelittlebarrestaurant.com

Our first stop for the day was an iconic little townie tavern called **The Little Bar**. It looks like a little house, and it's a place the locals love. This is a simple place where everyone comes, everyone knows your name and everything is good. The Little Bar also has tremendous history. The likes of Henry Ford and even Thomas Edison used to occasionally light up a libation there. The food is honest, the people friendly and if you like laughing with the locals, you'll have a ton of fun there.

To welcome me to the neighborhood and loosen me up a bit, they brought me what's called a mini beer. It wasn't really beer... it was very mini, and it made me feel mini funny. Even though the drink looks like a tiny beer, it's actually made with a vanilla liquor and some heavy cream. We laughed it off and were on our way. We had so much fun that it was a little hard to leave. A mini beer at the Little Bar in Marine City. It doesn't get much bigger than that.

The Heather House
(810) 765-3175
409 N. Main St. (M-29), Marine City, MI 48039
www.theheatherhouse.com

Next we went to an incredible bed and breakfast called **The Heather House**, and it's a must see to believe. I've stayed at a lot of bed and breakfasts in my life, but this one takes both the cake and the ice cream. Heather Bokram and her husband Bill own and operate this incredible place, and I don't think I've ever met people more genuine or charming. I felt more sophisticated and well mannered just being around them. Wonderful people!

Even though this 1885 Queen Anne style home is absolutely huge, it still feels quaint, comfortable and cozy. It's full of little nooks and crannies where you can tuck in, tune out and get lost in a good book. Some people have been there a dozen times and say they still discover things they never noticed before.

If you're a true bed and breakfast lover, you will love the Heather House. If you do go, could you please grab my glasses for me? I left them in a nook... or was it a cranny? Doh!

The Sweet Tooth Candy Shop
(810) 765-4070
335 S. Water St., Marine City, MI 48039
www.thesweettoothmc.com

Next Scott took us to a sweet place he knew we'd love, and he was right! **The Sweet Tooth Candy Shop** is owned by Todd May. He's a seventh generation townie who loved sweets and wanted to bring an old fashioned neighborhood candy store back to Marine City.

This place is total old school. You walk in, grab a bag and fill up on all your favorites from the past, present and even future. There are hard-to-find classic and retro candies, all your current favorites and even a few unconventional new twists, like dark chocolate covered bacon. Even though my brain said no, no, no, I tried some and my taste buds said yes, yes and yes.

Todd loves candy, loves this community and is bringing a sweet bit of nostalgia back to Marine City. If you're walking down Water Street and the mood for a mound of chocolate hits, don't say you don't know where to go.

Sea Snoopers Dive Club
www.seasnoopers.com

Did you know that not only is Marine City inhabited by land mammals, sea snoopers inhabit the waters there, and they don't even bite? That's because **Sea Snoopers** is a dive club in Southeast Michigan that loves to explore the waters around Marine City. From what they told me, apparently there are tons of cool artifacts on the riverbed there that are just waiting to be discovered. So if you're a scuba dude or dudette, check in with the Sea Snoopers and check out the waters around Marine City. I'll bet there's plenty of treasure to go around.

Marine City Fish Company
(810) 765-5477
240 S. Water St., Marine City, MI 48039
www.marinecityfishcompany.com

All that running around Marine City gave us a powerful hunger, and Sherpa Scott knew right where to take us. **Marine City Fish Company** is a smokehouse and eatery that attracts people from far and wide because of their friendly atmosphere and great food. Three guesses what they serve there. I'll wait. If you guessed fish, you're right. They specialize in seafood and actually a whole lot more.

Melissa Fisher and her husband Jeremy have made this place a destination for people who love fresh local fish. They also specialize in homemade pastas, house-smoked ribs, beef tenderloin jerky, smoked salmon, gourmet sandwiches, steak burgers and hand-crafted desserts. Getting hungry yet?

Well, Scott promised a great meal at the Marine City Fish Company and we had exactly that. He also made sure we had a blast discovering his home town. So if you're in the mood for a fun-filled day, fill the tank and head over to Marine City. There's more cool stuff there than you can shake an email at.

Story behind the name:
Mini Beer Makes Me Mega Funny

The start of season three and we hit Marine City for a mini beer. They're small but pack a wallop.

Chapter 28

Season 3, Episode 2

• Saginaw
• Clare

Saginaw is a city with great history, architecture, culture and awesome natural beauty. The park system is outstanding and the surrounding neighborhoods are full of active and involved people who love their city and like where it's headed.

Spatz Bread
(989) 755-5551
1120 State St., Saginaw, MI 48602

With **Spatz Bread**, you either get it or you just don't know about it yet. With me, I just didn't know about it. But if you mention Spatz Bread to some people, they talk about it like it was the best bread EVER MADE BY MAN! Joe Spatz is the owner, chief bread maker and probably the hardest working man in the baking business. This guy is like a machine. The day we were there, he worked the ovens like a prizefighter in the first round. Joe was covered in flour, full of good humor and almost never stopped moving. You could tell that Joe took this proud family tradition seriously.

People come from far and wide to get their hands on these lovable loaves. My next door neighbor grew up in Saginaw, and when he heard we were going to Spatz, he literally begged me to bring him a loaf. Which of course I forgot. Sorry, Jim.

Why is this bread so special? The original German recipe goes back in Joe's family more than 150 years. It's a coarse white bread with a hard crust that is especially good for making toast. They've never changed what's in it or the way they make it. And nothing at the bakery is automated. It's a simple, honest loaf of bread made the old fashioned way, by real people.

Some folks will tell you this stuff is the greatest thing since sliced bread, and others think it's just, well, sliced bread. So I double dog dare you. Go to Spatz and try some of their famous bread and make up your own mind. I'd tell you what I think, but that would take all the fun out of it.

Japanese Cultural Center
(989) 759-1648
527 Ezra Rust Dr., Saginaw, MI 48601
www.japaneseculturalcenter.org

As much as I love Michigan, I've always wanted to visit Japan. But honestly, who can afford that? So we did the next best thing: we went to the **Japanese Cultural Center** in Saginaw. It's a beautiful place that's all things Japan. The grounds there are beautiful, peaceful and a wonderful place to just stroll and collect your thoughts.

The temples and the tea house there were built by three specially trained Japanese carpenters who came in from Kyoto more than twenty-five years ago. The interior of the teahouse was amazingly constructed without the use of even one nail. It was assembled by these master carpenters using specially jointed pieces of wood.

I wanted to steep myself in the culture, so I decided to participate in a real Japanese tea ceremony. The ceremony was fascinating. The costumes were beautiful and the tea was authentic. If you're into experiencing different cultures or just need a reason to come explore Saginaw, check out the Japanese Cultural Center. You'll think you're turning Japanese. I really think so.

Next we hit Saginaw's old town, because we at UTR figured out real quick that's where cool restaurants are popping up all across Michigan. And besides, you know us—we like to eat.

Fralia's
(989) 799-0111
422 Hancock St., Saginaw, MI 48602
www.fralias.com

The locals told us that if you want a seat with your meal at **Fralia's**, you gotta get there early because it fills up quick. They also told us that if you like great food, this is the food to fill up on.

High school sweethearts Jennifer and Adam Bolt own, operate and orchestrate this finer diner. If you're looking for a hip place where they put heart and soul into some great sandwiches, this is it. Everything is fresh, from scratch and made with an artistic and creative twist. Adam was an art major who started cooking for his college roommates, dove into the culinary arts and hasn't looked back since.

Fralia's is the place where people meet, eat and exchange ideas in Saginaw. Jennifer and Adam's philosophy is simple, "Serve fresh, creative food from the heart, and creative and caring conversation will follow." And it's working. There really is a positive vibe about this place that makes you feel like you belong.

So if you want a whole community rolled up in a killer sandwich, frequent Fralia's. That's what the rest of Saginaw does.

A wise man once said, "Art will save us." I don't know who he was, but he must have known Eric Schantz. Eric is a street artist and muralist who is putting a positive and creative face on many of Saginaw's structures. His fascinating images and explosions of color instantly grab your attention. After he's got it, his hope is to convey a sense that people care and that progress is being made. City art is giving a lot of people in Saginaw renewed energy and hope for the future. It's all part of the renaissance that's happening there.

Eric's an artist who could go anywhere, but Saginaw is the city he loves, and he loves showing it with art. Next time you're there, look around. Eric just might put a smile on your face.

Saginaw is an awesome city and we had a blast there. You should really go check it out for yourself real soon. If you do, please let me know. I need you to pick up a loaf of Spatz bread for my neighbor Jim.

If you're looking for a beautiful Americana type town to live in, **Clare** is the Mayberry of Michigan. It's clean, quaint, comfortable and full of rich history and friendly folks. It's the kind of place where people are born, grow up and never leave because it's so darn nice. It truly is quintessential small town America where people aspire to live.

Cops & Doughnuts
(989) 386-2241
521 N. McEwan St., Clare, MI 48617
www.copsdoughnuts.com

You've heard the expression **Cops & Doughnuts**. Well, in Clare, it's not just a lifestyle; it's an actual doughnut shop and bakery right in downtown Clare that's owned and operated by nine of Clare's finest. You read right, the iconic town bakery, built in 1896, was about to go out of business, so all the cops down at the police station decided to get together, pool their money, buy it and save it. The town gets to keep its historic bakery, and the cops still have a place to get their daily doughnut fix. A win-win!

These are the nicest bunch of guys you will ever meet, and they have an absolute blast owning and running Cops & Doughnuts. Business is so good now that they've hired a new staff and even added a restaurant and gift shop. The restaurant features fun foods like the "Stool Pigeon Sandwich" and the "Misdemeanor Weiner," and the gift shop offers official Cops & Doughnuts wearables and even a men's cologne called "Under Suspicion."

People are coming from around the world to experience this fun-filled natural combination. So if you're one of those people who thinks there's never a cop around when you need one, you should check this place out, because at Cops & Doughnuts, you have the right to remain full and happy.

The Herrick House & Mulberry Café
(989) 386-6120
120 E. 5th St., Clare, MI 48617
www.herrick-house.com

After all those doughnuts, believe it or not, I had a powerful hankerin' for a piece of pie, so our next stop was a place everyone recommended called **The Herrick House & Mulberry Café**. And from what the locals told me, Mary Ann Shurlow's pies reign supreme.

Even though we went for the pies, this quaint little restaurant in a Victorian house serves a lot more than that. The front is a little home decor and gift shop with a wonderful assortment of things you suddenly realize you just can't live without, and in the back is a cozy little eatery that serves fresh, local and lovingly prepared foods. We tried a whole bunch of different plates and pies and decided the one thing we loved more than anything else was everything.

The Herrick House & Mulberry Café is exactly the kind of little eatery you'd expect in a town this nice. Mary Ann is really doing it right. Her attention to detail is incredible, and she totally made us feel right at home.

The Whitehouse Restaurant
(989) 386-9551
613 N. McEwan St., Clare, MI 48617

Mary Ann's pies alone were worth the drive to Clare, but to be honest, after all that sweet, we needed some meat. So we slid over for some classic sliders at the one and only **Whitehouse Restaurant**. We sure do a lot of eating on our show. Bonus!

On UTR we love small towns. We love small businesses, and we love burgers. Every town needs a little burger joint, and in Clare Denise Jenks has packed a whole lot of tradition into a place even smaller than UTR World Headquarters. This place is so classic. It was built in 1935, and when Denise bought the business (she is the seventh owner), it actually came with two employees: Julie (forty-three years at the Whitehouse) and Jackie (twenty-five years). These two ladies give the Whitehouse its personality and its get-up-and-go.

The food is also exactly what you'd expect: good, greasy and full of flavor from a well-seasoned grill. Diner perfection. So if you're looking for a little place with big flavors and an even bigger personality, go to the Whitehouse. Don't worry, you won't need security clearance. Just a few bucks in your pocket.

515 Gallery
(989) 386-4175
515 N. McEwan St., Clare, MI 48617
www.515gallery.org

Since we were full of good eats, I thought we'd top it off with some good arts. So we stopped by **515 Gallery** and found out that Kim Kleinhardt is teaching kids there to be more than just artists; she's teaching them how to own a gallery and run a business.

At 515, students from Claire High School do everything from writing the business plan to the accounting to picking the artists featured in the gallery. With training like that, they could eventually eliminate starving artists. The entire community loves and supports these efforts because it also brings a wide and diverse variety of art to town. From abstract oils to incredible stained glass exhibits, the students learn and the town expands its appreciation for the arts.

If you get a chance to stop by 515 Gallery, you'll see some of the talented young people who continue to put Clare on the map and make it one of Michigan's best small towns to visit.

Doherty Hotel
(989) 386-3441
604 McEwan, Clare, MI 48617
www.dohertyhotel.com

Speaking of visiting, when you do, check out the historic **Doherty Hotel**. It's been the cornerstone of Clare since 1924 and it's right smack dab in the middle of town. A J Doherty's grandfather built this great hotel in hopes they would come, and thanks to Michigan Highways 27 and 10, they sure did. Now three generations work together to keep the tradition alive and well.

My favorite part of the hotel is the Leprechaun Lounge just off the main lobby. Legend has it that an artist from Saginaw came to the hotel many years ago in need of a place to stay. In exchange for room and board, the artist offered to paint a mural that would wrap around the entire lounge depicting Leprechauns. Five months later he finished and was on his way. The mural is wonderfully weird and fun to study.

If you're looking for a place with great neighborhoods, good schools, a beautiful downtown and fun stuff to do, I have just one thing to declare… oh, I already said it… Clare!

Story behind the name:
I Lost a Quarter at the White House

With a floor that is sloped in four directions, that seemingly forms a bowl in the center, when you drop a quarter, it's gone. Tom still talks about that lost quarter like it saved him in the war. It was his favorite quarter, and now it's somewhere in Clare.

Chapter 29

Season 3, Episode 3

Grand Rapids

Every time we go to Grand Rapids we discover more of the cool people, places and things that make it a great American city. There's no shortage of talent, energy or interesting people there. So, why do we keep going back? Simple, to show you more.

Frederik Meijer Gardens and Sculpture Park
(616) 957-1580
1000 E. Beltline Ave. NE, Grand Rapids, MI 49525
www.meijergardens.org

I have a garden at my house, but after I saw this place, I'm not really sure what to call mine anymore. Once you go to the **Frederik Meijer Gardens and Sculpture Park** in Grand Rapids, you'll wonder the same thing I did. Why the heck have I never been here before? It's acre after acre of art, science and natural beauty that'll make you stop, think, wonder and dream.

Frederik Meijer of the famous Michigan-based Meijer grocery chain had a love of sculpture, and his wife Lena had a great love of horticulture. So they combined their dreams and created a magical place. In this 132-acre park you'll find an incredible and fun children's garden, a five-story high tropical conservatory with plants and birds from around the world and countless arrangements of fascinating foliage. You'll see vegetation from all around the planet there, from beautiful flowers to desert cactuses. They even have some exotic carnivorous plants. Lucky I'm not a bug.

The sculpture park is over thirty acres of beautiful terrain containing the most comprehensive collection of outdoor sculptures in the entire Midwest. Some of these incredible sculptures are mammoth in size. To say this part of the park is impressive would be a huge understatement.

What Fredrick and Lena Meijer built together really is something that everyone should see. So carve out a day, get to Grand Rapids and check this place out.

The next day we ran into a guy who doesn't like to admit it, but he's one of the coolest cats you'll find in the Grand Rapids area. As a matter of fact, if I was twice as cool as I am now, I'd still only be half as cool as he is. Think about it.

Geoff Hudson
www.gr-retro.blogspot.com

Geoff Hudson is what you might call a resident hipster in Grand Rapids. He's a Musician, a DJ, a tech guru and an amateur historian who's keeping a lot of Grand Rapids' history alive. Especially the 80s. We had a great time reminiscing with Geoff because he is the ultimate off-beat 80s expert. If it happened in the 80s, you can bet he's got a replica, photo or recording of it. He keeps in touch with other likeminded 80s enthusiasts on his blog.

I don't know what was more fun, clubbing with Geoff (aka DJ Jef Leppard) at the Pyramid Scheme or toolin' around Grand Rapids in his sweet vintage Pinto 'cruiser' Wagon (complete with back bubble windows). Yeah, Geoff may still be cooler than me, but at least I'm cooler now that I've met him.

Moxie Beauty and Hair Parlor
(616) 281-8699
1144 Wealthy St. SE, Grand Rapids, MI 49506
www.wix.com/moxiebeauty/home

Have you ever watched those old movies and wondered how the heck those ladies got their hair to do that? Well, I don't know how they did it back then, but I know how they're doing it now. **Moxie Beauty and Hair Parlor** is a flash from the past with a funky new twist. This place is the bee's knees. To get more authentic than this shop, you'd need a time machine.

Stephanie Strowbridge is the retro maven behind Moxie, and she specializes in hair styles from the 30s, 40s, 50s and 60s. Kinda like my closet. Stephanie got her love of classic, vintage and retro everything from her family. She grew up watching old classic movies with her dad, and her mom even makes the vintage dresses Stephanie wears to work.

Not only can you get a retro look at Moxie, you'll actually feel like you stepped back to a time when everything was a bit simpler. The Parlor is full of retro furniture, photos and even a classic 50s fridge full of ice cold soda pops. Moxie has so much vintage eye candy that it's fun just being there.

You'll find Moxie in the Wealthy Street district, an up-and-coming part of town that's home to a ton of new businesses and cool eateries. And for the record, at Moxie they'll even give you an ultra modern look, if that's what you want. So look no further. Whatever look you're looking for ladies, you'd love a Moxie look.

When you see the word "reserve" on something, it usually means it's pretty good. But in this case, it means it's REAL good.

Reserve Wine and Food Restaurant
(616) 855-9463
201 Monroe NW, Ste. 100, Grand Rapids, MI 49503
www.reservegr.com

There are two simple reasons we wanted to stop by **Reserve** in downtown Grand Rapids. One was the stunning décor. This award-winning restaurant has a modern, sophisticated and metropolitan feel that instantly tells you this is a place to see and be seen. Put Reserve in New York, L.A. or San Francisco and it would fit right in.

All the furniture in the restaurant was made locally, and the private rooms there are outstanding. The building was built in 1914 and was originally a bank. One of the private rooms even has the actual bank vault in it where the premium wines are stored.

Reserve is also known for its incredible selection of cheese and charcuterie. They take great care in selection, preparation and presentation. They source locally and serve seasonally, so it's a true gourmet Michigan experience. Everything about Reserve is exactly what you'd expect. It's a very cool place with great food and awesome people.

Not only is the food scene getting better and better every year, but Grand Rapids gets better and better every time we go there. It's a beautiful city that's got it all: great food, creative people and no shortage of stories to tell. If I were a bettin' man, I'd bet we'll be back again real soon.

Story behind the name:
Sweet Ride

Could Jeff's 1970s Pinto be any cooler? No, no it could not.

Chapter 30

Season 3, Episode 4

Glen Arbor
St. Ignace

Glen Arbor is one of those small towns that makes it on almost everyone's list of Michigan's most beautiful places. The people who live there love it. The people who visit there love it. And the people who haven't been there yet, well, they just don't know what they're missing. The town sits on the shores of Lake Michigan, just north of beautiful Glen Lake. It's a vacationer's and boater's paradise… and the western end of the lake takes you right up to one of Michigan's most famous natural wonders, the Sleeping Bear Dunes National Lakeshore. More than seventy thousand acres of giant sand dunes, pristine beaches and places to tire the kids out.

Cherry Republic
(800) 206-6949
6026 S. Lake St., Glen Arbor, MI 49363
www.cherryrepublic.com

We knew this part of Michigan was the cherry capital of the world, so we decided to visit **Cherry Republic**, a cottage industry in Glen Arbor that reinvents the cherry every single day. They do everything you can think of with cherries, and even some things you haven't thought of yet. From cherry wines, sauces, candies, pastries, jams, jellies and you name it, it's all there. From sweet to sour to savory and spicy, this is a cherry lover's bonanza.

If it has anything to do with cherries, founder Bob Sutherland is probably already working on it. Bob came from humble beginnings. He started it all back in college when he came up with a plan to make extra money. He printed up some t-shirts that summed up how he felt about this beautiful place where he lived. The shirts simply said, "Life, Liberty, Beaches & Pie." After selling over 3,500 of them, he thought, "Hey, I've got something here."

Now, five expansions later and a fan base of millions, Cherry Republic has become a destination location for cherry lovers around the world. When you're there, it almost feels like a little oasis with beautiful gardens, patios and cozy places to enjoy your cherry treats. After growing up and raising his family there, Bob put it best when he simply said, "I'm the luckiest guy in the world."

If you like cherries and you live in Michigan, consider yourself one lucky son of a… shut your mouth! I'm talkin' 'bout Cherry Republic. We can dig it!

Everyone will agree that there is a ton of natural beauty in Glen Arbor, with its beaches, sand dunes, forests and trails. But there's also no shortage of the man-made variety. Beauty attracts artists and artists attract other artists. Keep up this cycle, and before you know it, you have a bona fide thriving art community, and that's exactly what's happened in Glen Arbor.

Renowned painter **Hank Feeley, Becky Thatcher** of Becky Thatcher Designs and **Beth Bricker** of Forest Gallery are three artists who found their way to this area. Even though their art is all very different, they all came to Glen Arbor for the same reason: inspiration. They talked about the lakes, the colors, the surrounding natural beauty and how communing with nature is a great inspiration accelerator.

There are all kinds of art shops and galleries sprinkled throughout this community. So if you're looking to appreciate, buy or even create your own art, Glen Arbor should be on your short list.

Art's Tavern
(231) 334-3754
6487 Western Ave., Glen Arbor, MI 49636
www.artsglenarbor.com

There is a ton of art in Glen Arbor, but I think this Art was there first. **Art's Tavern** has been an institution in these parts for a lot more years than I've even been on the planet. If you're looking for a casual place to eat, drink and rub elbows with the locals, pull up your sleeves, because they're all at Art's.

Tim Bar is the proud proprietor of Art's Tavern (funny, a guy named "Bar" owning a tavern) and he's carrying on a great local tradition there. Since the 1930s, Art's has been the place all the locals went to. Tim worked there in the 70s, came back to buy it from Art himself and is only the third owner since prohibition.

In the olden days, cottage owners would come up on a Friday evening, turn on the heat at the cottage, and come to Art's for dinner and drinks while their places warmed up. Nowadays Tim said people punch a few buttons on their cell phones and their cottages warm up automatically. One thing hasn't changed though. They all still come to Art's for a good time.

Art's Tavern is one of those colorful little local hangouts where you can warm up, cool down, fill your belly, wet your whistle and meet or make good friends. We made a lot of new friends, left real full and plan to go back real soon.

Sleeping Bear Dunes
(231) 326-5134
9922 W. Front St., Empire, MI 49630
www.nps.gov/slbe/index.htm

Now as I mentioned earlier, this area is home to the **Sleeping Bear Dunes National Lakeshore,** and after we slept like bears at the homestead, we headed to one of the best under the radar hikes in the area, **Pyramid Point**. Even though it's a short, fun and easy hike, Park Deputy Superintendent Tom Ulrich went along with me, just to make sure I survived.

We started up the trail, and before I knew it, we were at the top. When you come over the crest of the dune, you're suddenly hit with an incredible jaw-dropping view of Lake Michigan and the surrounding islands. You're hundreds of feet above the water and the white sand dune falls almost straight down to the beach below. You're up so high and can see so far that you can actually see the curvature of the earth. If you do hike down to the beach at the bottom, please make sure you have the time and are in pretty good shape. It's far and very steep.

Park Deputy Ulrich told me that he has friends who work at many of the iconic national parks around the United States like the Grand Canyon and Yosemite. He went on to explain that when they visit, they say they had no idea this kind of immense and majestic natural beauty existed in Michigan, and that it gave them a new appreciation for this state.

On our show, the views looked great, but to be honest, cameras don't even begin to do this spectacular view justice. So I really think you need to get up there soon to see it for yourself. I honestly can't remember a time when I hiked so little and saw so much. The view from the top of Pyramid Point was something I'll remember the rest of my life.

And, if there's any question why Glen Arbor and this entire area should be at the top of your must see list, I hope we answered them all.

When you come to **St. Ignace**, don't just get on the ferry and go to Mackinac Island. Come to St. Ignace to see St. Ignace. Why, you ask? Because it's a cool, funky harbor town with great views, tons of things to do and a great Native American history. It's the first city of Michigan's Upper Peninsula... literally!

There really is so much to discover in this town that you almost need to talk to an expert before you start exploring, and that's exactly what we did. But, you know us, we found an expert who also happens to serve killer food.

Java Joe's
(906) 643-5282
959 N. State St., Saint Ignace, MI 49781
www.javajoescafe.com

If there's anything about St. Ignace you want to know, the place to go is **Java Joe's**. Java Joe's is a tuned-in, turned-on, psychedelic little café with great coffee and excellent food, and it's run by two of the most interesting and energized people you'll ever meet. Joe and Sandy Durm make this place go, go and then go some more. Just walking into this place is a trip. It's an explosion of color, content and creative stuff, and Sandy's wild collection of themed tea pots will amaze and delight you. All available for purchase… bonus!

As for Joe, he is such an interesting and intelligent character that I don't even know where to start. He's politically active, socially stimulating, philosophically fascinating and will tell you everything you need, want and should know about the area. Whether you agree with him or not, you have to respect the man's integrity and mental stamina. He's great fun to talk to, and he and Sandy are two of the nicest people you will even encounter.

If you want great food in a comfortable, casual, cozy and crazy environment, or you just need to know where in St. Ignace to go, it's all at Java Joe's. Don't 'cha know?

Manley's Famous Smoked Fish
(906) 643-8930
810 N. State St., Saint Ignace, MI 49781

What do you get when you cross a Green Bay Packers museum with smoked fish? No, it's not a trick question, it's called **Manley's Famous Smoked Fish**, and it's where everyone goes in these parts for the best smoked fish around. Even Detroit Lions fans!

Manley's is an authentic little smokehouse by the side of the road that's literally adorned with all things Green Bay Packers. It's so packed full of Packers paraphernalia that you're not sure if you should buy some smoked fish or look for your seats for the game.

Owner Don Wright bought Manley's from Manley himself and is continuing a tradition that started over sixty-five years ago. At Manley's the fishermen bring the fish in fresh almost daily. The fish are dressed (like what I don't know), washed, soaked in brine and then smoked to perfection. They smoke white fish, lake trout, salmon, menominee, herring—you name it. As they like to say at Manley's, if you'll eat it, they'll smoke it.

So whether you're a Packers fan or a Lions fan, if you like smoked fish, you're a Manley's man. Or lady!

Castle Rock
(906) 643-8268
N2690 Castle Rock Rd., St. Ignace, MI 49781
www.castlerockmi.com

There aren't too many places in this world where you can get a million dollar view for a buck, but just north of downtown St. Ignace, we found one. It's called **Castle Rock**, and it's a local landmark that you can actually climb to the top. It's good exercise, great family fun, the views are incredible and, yes, it's only a dollar.

This huge rocky outcropping has been in Mark Eby's family for generations. His grandfather Clarence bought it back in 1929, put in a bunch of steps to the top and it's been a great U.P. tradition ever since. It takes no time at all to get up top, and the views are spectacular. You can see from the mighty towers of the Mackinac Bridge to the great northern wilderness of the U.P.

Warning: at the bottom of Castle Rock is a huge gift shop that's so full of awesome kid stuff, you might be staying a bit longer than expected. There are more cool travel trinkets in this shop than you can shake a rubber tomahawk at. Me? I bought my fair share and had a blast!

Castle Rock totally rocked!

Mystery Spot
(906) 643-8322
150 Martin Lake Rd., St. Ignace, MI 49781
www.mysteryspotstignace.com

Our last stop in St. Ignace was the famous and mysterious **Mystery Spot**. It's one of Michigan's biggest and strangest tourist attractions. I went in twice that day and haven't been the same since. It's great family fun that your kids will talk about all the way home.

What exactly is inside the Mystery Spot? I can't tell you that. Then it wouldn't be a mystery, now would it? You'll just have to go see for yourself.

If you've never been to Michigan's Upper Peninsula before, St. Ignace is a great place to start. Not just because it's the first place you come to, but because it really is a great place to be!

Story behind the name:
I Can See Jim from Castle Rock

Settle in, this one will take some time:

When we were filming in St. Ignace, we got a call from Scott Brown. "How'd you like to go to the top of the Mackinac Bridge?"

We're not dumb. We know how rare of a question that is.

So, we jumped at it. Jim, who is not afraid of heights, was up for the task. Tom and Eric would continue to shoot the episode in St. Ignace, and Jim would take a camera to the top of the bridge.

Amazing views. Super Windy. Beautiful.

Tom and Eric were at Castle Rock with a great view of the bridge. They looked through those twenty-five cent binoculars at the bridge, and there at the top of the south tower, they were able to see Jim, in his lovely bright orange traffic vest. Pretty cool.

Chapter 31

Season 3, Episode 5

Southwest Detroit

Southwest Detroit continues to be one of Michigan's most diverse communities. Detroiters from a dozen different cultures live, work and play there, all with a unified plan to grow and prosper. These are passionate people who love to share their culture with food. They're also politically active, community minded and full of energy and hope for the future.

Café Con Leche
(313) 554-1744
4200 W. Vernor Hwy., Detroit, MI 48209
www.cafeconlechedetroit.com

If you're looking for a welcoming place where you can rub elbows with the people of Southwest Detroit that's also a real melting pot of coffee, I think we found your new hangout. **Café con Leche** is the place where hip Southwest Detroiters come to relax, dream, think and share ideas, all with a bite to eat and a great cup of coffee.

Giordi Carbonell came all the way from Barcelona, Spain to start a new life in Detroit, and he brought his sense of community with him. He told me he loves this part of Detroit because it reminds him of home. He loves the "city feeling" and how people from all walks walk into his café and instantly fit in. Students, professionals, princes and paupers all come together to share a cup of coffee and their connection to this great neighborhood.

Giordi serves a simple selection of Spanish and Latin American foods, and the walls are adorned with brilliant local art. It's the kind of cosmopolitan place where you feel like you're in any number of countries around the world. I may not know how to order food in different languages, but I do know that Café con Leche speaks the language of Southwest Detroit.

As for the name Café con Leche, it simply means "coffee with milk."

El Barzon
(313) 894-2070
3710 Junction, Detroit, MI 48210
http://198.171.52.19

With foods from all different cultures in Southwest Detroit, we couldn't decide where to go for lunch. The crew wanted Italian, but I wanted Mexican. So we settled on both at **El Barzon**. You heard right; one restaurant serving delectable dishes from two continents. It's all the handy work of Norberto Garita, a chef trained in classical Italian who happens to be Hispanic but definitely loves them both.

This is casual fine dining that is totally worth whatever your drive might be. No cans are being opened back in Norberto's kitchen; everything is made fresh and from scratch. Take his authentic Mexican mole sauce, for example. It takes twenty fresh ingredients and two full days to prepare. Mmmmmmm, mole! I asked him for his secret family recipe. He just gave me a polite, funny look.

Norberto must be doing something right, because he's growing, hiring, expanding and serving more great food than ever. I asked him which he serves more of, Mexican or Italian, and his response was, "Almost dead even." The menu is so varied and has so many classics from both continents that you just might have an anxiety attack trying to decide what to order. But once you do, you'll be pleased with the quality and care that goes into every meal.

Simply stated, if you love Italian and Mexican food, heck, if you love food period, you'll dig El Barzon. What does El Barzon mean? I don't know, let's eat!

The Alley Project
(313) 598-2050
9233 Avis, Detroit, MI 48209
www.youngnation.us

Food isn't the only thing that brings people together. There's also culture, community and art. Eric Howard is the founding father of Southwest Detroit's **Alley Project**, a living, breathing outdoor art environment that's smack dab in the middle of a neighborhood. He grew up in this neighborhood, saw a need and started a movement that has now made a big difference in the lives of so many young artists.

It all started in 2004 when a number of residents donated the use of their garage doors to give kids a place to develop their skills and express themselves artistically. Now this cool space has become an artistic outlet for artists across the region. Graffiti artists need a place to express themselves and this gives them an accepted, safe and legal venue to do just that.

The Alley Project is an outdoor modern art gallery that's constantly changing and evolving, and artists are now working in a variety of methods and mediums that make this space a visual adventure. If you're looking for an interesting place to experience real neighborhood street art, the Alley Project will not disappoint.

Detroit Soup
www.detroitsoup.com

In a lot of places, $5 will get you a bowl of soup and a salad. Not a bad deal. But at Detroit Soup, it gets you involved in your neighborhood and your city. **Detroit Soup** is a monthly gathering that raises money to fund community-oriented projects. It's kind of like a fun and funky dinner party where you show up, pay five bucks for a bowl of soup, and when the voting is done, all the proceeds go to an aspiring artist or business person who wants to improve and give back to the community.

Amy Kaherl is one of the passionate people who turns often-empty spaces into places where the community shares ideas and makes real change. She helps find local restaurants to donate the food, local bands to provide the entertainment and volunteers to turn it all into a successful soup.

When everyone sits down to break bread with their soup, the presenters, one by one, take the stage and make their presentation. The projects can be everything from a charity or a new business to a new playscape for kids or even a public art project, anything that will help improve quality of life in the area. The votes are tallied right then and there and the recipient of the funds leaves that night knowing they make a difference. The whole concept is simple, beautiful and clearly demonstrates what community is really all about.

The night we went to experience Detroit Soup was incredibly uplifting. The space was filled with passionate Detroiters who came to eat, listen, ask, vote and give back to their community. When all was said and done, another community project was off and running. If you like soup and you like Southwest Detroit, put the two together and there's nothing you can't accomplish.

Story behind the name:
Detroit is for Lovers

Jeordi moved all the way from Spain to Detroit for love. Sorry, Virginia, *Detroit* is for lovers.

Chapter 32

Season 3, Episode 6

Silver Lake
Midland

Silver Lake was nominated by Travel & Leisure as one of America's "Best Little Beach Towns," and when you go there, you'll see why. The town is surrounded by mountains of sand, miles of pristine beaches and tons of fun stuff to do and great places to stay. If you're looking to manufacture some marvelous family memories, this is a Michigan stop you must make.

I was so overwhelmed with the funness of this place that I decided to rename Silver Lake "Extreme Family Funville USA." From go-karts and mini golf to ziplining and jet skis, they have everything for family fun there, but the big attraction is the sand: miles and miles of it. It's like the world's coolest sand box surrounded by water, and it's all there for you to play in.

Believe it or not, these are also the only **sand dunes** east of Utah that you can actually drive your own vehicle on… now that's pretty cool. People from all over the world bring all kinds of customized (and even some not so customized) vehicles there to challenge the sand. Yep… believe it or not… this is in Michigan!

Mac Wood's Sand Dunes
(231) 873-2817
629 N. 18th Ave., Mears, MI 49436
www.macwoodsdunerides.com

The first thing we wanted to do was get a lay of the "sand," as it were, so we headed over to **Mac Wood's Dune Rides**. This is a great way to see some of the coolest dunes this side of the moon. The Wood family's been doing these rides for four generations now, and there's no other experience in the sand quite like it. You take off into the dunes with a tour guide and about twelve of your new best friends and go for an action-packed educational thrill-ride in the sand.

I tell ya, our Mac Woods adventure was like a roller coaster ride combined with some of the best views in Michigan. Add in all the fascinating facts and good humor you get from your tour guide, and you've got the makings of a pretty awesome Michigan experience.

When the ride was over, not only did I learn a ton about the dunes, my shoes were full of sand and my stomach hurt from laughing so much. It's good old fashioned family fun, and it's fun like this that makes the best vacation memories. Just don't forget who told you about it.

Hansen Foods
(231) 873-2826
3750 W. Polk Rd., Hart, MI 49420
www.hansenfoodshart.com

We heard a strange tale about an awesome specialty grocery store called **Hansen Foods** in a cool little town called Hart. The owner of this store was said to be a sausage making mad-man, and people told us that if you ask him nicely, he'll even cook up the sausage for you right there on the spot. Well, at UTR, we love food fables like this, so we found the store and met this mythical man of meat.

Around those parts, they call Dave Hansen the "Homemade Sausage King." They also call him Dave… go figure. If you like gourmet, handmade, artisan sausage, Dave is your royal highness. Sure, he and his family own a great grocery store, but in his spare time, Dave's in the back coming up with some of the most unusual and tasty tube treats you'll find anywhere. From his signature asparagus sausage to his beer-filled "meat and potato" brats, I guarantee you'll find at least a half dozen to love. He makes over thirty different kinds.

We came, we saw, we helped make some sausages, we helped eat some sausages and King Dave sent us on our way with more brats than you could shake a mustard bottle at. You know us; those brats never made it home.

Country Dairy
(231) 861-4636 ext. 118
3476 80th Ave., New Era, MI 49446
www.countrydairy.com

Remember when your parents used to tell you to stop having a cow? Well, if you get into the dairy businesses, you can have all the cows you want. **Country Dairy** is a first class dairy farm just outside Silver Lake, and it's all things cow. They make milk, cheese and ice cream, and they even give educational and fun family tours of the entire operation. And if that's not enough, they also have a restaurant right on site that serves tasty stuff you can wash down with regular (or chocolate) milk.

Seventy-five thousand gallons of milk are produced there every week, and the milk goes to over three hundred Michigan stores and to twelve Michigan school districts. It's a big operation that still has a down-home, warm, family-friendly atmosphere. It really is a great place to take the kids or even just go to for a tasty burger and ice cold glass of milk. So if you're near Silver Lake and you wanna have a cow, stop by Country Dairy. They won't mind. They have 'em all the time.

Parott's Landing Dune Rides
(231) 873-8400
8110 W. Hazel, Mears, MI 494236
www.parrotslanding.com

Well, before we left we had to take one last look the dunes. Jimmy Anderson from **Parrot's Landing** took us out for a wild ride, and we had the time of our lives. If you're into off-roading in the sand, this is totally the place to do it. Sure, you'll get more sand everywhere, but believe me, it's totally worth it. If you're floundering, trying to find a fantastically fun family vacation spot, try Silver Lake. You'll be able to tell how much fun you had just by the amount of sand in all your shoes.

Next we headed for what I'm now calling "the Middle Earth of Michigan." People told me I'd like **Midland**, and I really do. It's a sophisticated small city with first-class places to stay, a variety of businesses to explore and no shortage of places to get good food. And when you've got incredibly beautiful and historic neighborhoods right downtown, you've got a perfect place to park yourself. If you're looking for lifestyle, look no further.

Charles W. Howard Santa School
(989) 631-0587
2408 Pinehurst Ct., Midland, MI 48640
www.SantaClausSchool.com

Even though our show is about Michigan, in Midland, I got to go to the North Pole and meet Santa. Actually, to be more accurate, I met about two hundred of them. The **Charles W. Howard Santa Claus School** is the world's oldest institution completely dedicated to the art of being Santa. Once a year, jolly gents from around the world go there to spend three days learning all things Santa.

The school is right in downtown Midland, and you'll know it by the sea of Santas strolling up the twinkling front walk every October. The inside of the Santa House is almost surreal. It's like something out of a fairytale. Dozens and dozens of Santas singing carols, eating Christmas cookies and learning to be the best Santas they can be. This has got to be the coolest Santa house this side of the North Pole.

The school was started over seventy-five years ago by Charles Howard. Howard was the original Macy's Thanksgiving Day Parade Santa. He saw a need for better Santas, and the rest is history.

If anyone has the spirit of Santa in them, it's Tom Valent and his wife Holly (aka Mr. and Mrs. Claus). Together they run the school and are keeping the legend of this jolly man alive and well.

Whether you're a first-timer at the school or a seasoned Santa, getting together once a year like this is a great way for these guys to share and grow. These guys are the real deal. Real beards, real bellies and a real desire to keep the spirit of the holidays happy and pure. Now these guys may look just like Santa, but inside they're really just big kids with really big hearts.

With a little coaxing, tugging, shoving, tying and gluing, they even made me up to look like Santa. And you know, when I was done and everything was in place, I almost felt like the jolly old gent. Every one of these Saint Nicks was so nice. I was overwhelmed with their kindness and good cheer.

I'm sure Santa at the North Pole would be very proud of all these guys. They're helping keep the spirit of Santa alive and bringing holiday cheer to kids all over the world, some small and some not so small, like me.

Alden B. Dow Home & Studio
(866) 315-7678
315 Post St., Midland, MI 48640
www.abdow.org

If you're a fan of modern American architecture, the **Alden B. Dow Home & Studio** is a must, must see. It's twenty thousand square feet of fascinating form and function. Alden B. Dow was one of the most renowned and influential architects of the twentieth century, and this incredible structure was both his architectural firm and his family's home.

Talk about a live-work space: in the front of the building are the design studios where he and his staff would work. Then after a day at the office (so to speak), Dow would take a few short steps from his studio to a home the likes of which I've never seen before. Around every corner you'll find something that'll make you laugh, learn and love this place.

I like to describe Dow's work as Frank Lloyd Wright meets Walt Disney. His designs and spaces are colorful, playful and have a sense of whimsical humor that makes you smile at every turn. Dow actually studied with Wright, and they shared a great number of design philosophies. Both men believed that the places where we live and work should be extensions and expressions of the natural surroundings. Dow believed that true inspiration came from spaces that were fun to be in, and touring his home was just that: fun.

The Alden B. Dow Home & Studio has been preserved in order to share this great man's legacy with the world. I think the last time I said "wow" this many times in one day, I was at the Grand Canyon. And like the Grand Canyon, cameras really don't do this place justice. If you want to see what I mean, come tour the Alden B. Dow Home & Studio. Oh, and bring your wow counter… you'll need it!

Shari at the Willard Hillton
(989) 662-6621
1506 W. Beaver Rd., Auburn, MI 48611
www.Shariatthewillardhillton.com

Now, if you like restaurants that are scary good, have we got a place for you. It may be a ways out of town, but once you make the drive, believe me, you'll make it again. It's a genuine gourmet restaurant in the middle of nowhere called **Shari at the Willard Hillton**, and it's full of great food, fun folks and even a friendly ghost.

Chef Shari Rae Smith is the heart and soul of this eclectic eatery, and even though she studied culinary arts in California and New York, she came back to make her mark in Michigan. Almost a quarter century later, she has created a restaurant that is getting national attention. Shari describes herself as a "world chef" who sources local, cooks seasonal and serves from the heart. She has also assembled a knowledgeable and passionate staff that really understands the magnificence of a great meal.

This place also has both an illustrious and infamous history. Built in the 1800s, it's been a hotel, a bar, a general store, and yes, even a suspected brothel. As for the friendly ghost who resides there, many patrons and staff claim to have seen her. They all describe Sadie the same way (yes, her name is Sadie): petite with long red hair and a flowing white gown. I thought I saw her at table six, but it was just a nice lady from Flint.

Next time you're looking for somewhere incredible to eat, try the middle of nowhere at Shari at the Willard Hillton. And if you're looking for a great Michigan city to settle into, come to Midland. After all, Santa's even got a place there.

Story behind the name:
The Sand is EVERYwhere!

Ever tried to vacuum sand out of your car after a trip to the beach? Try it after a trip to the Silver Lake Sand Dunes. WITH TOM!

How does sand get on the head liner? Jim is still vacuuming his car out.

Chapter 33

Season 3, Episode 7

- **Marshall**
- **Colon**
- **Grand Haven**

If you want to step back in time, don't buy one of those expensive time machines off the Internet, do what we did: go to Marshall, Michigan. Marshall is so full of history and nineteenth century small town architecture that it's been given status as a National Historic Landmark District. Some families have done business there for generations, and it's easy to see why. This is a beautiful place to live, work and play.

The Marshall Carriage Company
(269) 781-8818
203 W. Michigan Ave., Marshall, MI 49068
www.Marshallcarriageco.com

The **Marshall Carriage Company** is a great way to see town, and Karen Hagerty from the Chamber of Commerce was the perfect person to have as our guide. Karen said it best when she described Marshall as "Norman Rockwell in a nutshell." The beautiful downtown is filled with incredibly cool historic buildings and the surrounding neighborhoods hold over 850 registered historic landmarks. It's a Michigan history lesson wrapped up in a town of seven thousand.

Marshall was also proposed to be the state capital until it lost out to Lansing in 1847. Karen was so full of fascinating facts about this community that, by the time we were done, my head was spinning more than the carriage wheels. When you meet passionate people like Karen, it's easy to see why so many people come to enjoy Marshall every year.

Schuler's
(269) 781-0600
115 S. Eagle St., Marshall, MI 49068
www.schulersrestaurant.com

In the restaurant business, they say you're only as good as your last meal. Well at **Schuler's**, they've been saying it right here in Michigan for over one hundred years. And from what people told us, they haven't been wrong yet.

When it comes to fine restaurants, Schuler's is an institution here in Michigan. They also pride themselves in being a benchmark for quality, with an emphasis on local and fresh. Hans Schuler comes from a long line of people who understand what a meal out really means to most people.

In 1909 his grandfather started with a small sandwich shop, and over the years, Schuler's has grown into one of the premier restaurants in the Midwest. Hans' father Win (short for Winston) perfected the fine art of hospitality that Schuler's lives by today. The food is fantastic, the surroundings are classic and comfortable and the 125 people who work there will bend over backwards to make sure you have an outstanding experience.

So if you've heard of Schuler's and their incredible attention to quality, atmosphere and hospitality, you're halfway there. To get the rest of the way there, you'll probably need your car.

The American Museum of Magic
(269) 781-7570
107 E. Michigan Ave., P.O. Box 5, Marshall, MI 49068
www.americanmuseumofmagic.org

Now if you've watched our show, you know that we do a lot of TV magic. So I thought it would be cool if we actually went and saw some. If you're into magic, history or you just want an incredibly cool place to hang out for a while, this is the place. It's **The American Museum of Magic**, and it's right in downtown Marshall. It houses the largest private collection of magic memorabilia that's open to the public in the entire world. There are over a quarter million rare and historical items in this collection, and many of the premier pieces are on display there.

The part that fascinated and impressed me the most was the crazy number of authentic and original magic show hand bills and posters on display. From the great Houdini to the Amazing Randi, you get a real feel for the mysteries of magic over the years. And because of the size of the collection, they are continuously rotating what is on display. Even if you're not into magic, the history of this art form is fun to explore. The American Museum of Magic makes boredom instantly disappear.

When we left the museum, we heard there was a big magic festival going on about forty-five minutes southwest of Marshall in the town of Colon. When we got there we found out that not only is Colon the official magic capital of the world, this was the seventy-fifth anniversary of their annual festival called **Magic Week**. Every year magicians and magic fans from around the world go there for one thing and one thing only… the love of magic.

If you're wondering how the tiny town of Colon became the official magic capital of the world, it all started back in 1929 when Harry Blackstone, Sr. was out touring with his big magic production. They came through Colon on their way from Chicago to Detroit and he fell in love with the area. Blackstone bought over two hundred acres of land, and from that day forward, he would bring in the whole cast during the summers to rebuild the show to take out again in the fall. He started inviting other magicians there from around the world, and the rest, as they say, is history.

The Fab Magic Company
(269) 432-4017
212 E. State St., Colon, MI 49040
www.fabmagic.com

The town was full of festival goers and magicians doing street magic. Our first stop was at **The Fab Magic Company**, where owner Rick Fisher gave us a few lessons in the art of illusion. Rick is a great guy, and when it comes to magic, he knows every trick in the book. The Fab Magic Company is a great place to pick up some simple to very complex magic tricks you can even perform yourself. It's amazing how quickly you can do some of these awesome tricks once you know the secret.

After enjoying a number of the street performers throughout town, we ended up over at another iconic magic shop called Abbott's Magic Manufacturing Company. Since 1934, Abbott's has been one of the world's premier places to get everything you need to amaze and mystify. The day we were there, they were putting on a magic show in their in-store theater. I can't even begin to count how many times I must have said, "How the heck did they just do that?"

We had a great time at Magic Week in Colon, and we also learned a ton about Michigan's rich history in Marshall. So if you wanna have fun and learn a ton, put Marshall and Colon on your list, and do it soon, before someone at Magic Week makes 'em disappear.

If you think life's a beach, wait 'til you come to **Grand Haven**. There life's a beach and then some. It really is one of Michigan's great places to live, work, eat, stay and play. Travel and Leisure rated the Grand Haven Beach as one of the best secret beaches in the entire world. Add great restaurants, shops and places to stay, and you've got a classic place for your next Michigan adventure.

Fortino's Italian Market
(616) 842-0880
114 Washington St., Grand Haven, MI 49417
www.fortinos-gourmet.com

If you're not Italian, even if you've never been to Italy, you'll love **Fortino's** in downtown Grand Haven. This classic little food store offers authentic old world shopping just like they do back in the old country. For four generations Margaret Michlitsch and her family have been serving up a little bit of Italy and a lot of personality.

Margaret's Grandfather opened this little store in 1911, and they've been providing the community with old world foods and candies ever since. As Margaret puts it, this place isn't pretend old, it's real old. It's in the walls, in the air and in the atmosphere. Not much changes there from year to year because the customers like it that way.

While we were there, it was a real treat and absolute pleasure to meet and spend a little Italian time with Margaret's lovely Aunt Mary Pontarelli. At the young and vibrant age of ninety-four, she still works at the store and is proof positive that the old-world way is the best way.

Next time you're in Grand Haven, check out Fortino's Italian Family Market. I guarantee when you leave, you'll be a lot happier and a little more Italian than when you came in.

Next we went to a place that was a little more "new" world.

Smokin' Mad Love
(616) 795-2642
5 N. 7th St., Grand Haven, MI 49417
www.smokinmadlove.com

Let me ask you something. Are you bored with your present life? Well, if you are, you won't be bored for long once you try a long board. **Smokin' Mad Love** is owned by Blair Butterworth and her husband Jon Butler, and their energy and ideas are putting Grand Haven on the map for long-boarders around the world.

If you're wondering what a long board is, it's simply a skateboard that's longer and made less for tricks and more for cruising and transportation. They're being used more and more by all kinds of people as a fun and fit way to get around. Because these boards are longer, your center of gravity is lower, making them easier and safer to ride.

Blair and Jon are designing and making their boards right in Grand Haven and now shipping them around the world. They also have long boarding clubs with participants from age six to sixty-six, so this sport truly is for almost everyone.

If you're wondering where the name came from, "I smokin' mad love you" is what Blair and Jon would affectionately say to one another. So with the passion they have for each other, what they do and where they live, it just seemed like a natural choice. I have to tell you, I don't think we've ever met people who simply love life more than these two. Their enthusiasm and positive energy really help connect and motivate their entire neighborhood. They really are a priceless part of that community.

Long boarding is both fun and easy. And if I can do it, it can't be that tough. So don't be bored. Get a hold of Smokin' Mad Love, get a board and board your boredom away.

Harbor House Inn
(800) 841-0610
114 S. Harbor Dr., Grand Haven, MI 49417
www.harborhousegh.com

If you're looking for a classic place to stay while you're checking out Grand Haven, you might want to check into the beautiful **Harbor House Inn**. This place is quite a sight to see, and it's right downtown with great views of the waterfront. It's a Victorian style structure that really has a comfortable but still cozy feel to it. We dug it the most!

Story behind the name:
Wanna See a Trick?

Illusions and trickery. It's all magic and when anyone in Marshall or Colon asks if you want to see a trick, the answer should always be a resounding, "YES."

Chapter 34

Season 3, Episode 8

• Southeast Michigan

I've got five great reasons for you to visit Southeast Michigan, and guess what? They all serve sliders. That's right, on this special episode of UTR, we sampled bite-sized burgers from five of Southeast Michigan's classic, iconic, little, white, slider diners. We also showed you three more great reasons why this part of Michigan is a great place to live, work, play and explore.

Telway Hamburgers
(248) 545-7962
27000 John R Rd., Madison Heights, MI 48071

The first of the five classic slider diners we visited was the iconic **Telway**. This little white tile monument has been a landmark in Madison Heights for over half a century. Owner Allen Owen's dad opened the Telway in 1944, so Allen literally grew up in this place. I asked him what made his sliders so good, and he simply said, "The spices."

We tried them. Tried a few more. Tried a few more and were on our way. But I have to tell you, the Telway was just what we expected. The great people, tasty burgers and retro atmosphere made for a classic slice of slider heaven. If you've got a big appetite for little burgers, try the Telway and tell 'em we sent 'cha.

Marvin's Marvelous Mechanical Museum
(248) 626-5020
31005 Orchard Lake Rd., Farmington Hills, MI 48334
www.marvin3m.com

Next we hit a place in Farmington Hills you simply have to experience to believe. It's called **Marvin's Marvelous Mechanical Museum**, and if you think the name is crazy, wait until you see what's inside.

When it comes to describing Marvin's, I don't even know where to begin. It's part amusement park, part arcade, part museum and completely insane. It's an incredible collection of bizarre, classic, vintage, modern and one-of-a-kind arcade games that you can actually play. And every bit of Marvin's is covered with something weird, fun, rare or just plain silly to look at. You can go there five times and still not see all the crazy stuff Marvin has packed in this place.

Marvin Yagoda is the man responsible for all these clinking, blinking, clanking, clattering contraptions. He started buying these machines years ago, and after just a brief conversation with him, I could totally tell how much passion he has for this place. Marvin was like a kid while showing us some of his favorites. This is a place where you can totally get carried away. And as you might expect, I totally did!

Marvin's is an experience that is uniquely Michigan, because I sincerely believe there isn't another Marvin Yagoda anywhere else in the universe. Marvin's Marvelous Mechanical Museum is mighty amazing. Even more amazing than what you just read!

Hunter House Burgers
(248) 646-7121
35075 Woodward Ave., Birmingham, MI 48009
www.hunterhousehamburgers.com

If you're cruising down Woodward Avenue in Birmingham and you suddenly smell the seductive scent of sliders, it's not your imagination. You're passing the legendary **Hunter House**. For sixty years, this iconic burger bungalow has served up classic sliders for all to enjoy. Susan Cobb's family has kept Hunter House humming for three decades now. Her family has owned Hunter House for literally half of its existence, and as she put it, "It's an honor to continue this tradition." The customers are so devoted and loyal that even when they move away, it's the first stop they make when they come home and the last stop they make before they leave.

You can just imagine what it must have been like back in the day with classic cars of the 50s and 60s rolling in and out of there. Susan told us that nothing has changed from those glory days, not even the burger recipe. She did divulge that other than the grind of the meat and the type of onions they use, the grill cook is the key to a great slider. And at Hunter House, these grill cooks are black belt level in my book.

We came, we saw and we chowed. After all, isn't that what a slider diner's all about? All I can say is Hunter House hit the spot.

Voodoo Choppers
(248) 299-8200
2720 Auburn Rd., Auburn Hills, MI 48326
www.voodoochoppers.com

You're gonna find this hard to believe, but I believe in Voodoo. **Voodoo Choppers** that is! Voodoo Choppers in Auburn Hills is where people from around the world come when they want a one-of-a-kind, custom-built chopper, and Eric Gorges is the man they see to make it happen. He combines art, metal, motion and mechanics to make motorcycles that do more than just get you down the road. They make a statement.

Eric started his adult life as an IT guy but wanted to do something that would feed his soul. So he took his love of motorcycles in a creative direction that's getting him noticed around the world. Eric explained that making a great chopper for someone is more than just understanding mechanics or even metal fabrication. It's also about getting to know the person you're building it for, so the bike becomes an extension of their personality. You really need to be one part mechanic, one part artist and one part psychologist.

Eric loves being in Southeast Michigan, because as he put it, being near the Motor City is the best place to set up shop. All the best talent and resources are in and around Motown. So, if you're in the market for making a statement on the highway, get a hold of Eric Gorges at Voodoo Chopper and let him do that voodoo, only he do, so well.

Motz's Hamburgers
(313) 843-9186
7208 W. Fort St., Detroit, MI 48209
www.motzs.com

If you've got a hunger for some slider history, this is the place for you. **Motz's** is one of the oldest continuously operated family-owned burger joints in the entire U.S. It's where sliders started for a lot of us in Detroit. Motz's Burgers are so revered, they even inspired a whole new generation of slider chefs. Just ask Jeremy Sladovnik; he owns Joe's Hamburgers in Wyandotte, and it was Motz's that inspired him to open his own slider diner.

The man at Motz's that inspired Jeremy is none other than owner Bob Milosavljevski, and if you can pronounce his last name correctly, you're a better man than I. Bob explained that it's the magic of these little burgers that has helped this landmark eatery survive the good and bad times in Detroit since 1929. A lot of slider aficionados literally consider Motz's to be the epicenter of the known slider universe. Bob claims this phenomenon is caused by three things: fresh ground beef, caramelized Spanish onions and a well-seasoned grill.

Next time you're in Detroit, do what Jeremy from Joe's Hamburgers in Wyandotte does, stop by Motz's for a quick slider refresher course. Actually, Jeremy stopped by while we were there, and I think we all had about four courses!

Airtime Trampoline Park
(248) 918-0909
662 E. Big Beaver Rd., Troy, MI 48083
www.airtimetrampoline.com

Life is full of ups and down, especially at **Airtime Trampoline Park** in Troy. Airtime is the perfect name for this place, because in the air is where you're gonna spend most of your time. It's an all-ages trampoline park that just might be the most fun you'll have, ever! This place is huge. It's about the size of a big grocery store and is wall-to-wall trampolines. You can jump from one end to the other uninterrupted. Crazy cool!

Pam and Will Wannamaker brought their energy and this great idea to Michigan for all of us to enjoy. They looked for a suitable place to open their first park, and after looking all over the United Sates, they picked Troy. Pam told us that they loved the people they encountered in Michigan and that they really wanted to be part of the bounce back of Detroit. Nice!

Not only will you find wall-to-wall trampolines at the park, they also have high-flying hoops you can play, a huge dodge ball court on tramps and even a giant pit of foam you can fly into with reckless (yet safe) abandon. The place is great for kids and couples, and believe it or not, they've even had a couple weddings there, jumping for joy as it were.

If you're looking to get silly and have a serious good time, hop on over to Airtime in Troy. Just don't eat fifteen sliders before you do. Just sayin'.

Bates Hamburgers
(734) 427-3464
33406 Five Mile, Livonia, MI 48154
www.batesburgers.com

If you live, work or play in Southeast Michigan, you've probably driven by **Bates Hamburgers** about eleventy billion times. And guess what? That's almost the exact number of sliders they've served. Bates is a Livonia tradition and a family tradition for owner Laurie Johnston. Her grandfather started it in 1955, and it's been in the family ever since.

You can tell Bates serves a ton of sliders because there were almost as many people working behind the counter as there were enjoying burgers. Bates was also the only slider restaurant we went to that had bottles of secret sauce on the counter. I'd tell you what's in it, but I've been sworn to secrecy. All I can tell you is that a ton of it ended up on my burgers.

Another thing you get at Bates is a real sense of community. Everyone on both sides of the counter was on a first name basis, and that makes for a great sense of place and a great place to get a slider. So if you're in the mood for a classic, quality slider, head to Livonia and grab a bag of Bates. Just do me a favor. Save me a couple.

Greene's Hamburgers
(248) 474-7980
24155 Orchard Lake Rd., Farmington, MI 48336

Well, we finally reached the last stop in our slider fun fest. At **Greene's Hamburgers** they're serving up what they like to call "The All-American Slider," and since I'm an all-American kind of TV show host, I thought I'd give 'em a try. These little burgers are the slider pride of Farmington, and from what I heard, ya can't eat just one. Owner Debbie Sutton told me that the right way is the Greene's way.

Three generations of her family have been flipping and frying these little burgers for all to enjoy. Everything is fresh and bought local. Debbie also explained that Greene's is also very green and produces very little waste.

When all was cooked, served, said and done, we had a great time with the staff at Greene's. We met great people on both sides of the counter and experienced another yummy slice of slider heaven.

We went to five of Southeast Michigan's classic, iconic, little white slider diners. Which one did we like the best? Well, I'm not gonna tell you. You need to go out, make an adventure of it and taste them all for yourself.

Go get full on sliders and explore Southeast Michigan, because the more time you spend there, the more time you'll want to spend there. I guarantee it!

Story behind the name:
burgermeisters,
Meisterburger

You know we can eat on UTR. But when you try to hit five iconic slider joints in Metro Detroit, the cardiologist is going to call after viewing the episode just to make sure you're okay.

We are the burgermeisters. We ate a ton of burgers.

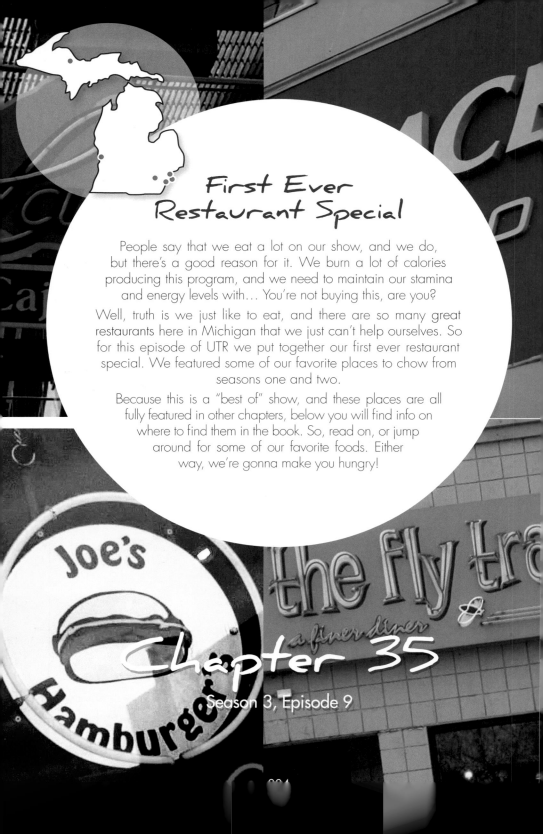

First Ever Restaurant Special

People say that we eat a lot on our show, and we do, but there's a good reason for it. We burn a lot of calories producing this program, and we need to maintain our stamina and energy levels with… You're not buying this, are you?

Well, truth is we just like to eat, and there are so many great restaurants here in Michigan that we just can't help ourselves. So for this episode of UTR we put together our first ever restaurant special. We featured some of our favorite places to chow from seasons one and two.

Because this is a "best of" show, and these places are all fully featured in other chapters, below you will find info on where to find them in the book. So, read on, or jump around for some of our favorite foods. Either way, we're gonna make you hungry!

Chapter 35
Season 3, Episode 9

Hold on to your napkin and get ready for a Mardi Gras of Cajun and Creole flavors at **Lagniappe** in Marquette on page 21.

Next we headed to **Mia & Grace** in Muskegon for food passion the likes of which we had never seen. Oh, you may find them on page 101.

Now it's time for one of Jeremy's sensational sliders at **Joe's Hamburgers** in Wyandotte. Why not try page 81?

You guys getting hungry yet? Good, because now we're gonna trap your appetite at the one and only **Fly Trap** in fabulous Ferndale. You can get stuck on this place on page 150.

When we went to **Good Girls Go To Paris** in Detroit, we discovered three things. The owner is awesome, the food is fantastic and, oh, yeah, boys go there too. Boy or girl, go to page 59.

Now, even though we went there in the morning, this next place has been delighting diners in Ann Arbor for generations. For some **Afternoon Delight**, go to page 43.

Well, I hope you enjoyed jumping around the book finding all the great eateries from our first ever UTR Restaurant Special. Get out there and make your own food adventure and explore Michigan's great restaurants. Now, if you'll excuse me… I gotta get something to eat. This chapter made me mighty hungry!

Story behind the name:

Hungry, Hungry Hippos

Ah, a look back on some of the restaurant segments from episodes in seasons one and two. Fun stuff and great people. Plus, we love the game HHH. Not easy to play in the car, but fun.

Chapter 36

Season 3, Episode 10

•Chelsea
•Harbor Springs

Chelsea is one of those towns that, whether you live there or not, when you get there, you're home. It's small town America done right, with just the right amount of great people, places and things to do. If you don't like it in Chelsea… well, you just ain't right!

Jiffy Mix / Chelsea Milling Company
(734) 475-1361
201 W. North St., Chelsea, MI 48118
www.jiffymix.com

What do you get when you mix flour, eggs, sugar and salt? Another great Michigan company, that's what. **The Chelsea Milling Company** is a true American icon, and I honestly had no idea that the Jiffy Mix our entire country grew up on was made right in the heart of downtown Chelsea. Let's face it, that little blue box is in almost every kitchen cupboard in America.

For 120 years Howdy Holmes' family has been milling flour in Chelsea. His great grandfather started the company, and it was his very own Grandmother Mabel who invented and named the prepared Jiffy Mix that we all still use today. Up until that time, all baking was done from scratch, so having a pre-prepared baking mix in the cupboard was a liberating thing for anyone who had to prepare daily meals. Today, the Chelsea Milling Company brings quality and affordable baking mixes to the masses all around the world.

Howdy took us on a personal tour of the plant, and we were amazed. Not only by how cool all the machines were or how many people they employ, but by the fact that 1.6 million little blue boxes of Jiffy Mix come out of this mill every single day. If you'd like a tour of the factory, be sure to call ahead, because they do it by reservation only.

So next time you take that little blue box of Jiffy Mix out of the cupboard, think of Howdy, Chelsea and me. Well, skip me. You don't wanna spoil your appetite.

Ugly Dog Distillery
(734) 433-0433
14495 N. Territorial, Chelsea, MI 48118
www.uglydogvodka.com

If you're the kind of person who occasionally needs a little hair of the dog, have I got a vodka for you! Ruger, a German shorthaired pointer, is the inspiration and namesake for **Ugly Dog Vodka**, an award-winning spirit that's made right in Chelsea. Now, even though Ruger helps out quite a bit, he doesn't actually make the vodka. That's the handy work of Jon Dyer. When Jon's not spending quality time with Ruger he eats, sleeps, makes, thinks and drinks vodka.

It all started a while back when Jon was out bird hunting with Ruger and some of his best buddies. While sitting around the campfire (as Jon says, "tellin' lies and stories") one of his buddies dared him to try and make some whisky. Well, you know how us guys are; we'll do almost anything on a dare. So Jon went out and bought a coppersmithing book published in 1865, hand hammered his own copper stills, built the electronics and commenced to makin' mash.

Not only do they make premium vodka, rum, gin and even a bacon flavored vodka (great for Bloody Marys), Ugly Dog Vodka is winning awards and showing up in restaurants and retail locations everywhere. If you want a great locally made spirit, just look for the ugly dog on the label. Oh, and in Ruger's defense, I think he's a handsome fella!

The Common Grill
(734) 475-0470
112 S. Main St., Chelsea, MI 48118
www.commongrill.com

If you're looking for an uncommon dining experience, **The Common Grill** in downtown Chelsea is the place to get it. It's an award-winning eatery where all the dishes are so well thought out, all you have to do is think about which one you want to eat.

Award-winning Chef Greg Common has spent twenty years perfecting his version of a great restaurant. In 1990 he came to Chelsea from Dearborn, fell in love with the town, and has been pleasing palates there ever since. Greg is a self-taught chef who truly believes that not only food, but customer service is the difference between a good and a great restaurant. It's fine, but casual dining, and the menu is what I like to call classic, classy American.

When we spoke to the people dining that evening, it was amazing how much love folks give this place. We ran into one gentleman who actually drove sixty-five miles one way just to have dinner there. WARNING: Be careful with the rolls they serve at the Common Grill. They're so darn good, you might not have room for dinner.

If you're looking for a new go-to restaurant to go to, go to the Common Grill. You won't be disappointed. And if you're going to go to Chelsea, just remember, if you lived there, you'd be home by now.

Harbor Springs really is one of those iconic harbor communities that people think of when they dream of vacationing in Michigan. It's become a tradition for families across the Midwest to come back, have fun and relax there every year. And if you ask the people who live there, they'll tell ya there's no place they'd rather be.

Turkey's Café & Pizzeria
(231) 526-6041
250 E. Main St., Harbor Springs, MI 49740
www.turkeyscafeandpizzeria.com

If you like pizza topped with history, community and special sauce, you're gonna love Turkey's. Even though **Turkey's Café** is known for their excellent pizza, they also serve a ton of other great edibles. It's where the locals go to connect and share good food.

Turkey's is also known for how much owner Jeff Graham is connected to this great community. In 1903 his grandfather came to Harbor Springs fresh out of the University of Michigan and opened a dentist office, and today the Graham family continues to serve this community. In Jeff's case, it's with great-tasting pizzas. Jeff opened Turkey's in 1975 and hasn't looked back since.

If you're wondering where the name came from, when Jeff played football back in the day at Harbor Springs High School, he got two sprained ankles in one week. The coach yelled out to him on the field, "Hey, you're walking like a turkey out there," and you know high school kids; the name stuck.

Unlike a lot of the businesses in a resort community, Turkey's is open year round, and it's one of those wonderfully versatile places that is many things to many people. It's a pizzeria, sub shop, café, coffee shop, and in the evenings it even becomes a pub. The pizza there really is excellent, and they bake all their own bread daily. The day we were there, Jeff whipped up one of his famous "everything" pizzas. Mmmmmm, everything!

You're gonna like Turkey's because it's a comfortable place with good food served by longtime locals who love where they live. And if anyone is helping to create a sense of place in the community, it's Jeff. Besides, what's not to love about a pizza place called Turkey's?

You know, my mom used to make cookies for me all the time, and they were pretty good, but I don't remember her having a store in Harbor Springs...

Tom's Mom's Cookies
(231) 526-6606
267 S. Spring St., Harbor Springs, MI 49740
www.tomsmomscookies.com

Tom's Mom's Cookies are award-winning homemade cookies that are baked right in a cute little house in Harbor Springs and shipped literally around the world. If you're looking for a big cookie that tastes like my mom used to make, you've come to the right little place. Believe it or not, during the summer as many as 1,500 homemade cookies will go out the door of this little house and into eager tummies. All made from scratch. And the chocolate chunks they use are as big as your fist.

The day we stopped by, Zen Cookie Master Kelly was at the oven making Tom's Mom's Cookie magic. She's made more cookies there than most of us will eat in a lifetime. When I asked her to name off all seventeen varieties they bake, she did so with great enthusiasm and rapid fire.

Here they are, exactly as she recited them: Chocolate Chunk, Chocolate Pecan, Chocolate Walnut, Chocolate Macadamia, White Chocolate Macadamia, Chocolate Cherry, White Chocolate Cherry, Cinnamon Sugar Dark, Cinnamon Sugar White, Chocolate Almond Coconut, White Original, Plain Peanut Butter, Chocolate Peanut Butter, Molasses, Oatmeal Raisin, Chocolate Oatmeal and Oatmeal with Butterscotch. Wow! And who knows, they may have added a few since we were there last.

People really do love these cookies. We even ran into a guy that claimed to be there all the way from Key West, Florida for his Tom's Mom's Cookie fix.

So next time you're doing a little too much talking (like me) I highly recommend filling your mouth with some Tom's Mom's Cookies. By the time you're done eating them, you just might forget what the heck you were talking about in the first place. I do it all the time.

Tunnel of Trees
M-119, Harbor Springs, MI 49737

The **Tunnel of Trees** is a beautiful twenty-mile stretch of road on M-119 that takes you from Harbor Springs north to historic Cross Village. And even though the road's covered by a thick canopy of trees, you occasionally get these breathtaking views from high atop cliffs that overlook Lake Michigan. It's a uniquely Michigan experience that'll totally remind you why you live here. Now, the road's pretty narrow and the scenery pretty awesome, so we took our time, and at the end of the drive was a place, well, you just have to see to believe.

Legs Inn
(231) 526-2281
6425 N. Lake Shore Dr., Cross Village, MI 49723
www.legsinn.com

If you're just like me and you've heard of **Legs Inn** your whole life and never been there, well, you're just like me. But now that I've been there, we're just a little bit different.

The historic Legs Inn is literally like something you'd see in a fairy tale, but a fairytale where they serve great Polish food and Michigan draft beers… bonus! It's stone on the outside, hand-crafted wood on the inside and probably one of the coolest places you'll ever walk into. The inn is located at the end of the tunnel of trees drive in Cross Village, once a thriving fishing and lumber town.

George and Kathy Smolak, along with their two sons Mark and Chris, make up two of the four generations who continue to care for this great Michigan landmark. George's Uncle Stanley, who was born in 1887, emigrated from Poland and built Legs Inn. Now people go there from around the world to see the incredible wood carvings inside. It's called Legs Inn because of the inverted stove legs Stanley decided to use on the roof in the front of the building. Wonderfully weird!

Legs Inn is so much more than just a great restaurant; it's a pure Michigan destination. People who go there describe it as a unique museum, art gallery and monument to nature. If you're lucky enough to get a table out on the patio, the views of the sunset over Lake Michigan are breathtaking. Great atmosphere, great food, great beer, all smothered in Smolak hospitality.

The Legs Inn was a great way to top off our trip to Harbor Springs. It was a one-of-a-kind experience that even if you do it two and three times, it will still feel special. Michigan truly is a special place, and that's why it's the place I always return to.

Story behind the name:
Hey Buddy, Can I Get a Ride?

When we were filming up at the Legs Inn, the owners had a friend there who owned a Ferarri. When you're offered a ride in a Ferrari, you take it. When you can work it into your TV show, you do it.

That car cost more than most of our houses and it handles better.

As Ferris Bueller said, "If you have the means, I highly recommend picking one up."

Chapter 37

Season 3, Episode 11

• Mackinac Island
• Jackson

Most of us are used to seeing Michigan's beautiful Mackinac Island in the summer when everything is green and lots of fudgies are having tons of family fun in the warm summer sun, but we decided to hop on the ferry, brave the winter winds and find out what it's like for the five hundred people who actually live on the island year round.

On the blustery boat ride over, we were lucky enough to run into the **Mackinac Island girls' high school basketball team**. While we were going on an adventure, they were simply going home. In just a few short minutes, these kids told me how much they truly love living on the island. You'd think that nowadays, kids that age would feel isolated or cut off from modern pop culture, but with the Internet and today's modern modes of communication and transportation, these kids are as connected as anybody. Probably more than me!

Once we got onto the island, what surprised me was how different this place is when all the tourists are gone and the traditional fudge and souvenir shops close down for the winter. The island turns back into a small community. But lucky for the locals, if you still want a good meal out, the Mustang Lounge and Cawthorne's Village Inn are open year round.

An even bigger surprise for me was the fact that even though motorized vehicles are normally not allowed on the island, in the winter, things get real, all bets are off and the snowmobiles are on. It's how the islanders get what they need during the long, cold winter months. It was so strange to see entire families go zipping by in the snow on their snowmobiles.

Mackinac Island Christmas Bazaar
www.mackinacisland.org/event/mackinac-island-christmas-bazaar

We were lucky enough to be on the island during the **Mackinac Island Christmas Bazaar**. It's the islanders' big Christmas celebration that happens every year in early December. The entire island shows up at the old town hall to sell handmade crafts, eat good food and auction off unique island items, and it's all to raise money for the island hospital and school. Walking into the bazaar was like stepping back to a time in early America when people got together to share everything they made. From hand-crafted gifts to homemade foods, the bazaar was a true reflection of this close island community.

The Cottage Inn
(906) 847-4000
7267 Market St., Mackinac Island, MI 49757
www.cottageinnofmackinac.com

Now, if you're looking to come up and experience a real Mackinac Island Winter, remember, not all hotels and bed and breakfasts are open, so do your research. We stayed at **The Cottage Inn**. It's right in town, and Innkeeper Rich Lind will make sure you stay warm, fed... and have a ton of fun. You honestly won't find people more passionate about the island than the great folks at The Cottage Inn.

Doud's Market
(906) 847-3444
7200 Main St., Mackinac Island, MI 49757
www.doudsmarket.com

We were staying on the island for a couple days, so the next stop was for provisions, and for that we went to America's oldest family-owned grocery store, **Doud's Market**. It's right on Main Street, and they've got everything your appetite needs for an island stay. The market has been in continuous operation since 1884 and it's where the islanders go for what they need. While you're there, take a look at some of the old photos hanging on the walls. They'll give you a real sense of the history of this classic little market. We found everything we were looking for to survive and then some. And you know me, the "then some" is my favorite stuff.

Mackinac Island Carriage Tours
(906) 847-3325
7278 Main St., Mackinac Island, MI 49757
www.mict.com

If you've watched our show, you know that I like to horse around, and there's no better place for horseplay or work than Mackinac Island. The horses there literally make the island run, and other than bicycles, they're the only form of transportation on the island during the tourist season. The island means everything to these horses, and these incredible animals mean everything to Dr. Bill Chambers. Dr. Chambers owns and operates **Mackinac Island Carriage Tours**, and his family's been handling horses on Mackinac a lot longer than they've been selling fudge there.

They started giving carriage tours of Mackinac Island way back in 1869, and in 1948 the carriage men of the island officially established Mackinac Island Carriage Tours, Inc. The founders of Mackinac Island Carriage Tours have had a very important role in making Mackinac Island Michigan's most popular tourist attraction. It was the carriage men, led by their president, Thomas Chambers (Dr. Bill Chambers' great grandfather), that petitioned the Village of Mackinac Island to ban the automobile from the island. Today, Mackinac Island Carriage Tours, Inc. is the world's largest, oldest and longest continually operated horse and buggy livery, with approximately one hundred freight and passenger carriages put in motion by over four hundred horses.

These horses are very well cared for. They're fed well, brushed, rested, given top notch medical treatment and treated with great respect. Heck, most of them even get to vacation in the U.P. during the winter. I've done that. It's fun!

I think the horses will always be my favorite thing about Mackinac Island. When you travel by horse, it forces you to slow down and gives you more time to think. Which, for me, is a bonus!

As for Mackinac Island in the winter, if you want to meet the real people of the island, this is the best time to go there. Sure it's cold, but life in Michigan is an adventure. And besides, the warm welcome you get will totally make it worth the trip.

This was my very first trip to **Jackson**, and after spending some quality time there, it won't be my last. The city's that walkable size I love. There are plenty of great shops and eateries, and the classic big city architecture you'll find makes you feel like you're in a place where cool things happen.

Jackson Union Rail Station
(800) 872-7245
501 E. Michigan Ave., Jackson, MI 49201

Driving there is easy enough, but there's a great reason to take the train. **Jackson Union Station** will take you back to a time when your choice was either the train or some sort of four-legged land mammal. It's a classic structure that will take your mind way back in time.

Lead Station Agent Brian Karhoff has spent five decades keeping this travel treasure in tack, and he gave me a tour of the station that really opened my eyes to its importance to this region. It's a landmark that has helped supply and settle this part of Michigan, and it has also seen multiple generations go off to and return from war. It's the historic gateway to this city, and preserving it is so very important.

Now an Amtrak station, ir was originally built in 1841, rebuilt in 1872 by the Michigan Central Railroad and in 2002 was added to the National Register of Historic Places. Even if you don't take the train to Jackson, the Union Station is totally worth a visit. It's a great place to experience a little bit of Michigan's great railroad history.

If you're a fan of authentic West Texas style barbeque and you live in Michigan, you probably thought you were plum out-a-luck. Well, in Jackson, Michigan, your luck just changed.

West Texas Barbeque Company
(517) 784-0510
2190 Brooklyn Rd., Jackson, MI 49203
www.westexbbq.com

If you're familiar with West Texas style barbeque, you know that it means no frills, down home, real deal barbeque, and that's exactly what **West Texas Barbeque Company** is. Dan Huntoon and his son Justin make magic at this place, and quite simply, these meat men are the men to meet. They took a chunk-a Texas... slow smoked it... and brought it all the way to Michigan for all y'all to enjoy. And all I can say is, them's some good eats!

You can carry out, or if you like, have a seat at their "BBQ Joint" right on the premises. This is authentic Texas style pit barbeque and the pits are fired using only seasoned oak and hickory. They don't use gas, electricity or charcoal, and they never rush what they're cooking. They always cook it "low and slow." Getting hungry yet?

Even though this place is a bit under the radar, barbeque lovers from all over are finding it, and they're also finding it to be just the place they've been looking for. These guys can caramelize the fat on a beef brisket like there's no tomorrow, and their ribs, BBQ turkey and smoked sausages are (as my foodie friends would say) "to die for." Dan spent time with some of the best pit-men in Texas, perfected what he learned and brought it up north for us Yankees to munch on. So un-restaurant-chain your brain and come meet some real barbeque people. In the vernacular of the West Texas countryside... it don't git nun not no better.

Historic Prison Tours of Jackson
(517) 817-8960
100 Armory Ct., Jackson, MI 49202
www.historicprisontours.com

Most normal people try to stay out of prison, but then again, I never claimed to be normal.

The best way to go to prison, so to speak, and learn about Michigan's fascinating prison history is to take the **Jackson Historic Prison Tour**. The tour is absolutely fascinating and will take you from the prison's notorious past to the modern and efficient methods of today.

The tour starts at the historic Michigan Theatre where, through a combination of film and live storytelling, you get to hear and see the fascinating history of Michigan's First State Prison established in 1839. You'll hear all about prison life, colorful inmates, wardens, night-keepers, punishments, solitary and secret tunnels. You even get to board a bus and visit 7-block, a fully intact but now closed cellblock that was in operation from 1934 until 2007. In the prison yard you also get to hear stories about riots, reforms, guards, infamous prisoners and the one-and-only helicopter escape. You even get to eat a catered lunch right where the prisoners used to eat.

After your escape from the prison, the bus takes you to a very cool and eclectic gallery and mall called ART 634. In the 1850s the Art 634 building was a wagon and carriage factory adjacent to the prison. This historic building has been reborn into a place of creativity. There you'll find music, dance, photography, painting, sculpture, jewelry, pottery and community theater. Oh, and the prison tour gift shop… bonus!

So, if you're looking to get locked up in a classic Michigan experience, take the Jackson Historic Prison Tour. And if you're looking for a cool Michigan city to explore, take the train to Jackson. Or drive. It's totally up to you.

Story behind the name:
Corn Nutty Professor

Corn nuts are the official snack food of UTR (at least, until someone buys that sponsorship package).

So when we hit the road for Jackson, a spilled bag of corn nuts got Tom thrown out of the UTR mobile with Eric and Jim. Then he hopped the Amtrack with a duffel bag filled with Corn Nuts, those spilled, and that's what got him thrown off the train, just in time to hit Jackson.

NOTE: Corn Nuts are easier to vacuum up than sand, but it feels like a waste of salty, corny goodness.

•Restaurant Special 2

In this episode (and now chapter) of UTR we took viewers to more of our favorite restaurants we discovered in our first two seasons. We even gave it a catchy name. We called it (drum roll please) UTR Restaurant Special 2. Pretty nice, huh?

Because this is a "best of" show, and these places are all featured in other chapters, below you will find info on where to find them in the book. We found them first, now you get to find them. Go!

Chapter 38
Season 3, Episode 12

First up is Flint and **Hoffman's Deco Deli**, where we had as much fun as we did food. This one-of-a-kind place is the kinda place we love here on UTR… you can check it out on page 104.

Next we headed to Harbor Country in extreme southwest Lower Michigan to a place called **Mesa Luna (formerly The Soe Café)**. There we found great food and even a few folks from Michigan. You can find it on page 89.

You've heard the expression, fast, good and cheap—pick two. Well at **Zumba Mexican Grille** in Royal Oak, you can have all three… and that's muy bueno! Ir a la página 4.

Next we blasted off to Charlevoix and landed at **Roquette Burger Bistro**. And on a scale from one to ten, their burgers are, well, to infinity and beyond. You can land your rocket ship on page 108.

Next, our culinary caravan took us to a place called **The Brass Café** in Mt. Pleasant. They're doing it right, right in the middle of the mitten. You can find them right on page 134.

There are people who eat to live, and people who live to eat, and if you've ever eaten at **Zingerman's** in Ann Arbor, you know which one you are. Find out if you are on page 44.

Now, we're back in Royal Oak on 2nd Street for **Second Street Sub Shop**, which will really fill you up. So make sure to bring your appetite and your sense of humor. Take them both to page 3.

Well, that wrapped up our second UTR restaurant special. Hope you made it to all of them in the book, and I hope we made you hungry enough to try some for yourself. Remember, I don't always eat out, but when I do, I prefer to do it in Michigan. Stay hungry, my friends.

Story behind the name: Pretty in Pink

Another restaurant special and another chance to show Tom off in the pink apron he was wearing at Sweetie-licious. He still has that apron. Never returned it. Thief.

Chapter 39

Season 3, Episode 13

ᐧDetroit

Well, I may not be the sharpest tool in the shed, but I do know that Detroit really is becoming the city of tomorrow. There are so many possibilities and opportunities available that tons of young people are going there from all over to build their tomorrows. Up is where Detroit is headed, and young people are taking it there.

Tashmoo Biergarten
1416 Van Dyke, Detroit, MI 48226
www.tashmoodetroit.com

Have you ever been walking down the street and a beer garden just spontaneously popped up? Well, it happened to us, and we loved it. There's a lot of things you could call this spontaneous celebration, but in Detroit's West Village they call it **Tashmoo**. It's a pop-up beer garden that happens a few times every fall and features the best of Michigan brews and great locally made foods. It's a family-friendly celebration that's all about the rebirth of this great Detroit neighborhood.

Suzanne Vier and Aaron Wagner combined their talents and love of Detroit to bring a real sense of community back to this part of the city. They find a vacant lot, the word goes out and people from all walks walk into a party atmosphere of caring and sharing. You'll see families playing games, urbanites exchanging ideas and a community coming together to make change.

When you mix motivated and compassionate people with a great idea, and you can have fun and make positive change all at the same time, you're doing something right in this book.

What an awesome way for people to get together and eat, drink… and think. So next time you're in Detroit's West Village and a spontaneous beer garden pops up (aka Tashmoo), pop in. I guarantee you'll leave full, happy, inspired and with a great new sense of what's "really" happening in Detroit.

The Detroit Design Center
(313) 330-2259
6100 Michigan Ave., Detroit, MI 48210
www.detroitdesigncenter.com

If you're a fan of art that has both form and function, I've got a couple of heavy metal dudes you just have to meet. Eric Nordin and his brother Isreal are brothers bound by birth, business and their never-ending mission to create some of the coolest and most unique heavy metal art on the planet. They own and ARE **The Detroit Design Center**.

The Nordin brothers grew up working in an industrial steel plant, wondering all the while what else these steel objects could become. Now their art is on display in some of the most prestigious homes, businesses and public spaces in Detroit. These two raw and real guys work with their clients to create some of the most refined, one-of-a-kind creations you'll ever experience.

In 1999, the Nordins started the Detroit Design Center in order to create a hub where people could find things for their homes and businesses that they couldn't find anywhere else. They call themselves "artists that create objects for spaces," and together they create fine art and functional objects with steel, glass, wood, stone and other mediums. Eric and Isreal's styles and approach to their art are totally different. So, together they push, pull, collaborate and negotiate with each other to come up with fine art you just have to see to believe.

Eric and Isreal really do personify the comeback of Detroit. They're two young guys expressing themselves and building a dream in a landscape that right now presents a ton of opportunity for people willing to be part of the renaissance. More world class art and innovation made right here in Michigan.

Groovebox Studios
(313) 444-8980
1604 Clay Ave., Detroit, MI 48221
www.grooveboxstudios.com

If you're an aspiring musician or band and you're looking for a box to put your groove in, have we got a place for you. **Groovebox Studios** is in the heart of Detroit's rustic Russell Industrial Center, and it's a place that helps artists from all over get their careers off the ground. Jeff Wenzel and Shawn Neal are band-mates who turned their frustration with the endless maze of the music industry into a pretty ingenious way to help other musicians.

At Groovebox Studios, if you've got what it takes and you want to take your music career to the next level, they can definitely help. Groovebox is a production studio alright, but it's a whole lot more. Sure, Jeff and Shawn will record your band and even shoot a professional video for you, but here's where Groovebox goes the extra mile. They'll also help musicians execute a crowd-sourcing campaign to help pay for it all and give them a platform to have their video seen and heard. Groovebox offers a real network for independent artists who are trying to get noticed in today's crazy music business. Not only do Jeff and Shawn really know what they're doing, they're really nice guys who make all the parts of this process a pleasure.

To give us a real feel for what it's like to record at GrooveBox, Jeff and Shawn offered to do a session with the band I play in. Needless to say, we totally jumped at the chance and even invited friends and fans down like they do in the real sessions. When all was said and done, we learned a lot, had a blast and discovered yet another cool thing happening in Detroit. I'm not sure how much of a groove we laid down, but if Jeff and Shawn find it, I'm sure they'll put it in a box for us.

Green Dot Stables
(313) 962-5588
2200 W. Lafayette, Detroit, MI 48216
www.greendotstables.com

I was told that if you want a really good gourmet slider hamburger at a great price, you need to go to **Green Dot Stables** in Detroit. Now if something seems very wrong with that statement, believe me, once you go there, it will all seem very right. That's because there are no horses or jockeys at Green Dot Stables. There are just hip Detroit foodies enjoying an array of little gourmet burgers filled with incredibly fresh and tasty ingredients. From the Cuban and Korean burgers to the gyro and even the mystery meat burger, this place rocks. They're little and inexpensive, so try a handful with your favorite Michigan brew.

Jacques Driscoll is the owner and the man with the plan to make gourmet food not only affordable but easy to hold. He saw a need, found this funky, old, iconic Detroit eatery, kept the strange name and retro ambiance and started serving sliders. It's cooky, clean, comfortable and casual, and it totally works. Chef Les Molnar is Jacques culinary coconspirator, and he's a big part of the reason these little gourmet sliders take your taste buds to infinity and beyond. Everything is fresh and prepared with great care.

Word of mouth on Green Dot Stables has been extraordinary in this area, and now we know where all the mouths are coming from. The day we were there, the place was packed with all kinds of people enjoying all kinds of sliders. I also love the atmosphere at Green Dot. It's almost like you're in your buddy's rec-room having a beer and burger with all your best friends.

So if you like friendly people, lots of Michigan brews, a horse theme and your gourmet food in the form of a slider (and who doesn't?) giddy up on down to Green Dot Stables. It's so weird... it's wonderful!

The Craig Fahle Show
(313) 577-1019
www.craigfahleshow.com

If you really want to know about what's happening in and around Detroit, one of the best places to tune into is **The Craig Fahle Show** on Wayne State University's Public radio station, WDET. With a bit of an invitation, we invaded his studio to find out a little bit more about the man behind the microphone. What we found was one of the most prepared and informed radio show hosts on the planet. We also encountered a man who deeply cares about Detroit, the people who live there and the success of the entire region. He also happens to be one of the nicest guys you'll ever meet.

I asked Craig how he always seems to know everything about what's happening in the world. He told me his secret. He reads everything he can get his hands on and talks to everyone and anyone who's making a difference in the community. He went on to say that education and information is the key: "If you investigate and get good, accurate information, you can form clear opinions."

Another thing I really appreciate about Craig is that he is very fair and even-handed with his presentation. He presents the listener with the facts and then lets them form their own conclusions. He fills your mind and lets you mind the rest. Craig is what I like to call a clear thinker, and this world could certainly use a few more of those.

If you really want to engage yourself with the renaissance of a great city, come to Detroit. And if you want to stay in the know, listen to the Craig Fahle show on WDET... unless of course you're watching my show. Then all bets are off. :-)

Story behind the name:
Area Code

This was a complete accident. Episode 313 turned out to be on Detroit. That either is a cool coincidence or it shows how little we pay attention to things. Either way, it was a perfect way to tie in the area code of Detroit to the show name.

Chapter 40

Season 3, Episode 14

•Traverse City
•Mt. Clemens

Traverse City really is one of those Michigan cities that has everything. They've got an exploding food culture, thriving business climate and an international wine and beer scene, and it's surrounded on all sides by an incredible natural paradise. And as Goldilocks would say, "It's not too big, and not to small… it's just right."

Grand Traverse Resort and Spa
(800) 236-1577
100 Grand Traverse Village Blvd., Acme, MI 49610
www.GrandTraverseResort.com

When we got to town, we dropped anchor at the **Grand Traverse Resort and Spa**. Why? Because you know what they say, when you're in a nice place, it's nice to stay at a place that's nice. And, this place is nice! The resort has more than nine hundred acres of something for everyone. Whether you're in Traverse City to dine, visit the vineyards, swim, ski, shop, sail, golf or just get away, Grand Traverse Resort has all kinds of accommodations. Even the kind TV crews like… bonus!

Now for those of you who embrace winter and aren't afraid to get out and have fun in the snow, have we got a new sport for you. Fat-tire biking is one of the fastest growing sports in Michigan right now. What are fat-tire bikes? Simple, they're just what they say they are: bikes with big fat tires. But when it comes to riding in the winter, through sand or off the beaten path, these tires make all the difference in the world. Most normal bike tires are around two inches wide, but on a fat-tire bike, you're riding on tires four to five inches across.

Einstein Cycles
(231) 421-8148
1990 U.S. 31 N., Traverse City, MI 49686
www.einsteincycles.com

We were dying to give these bikes a try, so we met up with Jason Lowetz at **Einstein Cycles**. Jason rents them, sells them and knows all the best places in and around Traverse City to ride them. Jason suggested a great system of trails not far from his shop, so off we went. Once we got out and on the trail and in the deep snow, I was simply amazed. The trails were completely snow covered and hilly, and we had a ton of fun on the fat-tire bikes. It was unbelievable how smooth the ride was and how stable they were in the snow. I'm an avid cyclist during the summer months, so to be able to get out and ride like this in the winter was a real treat.

If you're looking for a new winter sport or just a bike you can ride through almost anything, fat-tire bikes are a blast. And believe me, you'll pick it up quick. After all, it's just like riding a bike!

The Cooks' House
(231) 946-8700
115 Wellington St., Traverse City, MI 49686
www.thecookshouse.net

Have you ever had a meal that was so good, you felt like you literally went to a cook's house for dinner? Well, guess what? We did! That's because it's a restaurant called **The Cooks' House**, and not only is it actually in a house, this funky restaurant is serving some of the best food you'll find this side of the Milky Way. Chef Eric Patterson, his wife Teresa and Chef Jennifer Blakeslee have created an intimate dining experience that will make you feel like you're part of their foodie family. And when I say intimate, I mean intimate. This cozy little eatery only seats about twenty-five, so it really is like you're sitting in someone's hip little home having supper. It's casual, comfortable and the perfect place to meet other people who appreciate great food.

In all the conversations I've had with chefs and restaurant owners across the state, I don't think I've ever met people more passionate and dedicated to their craft, their staff or their patrons. Every single person we encountered there was genuine and the real deal. They source locally, cook seasonally and have a great philosophy about how they create their meals. They don't just think up a dish and then try to find ingredients for it. They take whatever fresh ingredients are available and create something around them. It really is art in the kitchen.

Well one dish and glass led to another, and before we knew it, we were full, filled with great stories and already planning our return. If you want a great Michigan-made meal, just walk right into The Cook's House. You don't even have to knock!

Folgarelli's Market
(231) 941-7651
424 W. Front St., Traverse City, MI 49684
www.folgarellis.net

Every time we come to Traverse City, we always stop by **Folgarelli's Market** for a great sandwich, so we figured it was about time we actually featured them on the show. Even though the sandwiches there are so good you'll miss them when they're gone, Folgarelli's is much more than just a place to get an incredible sandwich; it's a foodie's paradise for gourmet cooking supplies, great wine, fresh roasted coffee and hard-to-find specialty items.

The Folgarelli family has been a big part of the Traverse City food community for over thirty-five years. They have literally created a food destination with their store. This place has so much personality and old world charm that you'd swear you were back in the old country. And speaking of old, the building has settled so much that there's about a foot difference in elevation from the front of the store to the back. That kind of authentic environment is hard to find. So will your can of peas be, if you drop them. Roll, baby, roll!

So if you're looking for a great place to fill up, stock up and get your foodie fix, Folgarelli's will fix you a fantastic sandwich and a whole lot more.

The city of **Mt. Clemens** may not have a mountain, but it does have cool people, places and spaces to explore. It's another one of those Michigan cities that felt good just driving into. Mt. Clemens is also the County Seat of Macomb County, so it's got that historic big city feel, but it's still a size that's easy to explore.

Weirdsville Records
(586) 431-0035
61 Macomb Place, Mount Clemens, MI 48043
www.weirdsvillerecords.com

Let me ask you something. Are you weird? Yep, me too. That's why **Weirdsville Records** is the perfect place for people like us to hang out. Even if you're not weird, you will be when you leave this place. It's a wonderfully strange collection of vinyl records, books, art, toys, games and just plain cool, weird, retro stuff. I'm telling you, this place has everything a genuine weirdo like me could want. I even found The Complete Idiot's Guide to Being a Good TV Show Host… bonus!

It's all the doing of Dave and Lisa Taylor. They are Mt. Clemens favorite purveyors of the crazy cool. When Dave isn't playing lead guitar in his intergalactic heavy metal surf band "The Amino Acids" (featuring loudness, Fender tube amps and reverb) he's out in search of fun, funny and unusual items that you didn't even know you wanted until you saw them. Lisa, on the other hand, specializes in finding and selling interesting and unusual books on all subjects. Together they make up the wonderful weirdness that is Weirdsville Records.

There's more bizarre stuff and interesting eye candy crammed into this small store than you can possibly comprehend in one visit, so I suggest a few. If Dave doesn't have what you're looking for in the store, he's probably got it in storage, at home, or he knows a guy who knows a guy. You should also know that Dave and Lisa are great people as well. Fun place!

So if you're tired of the usual, enter Dave and Lisa's world of the unusual at Weirdsville Records. It's a record store… and a whole heck of a lot of weird more!

The Mitt Restaurant
(586) 493-0500
143 N. Main St., Mount Clemens, MI 48043
www.themittrestaurant.com

We love Michigan and we love to eat, so we went to a place that brought the best of both right to our table. **The Mitt Restaurant** is the place to go if you want to put your love of Michigan where your mouth is. It's all things Michigan, from the food to the furniture, and Owner Ken Leonard is walking the walk when it comes to truly serving locally.

Ken describes his food as Michigan comfort food. Almost every single thing served is from here, and nothing is processed. Everything is homemade and made with stuff grown locally. From the monumental meatloaf and chicken pot pie to Ron's Country Spaghetti, both the menu and the portions are huge. Come hungry, get comfortable and put the best Michigan has to offer where your mouth is. The crew loved it there because the food was so good, I actually stopped talking for a while.

The Mitt Restaurant really goes beyond being just a restaurant. It's almost a state of mind. And what better way to feed your mind than with Michigan comfort food?

Frank's Eastside Tavern
(586) 463-4223
129 Avery, Mt. Clemens, MI 48043
www.frankseastsidetavern.com

If you're the kind of person who likes to keep your friends close and your beer even closer, we've got just the place for you! **Frank's Eastside Tavern** is unusual because it's a real, legal and fully functioning tavern that's in Frank's house. You read right; it's in his house. Actually, it's down in his basement, and believe it or not, they've been serving adult beverages down there for more than a hundred years. Back in 1909 you could get a glass of beer at Frank's for two cents. It must have been happy hour 24/7 back then.

Owner Frank DeBruyn is a great old guy who orders the beer, cooks the burgers, keeps things lively, and when he's done for the day, his commute is up the stairs and then he's off to bed. Even though Frank's is a tiny place (you won't be playing darts at Frank's), believe it or not, on weekends they actually have live music.

This place gives the phrase "up close and personal" a whole new meaning. Frank's is a small place with a big heart. All are welcome, and after literally rubbing elbows with the locals, you're instant family. WARNING: if you're more than six feet tall, you'll need to mind your head at Frank's. Come in, stay low, say hi and order a beer. That's how they roll at Frank's.

To have a good time at Frank's Eastside Tavern, all you have to do is let down your hair, walk down the stairs and you're instantly everybody's best friend. It's real people, real small and really a lot of fun. It's the kind of place where they make you feel like you belong.

And speaking of belonging, if you're looking for a cool Michigan city where you can be yourself and have everyone love you for it, you belong in Mt. Clemens.

Story behind the name:
Watch Your Head

Frank's East Side Bar is in the basement of a house with six-foot ceilings. You're going to bump your head on something. Good thing they don't have ceiling fans in there.

Chapter 41

Season 3, Episode 15

• Hemlock
• Escanaba

Well, it was time for another UTR U.P. adventure, so we loaded up the car, headed north, and, well, you know us—we got hungry. So we pulled off I-75 around Saginaw (we think)… got lost… (not unusual)… almost ran out of gas (pretty typical) and stumbled onto a place near Hemlock that's as unique as it is good.

The Maple Grill
(989) 233-2895
13105 Gratiot Rd., Hemlock, MI 48626
www.themaplegrille.net

You know, most restaurants bring food "into" their kitchen to cook for you. Well, here's a guy who took his kitchen outside to where the food is. It's called **The Maple Grille**, and it's a modern twist on the way things were done way back when. No freezers, no microwaves and no ovens, just fresh, local food cooked over a wood fire, right in front of you.

Josh Schaeding is the young chef who's turning heads and filling stomachs right by the side of the road. This truly is one of the most unique dining experiences we've ever had doing the show and one of the best. Josh depends on local farms and ranchers for the flora and fauna he serves up, and he even grows a lot of it himself. Imagine food so fresh that the chef just went right out back and picked it for your meal.

Even though the menu changes daily, depending on what's available, one thing stays constant at the Maple Grille, and that's family. With their help, Josh built the modern yet earthy structure that makes up both his outdoor kitchen and the dining area. It's funky, cool and right out in fresh air… perfect!

We dined on rib eye with secret sauce, lake trout, rabbit confit, colette steak, tri tip, grilled redskins, spaghetti squash and homemade cornbread. Hard to believe, but I was speechless.

So if you're looking for a unique dining experience with fresh local food and great people, the Maple Grille is only a drive away.

Note: Since our first visit, the Maple Grille has also opened an indoor dining area. Great news for those days Mother Nature is having one of her moods.

After filling up both our tummies and the car, we headed north and in no time at all we were crossing the mighty Mackinac Bridge. It's there that we made our decision where we were going in Michigan's beautiful Upper Peninsula. We decided that since Escanaba was only two and a half hours west, that's where we'd head. Remember, nothing is too far if you're having fun in the car.

If you never saw the movie or play "Escanaba in the Moonlight," don't worry about it because we're gonna show you what it looks like during the daylight.

Escanaba is another great reason to love Michigan's Upper Peninsula. It's eleven city blocks of great businesses, shops and restaurants that lead right down to the beautiful shores of Lake Michigan. It's the good life, U.P. style. Now a lot of people are opening new breweries here in Michigan. Well, we met someone who's using an old brewery to help change an entire town.

The Lofts on Ludington
(906) 420-3152
1615 Ludington St., Escanaba, MI 49829
www.loftsonludington.com

The Lofts on Ludington is an old building that's been made new again to create multi-use space that's helping attract a new business and energy downtown. The building features unique apartments and great new businesses. Matt Sviland and his wife Beth had a dream to convert this classic structure, and thanks to their vision and dedication to this building, business in Escanaba is good.

And speaking of business, three young female entrepreneurs who have new businesses in the Lofts on Ludington came together to promote themselves and are now known as The Lofty Girls. Ashley Westlund is helping to beautify Escanaba with her Salon West and Spa. Lofty Girl Rachel Miron is helping accessorize Escanaba with her Pink Sugar Boutique and Holly Nylund is helping capture Escanaba on film in her live/work photography space. The Lofts on Ludington is attracting young and talented people like the Lofty Girls, and now these three talented young ladies are helping Escanaba's economy grow. I call that a lofty goal.

Sayklly's Candies
(906) 786-1524
1304 Ludington St., Escanaba, MI 49829
www.UPcandy.com

While we were in Escanaba, we also had the chance to visit a place that's been making candy longer than Willy Wonka. Mike Kobasic and his family have been making great candy at **Sayklly's** since before there was TV, household refrigerators and even me.

In 1906, Joseph Sayklly, a young Lebanese immigrant, came to this country to pursue the American Dream. He settled in Escanaba, opened a small grocery store, started making and selling homemade candies and the rest is history. Three generations later, Sayklly's Candies is still using old-country recipes to make candies that are now an Upper Peninsula tradition that's known around the world.

Making candy is something I always thought was done by machines, but I quickly discovered that a lot of the good stuff is actually made by hand. So you know me, I had to try my hand at it. After a couple hours of rolling, pouring, mixing, dipping and of course taste testing, I almost got the hang of it. Well, at least I got pretty good at the tasting part.

I promise you won't be buying any of the candy I made, that stuff we ate before we even left town, and I can also promise that if you like candy, you'll love Sayklly's. Not only was their candy wonderful, they were the sweetest people I've met in a long time. Pun intended!

The Swedish Pantry
(906) 786-9606
819 Ludington St., Escanaba, MI 49829
www.swedishpantry.com

I've always dreamed of a place where I could get a decorative violin, a stuffed monkey, a vintage cuckoo clock, a ceramic duck, oh, and the best Swedish food in town. Well, at **The Swedish Pantry**, I finally found it. This wonderfully wacky place is one of the most eclectic restaurants you'll ever walk into. It's a gift shop, bakery, art gallery and eatery all rolled into a place that serves some of the best homemade Swedish food this side of the big pond.

How did we know the food was so good? Well, not only did we taste a ton of it, the words, "Best Food In Town" are also plastered all over the front of the building. But it works because the Swedish Pantry truly is a destination in these parts.

People come from around the world to sample their traditional Swedish dinners, and everything is homemade using traditional family recipes that include fresh homemade bread and butter. Mmmmm butter! If you love authentic Swedish meatballs, potato sausage, rutabagas and ham-stuffed potato dumplings, you're gonna love this place. Heck, they even serve lingonberries. I'll wait while you Google that.

So if you like a side of eye candy with your comfort food, check out the Swedish Pantry. It's mmm, mmm, man is there a lot of stuff in here!

The House of Ludington
(906) 786-6300
223 Ludington St., Escanaba, MI 49829
www.houseofludington.com

The House of Ludington is a landmark that's been a part of Escanaba's landscape for well over a century. This historic inn has hosted royalty, celebrities and dignitaries dating way back to the middle 1800s. Suzelle Eisenberger and her husband Ed now own the inn and are lovingly (and single handedly) bringing this icon back to its glory days, one room at a time.

The building almost looks like a castle and has been known for years as the Great White Castle of the North. If you do spend a day or two there, Suzelle and Ed can tell you many fascinating stories about the house and the illustrious people who have stayed there.

When we visited, they were still deep into parts of the renovation, so best to call ahead and see what is available. But the House of Ludington is an extraordinary landmark in Escanaba and is totally worth a visit and more research. Discovery is half the fun!

The Stonehouse
(906) 786-5003
2223 Ludington St., Escanaba, MI 49829
www.StonehouseEscanaba.com

They say if you want a great meal in Escanaba, you have to hear these words first: "You came to the right place." And where you'll hear them the most is at **The Stonehouse**.

It's no secret why this place is called The Stonehouse; it's a house that's made of stone. But according to owners John and Starr Romps, the secret to their success is family, great employees and the new food culture they're helping create there. If you've got friends, family or even clients coming in from out of town and you want to impress them, this is where you take them.

The restaurant is also a come-as-you-are kind of place where you can still enjoy fine dining. And their attention to quality and detail is second to none. If you want to have a fancy night out without getting all gussied up, The Stonehouse is your place.

John, Starr and their sons, John and Matt, are a great Michigan success story because they're doing things right, right in the U.P., and all of Escanaba is glad to have them.

Rosy's Diner
(906) 786-1983
1313 Ludington St., Escanaba, MI 49829

The next morning we started the long journey home, but not before stopping at **Rosy's Diner**. It's Escanaba's go-to place for a quick breakfast or lunch, and Rosy is a genuine character who makes you feel right at home. If you like a pound of opinion and a side of good humor with your meals, Rosy cooks it up just the way you like it. This is classic American Diner done right, and right in your face. We laughed, we ate, we laughed some more and left. Rosy's Diner is the real deal!

As for Escanaba in the sunlight, what more can I say? It's another great Michigan place to be!

Story behind the name:
When Can We Stop?

You know that here at UTR headquarters we like to eat. On this trip up to the U.P., we hit the road and no sooner were we just past Flint, but the calls from the backseat were, "I'm hungry" and "When are we going to eat?"

So we pulled the car over and found ourselves in Hemlock. The rest is TV history.

Chapter 42

Season 3, Episode 16

·Southeast Michigan

On this episode of Under the Radar Michigan, we hit five great spots in Southeast Michigan, all proof positive that Southeast Michigan is one of the greatest places to be on Planet Earth.

Lafayette Place Lofts
(248) 758-9925
151 Lafayette St., Pontiac, MI 48342
www.lafayetteplacelofts.com

If you can take something old and use it to help make an entire city new again, you're doing something right in my book. And that's exactly what they did when they opened **Lafayette Place Lofts** in Downtown Pontiac. They took an old building and turned it into cool, multi-use urban apartments and retail space that's turning heads all across the region.

This totally renovated building originally opened in 1929 as a Sears Department Store. After servicing the community for many years, the eighty-thousand square-foot building's exterior has been historically restored while the interior has been modernized, LEED certified and turned into upscale urban apartments where almost everything you need is at your fingertips.

If you're looking for a shining example of urban renewal and revitalization, this is it. At Lafayette Place they've got all the amenities the new urban dweller needs right in the building, from a gourmet fresh foods market and fitness center to banking and entertainment.

Lafayette Place lofts has also partnered with Grace Centers of Hope, a faith-based outreach organization that helps homeless and disadvantaged individuals and families. Together they employ many of those less fortunate in our society, giving them a chance to renew their lives and reclaim their place in the community. A noble act indeed!

Like a lot of cities in America, Pontiac fell on hard times, but now, thanks to recent developments like Lafayette Place Lofts, the time is right to reconnect with downtown Pontiac. Young professionals are moving in, and this part of Michigan is moving up.

Ernie's Market
8500 Capital St., Oak Park, MI 48237
(248) 541-9703

Next, we went to Oak Park to meet a guy I guarantee you will love, or my name ain't Baby. When you walk into **Ernie's Market**, you can't help but feel the love, because for decades Ernie's been at the heart of this neighborhood, and for good reason: he fills your tummy and feeds your soul. Also, be prepared to take on a new identity, because the second you walk in, your name will instantly be changed to "Baby," because that's Ernie's endearing term for all he meets.

At Ernie's, it's all about two things: feeling good about yourself and a good sandwich for a great price, and people come from far and wide for both. They say you should never eat anything bigger than your head, but at Ernie's, if you get a #6, get ready to smash that rule. And, if you've never been to Ernie's before, you can't get your sandwich cut in half. As Ernie says, "If it's your first time, you gotta fight it, Baby!"

Ernie truly is a bigger-than-life, one-in-a-million personality who makes even bigger deli sandwiches to order. His place is simple, real and takeout only. Everyone in the neighborhood knows Ernie and he knows them. His philosophy is that people in a community should help each other, watch over each other and care about where they live. The bonus with Ernie is that you get a great sandwich while he's caring about you.

If you do go to Ernie's, get ready to be called Baby. Get ready for a man with more positive energy than the sun with a smiley face painted on it. And get ready for a sandwich that will most likely hold you until tomorrow. Believe me, until you meet this extraordinary man, you won't know what you're missing. Now, what do you want on your sandwich, Baby?

The Wurst Bar
(734) 485-6720
705 W. Cross, Ypsilanti, MI 48197
www.wurstbarypsi.com

Since you're so used to us telling you about some of the "best" places in Michigan, I thought we'd tell you about **The Wurst Bar** in Ypsilanti—for real! It's the Wurst Bar alright, and it's a funky, cool watering hole and artisan sausage eatery that's attracting foodies from all over Michigan.

From the bizarre to the sublime, Jesse Kranyak and his business partner Jim Seba have put together one of the most unique dining and drinking experiences we've been to in a long time. And if you're looking for a creative chef who's totally committed to his craft, Dan Klenotic in the kitchen is your guy. He's the reason the seasonings at this place will blow your mind. It's the first restaurant I've ever been to where they talked about food in "flavor profiles."

The best thing about the Wurst Bar is that the wurst food is the best. They do things with sausage I didn't even think was possible. The menu offers everything from traditional to even snake sausage, and what they do with gourmet burgers is monumental. They even serve homemade regular or sweet potato tater tots, all offered up with a great selection of Michigan brews.

The Wurst Bar also has a great atmosphere. The funky furnishings and light fixtures make for a cool and eclectic environment. You'll also meet people from all walks there who share an appetite for adventurous and delicious food. But don't be afraid to bring the kids. There's plenty there for them to love.

So if you're looking for some exotic flavor profiles that'll tickle your taste buds, the best place to go is the Wurst Bar in Ypsilanti. Besides, what's the wurst that could happen—exactly!

Tollgate Farm
(248) 347-0269
28115 Meadowbrook Rd., Novi, MI 48377
www.ExperienceTollgate.com

Finally, a chance for me to feature something that's even sappier than I am! You read right, I said sap, and if you've always wanted to know what it's like to make real maple syrup, **Tollgate Farm** and Educational Center in Novi is the place to go. They know everything there is to know about tapping and sapping the mighty Michigan sugar maple.

First of all, when you visit Tollgate Farm, I highly recommend doing it with a bunch of kids, because you really start to feed off their energy and excitement. Watching them learn and discover is a real treat. Plus, it gives you the chance to pretend like you already knew it all.

The process of making syrup is a little bit of science, a little bit of magic and a whole lot of fun. We went with a wagon full of kids into the farm's maple forest, learned how and why the sap flows, actually tapped some trees and then made our way over to a real Sugar Shack to boil down the sap into delicious syrup. A guide was with us the entire way making sure the kids learned all about the process, because remember, I already knew it all… ha!

This was honestly the most fun I'd had in a long time. The kids were excited and wonderful, I actually did learn a lot and when all was said and done, I had some freshly made syrup for my pancakes the next day.

Please note that the maple tapping season is in the spring and is very short and unpredictable, so by all means, call ahead to see when they'll be tapping and sapping.

Even though we went there for the experience of making real maple syrup, Tollgate Farm is owned and operated by Michigan State University and is a real working farm with all kinds of activities and animals for the kids to see. They also offer an entire range of educational opportunities including youth education programs and camps, so I invite you to explore more about what this outstanding facility has to offer.

The Detroit Zoo
(248) 541-5717
8450 W. 10 Mile Rd., Royal Oak, MI 48067
www.detroitzoo.org

Next we went to **The Detroit Zoo** to see an exhibit I had heard about and always wanted to see. I'm telling you right now, this exhibit is so incredible that whether you're six or 106, you'll BEARLY be able to contain yourself.

It's called the Arctic Ring of Life, and it's North America's largest polar bear exhibit. What's also cool about this exhibit is that it's a complete four-acre arctic habitat that also houses arctic foxes and seals.

My favorite part about the experience is the spectacular seventy-foot-long Polar Passage, a clear tunnel that winds through a vast underwater marine environment. It's a twelve-foot-wide, eight-foot-tall tunnel that takes you underneath diving and swimming polar bears and seals!

For safety's sake, and to keep everyone in one piece, the bears and seals are separated from each other by a transparent barrier, but it totally looks like they're sharing one aquatic environment.

The Arctic Ring of Life was actually named the Second Best Zoo Exhibit in the U.S. by the Intrepid Traveler's guide to "America's Best Zoos" and is open year round. So whether it's winter, spring, summer or fall, if you get the call of the wild, spend some quality time with your furry and feathered friends at the Detroit Zoo. Don't worry; they'll be waitin' for ya.

Story behind the name:
Yeah, Baby!

One word: Ernie. This guy knows how to welcome people to his store. We should all be this excited to see people.

Chapter 43

Season 3, Episode 17

·Kalamazoo
· Milford

Kalamazoo is one of my favorite cities in Michigan, and for good reason. It's a place that's known for its art, innovation and friendly people. And the downtown is full of history, classic architecture and a great variety of places to eat, drink and even think. And Western Michigan University and Kalamazoo College give this town a constant positive energy and creative vibe.

The Rickman House
(269) 903-2885
345 N. Burdick St., Kalamazoo, MI 49007
www.medallionmgmt.com/propertyindex.aspx

What do you call it when you beautify a city, preserve history and give people with special needs a wonderful new place to live? In Kalamazoo they call it **The Rickman House**. Let's face it, some folks in our world just need a little extra help, and at The Rickman House, people with special needs are given a place to live with both dignity and a great sense of place in their community.

The Rickman House is an iconic, century-old eight-story building that has been renovated into efficiency apartments for low-income adults who have special needs. Support staff is on site twenty-four hours a day, and residents pay no more than thirty percent of their income. This wonderful building helps support so many of the people society tends to either forget about or simply turn its back on.

I was lucky enough to spend some quality time with some of the residents at The Rickman House. Not only did they tell me some great old stories about the neighborhood, they also told me how touched they were that people cared enough about them to give them this wonderful, beautiful and safe place to live.

It's times like these that really make you appreciate the human spirit and what people are willing to do for each other. The Rickman House is right downtown, nice to look at and the right thing to do for these special people. Every town should have a Rickman House!

Food Dance
(269) 382-1888
401 E. Michigan Ave., Kalamazoo, MI 49007
www.fooddance.net

Well, I'd heard of the moon dance, the victory dance and even the enchanting Under the Sea dance... but "**Food Dance**"... now that's one I was willing to learn!

Don't worry guys, this segment's not about dancing, because Food Dance is actually a restaurant. That's right, we went there to eat! If you're looking for who helped invent the whole farm-to-fork movement here in Michigan, Julie Stanley just might be your mother of invention. She's been serving fresh and buying locally since way before it was cool. The restaurant is also seasonal. So when something is out of season, you miss it and absolutely love it when it comes back.

Julie is a locavore and believes in enjoying foods that are sourced locally, which to a locavore means no farther than fifty to one hundred miles away. That ensures the foods are fresh and more nutritious. It also makes sure you're supporting the local agricultural economy.

The restaurant also has a very unusual atmosphere. Cool art, great murals and even an artistically recreated giant stand of corn stalks that take you from one dining room to the next. If you look closely, you'll even see food fairies lurking about.

People from far and wide put Food Dance on their dance card because of the great food and the exceptionally artistic atmosphere. And our tummies dance all through dinner, so if you can't dance, don't worry about it. At Food Dance, they'll do all the dancing for you. And believe me, they know a step or two!

You know, sometimes your bartender can be the wisest person in your life, and when we were in Kalamazoo, we met one whose mantra is, "Eat, Drink, and Be Michigan." Sounds pretty wise to me!

The Old Dog Tavern
(269) 381-5677
402 E. Kalamazoo Ave., Kalamazoo, MI 49007
www.olddogtavern.com

Now, first things first. If you want to meet up with a great bartender, you gotta start with a great bar, so we headed on over to **The Old Dog Tavern**. The Old Dog is one of those places that no matter how much you drink, you'll never forget it. It's relaxed, raw, real and it's the right place to be if you want great music, good food and laid-back friends. The owner Sean Smith put his heart, soul, blood, sweat and tears into this old historic building, and when you walk in, you can feel the friendliness.

Angie Jackson
www.elixirmixernews.blogspot.com/p/elixir-fixer.html

As for our bartender, we didn't just meet up with any mix maker. We were about to get our Michigan drink on with the one and only "Mighty Mixologist," the "Elixir Fixer" herself, the one and only **Angie Jackson**. She's a certified master of mixology who prides herself in making unique libations using locally grown fixers, mixers and liqueurs. With Angie, you don't just get a tasty cocktail, you get an education, an entire floor show and a genuine sense of community.

Angie takes her mixology demonstrations to a variety of establishments, and if you're lucky enough to catch her show, it's a blast. I helped out with her demonstration the night we were at The Old Dog (sort of). I may not be a very good elixir-mixer-drink-fixer guy (actually, I'm more of a muddler) but what Angie and I did have in common is a great love of where we live.

So thanks to Angie, at The Old Dog, I learned some new tricks. I also learned that no matter where you're from, when you're in Kalamazoo, they make you feel like you belong.

Nice is the word, and **Milford** is the town. It's one of those rare places that feels like home, even your first time there. The downtown is full of great shops and cool restaurants, and you're surrounded on all sides by awesome green space and beautiful historic homes and neighborhoods. One walk through the winding downtown, and we were sold.

Just up the road from Milford in the beautiful little town of Highland is a market. Now there are markets, and there are markets. But, this market was, well, you have to go there to believe it. If I were you, I'd put it on your calendar and mark it!

Colasanti's Market
(248) 887-0012
468 S. Milford Rd., Highland, MI 48357
www.colasantis.com

One walk through **Colasanti's Market** and you'll wish you lived right down the street. It's old-world wonderful and goes way beyond just being a market. Ken Snook visited years ago as a butcher and loved the place so much, he bought it. His love for tradition and attention to detail has kept Colasanti's near and dear to the hearts of all the people who have come to depend on this wonderful place. Not only does the market provide the residents with so much of what they need to enjoy life, it also creates a sense of place for this entire community.

Now, the only way to accurately describe Colasanti's is to simply tell you what it is. Are you ready? It's a wonderfully diverse, old-world gourmet market, a butcher shop, an artisan cheese shop, a garden shop, greenhouse, organic produce stand, a wild exotic parrot sanctuary, a culinary educational center, a zoo, a bakery, a wine shop, a flower shop, deli and gift shop. Heck, they even have a super cool antique train that travels around the store high above the merchandise and beautiful murals that illustrate the history of the market. It really is one of those unique places that you have to visit many times before you can take it all in, yet it's still small, friendly and welcoming.

So whether you're looking for something for your yard, your home, your head, your heart or your stomach, Colasanti's Market will not disappoint. The only disappointment might be that you don't live right down the street.

Your Nesting Place
(248) 685-7314
332 N. Main St., Milford, MI 48381
www.yournestingplace.com

If you're looking for a place that's got cool stuff for your place, don't worry, we found just the place. If you're into funky, cool, eclectic, reclaimed and creative interiors, place this place on your list. It's called **Your Nesting Place** and owner Chris Meredith is helping put personality back into the places people live. She finds eclectic-style furnishings that turn a house into your home.

Chris is one of those rare and talented people who can go out, find a couple cool and unique things and turn them into a theme that gives an entire room a personality. She specializes in making your home reflect you. She has everything for every taste, everything from the expected to the cool and funky unexpected. Believe me, this girl has a black belt in feng shui.

Chris' mantra is simple and brilliant... There are no HAVE TOs! Buy what you love and build around it! "It can be as simple as a pillow, your Grandmother's dishes or a pair of lamps," she said. "That's what makes an interesting room. A home tells a story and it takes time for that story to evolve. It can't be done by just purchasing a showroom of furniture." Wise and creative words indeed.

So if you're looking for that certain something to make your home different, Your Nesting Place is certainly something you should consider.

Milford House Bar & Grill
(248) 684-2226
113 E. Commerce, Milford, MI 48381
www.themilfordhouse.com

Every community needs a gathering place, and if that gathering place happens to be a restaurant that serves homemade food—bonus! Three generations of the Sinacola family have worked hard to turn **The Milford House** into the "go-to" place for comfort food, comfortable surroundings and a place where the locals connect.

Perry Sinacola has worked hard to turn this place into "the place to be," and his philosophy is pretty simple: keep the food real, the surrounding comfortable and treat your guest like your neighbors. And that's exactly who they are. If you want to meet your friends for a bite to eat, it's the Milford House. If you want to meet the gang to watch the big game, it's the Milford House. Whether you're meeting someone to talk, eat, drink or just think, the key word is meet, because that's what the community does at the Milford House.

And speaking of meat, if you get a chance, order some of the real Italian meatballs, because Perry's mom Maria is back in the kitchen making her family recipe from scratch. Both Maria and the meatballs were Italian-awesome! And she liked me so much, she even let me help... sort of. Don't worry; they didn't serve the ones I made.

So if you're looking for a casual, comfortable place to eat AND connect with your fellow man, man, you have to go to the Milford House.

And if you're looking for a new town to live, work or play in... Milford will make you feel right at home, every time you come back.

Story behind the name:
I'll Make Mine a Triple

There must be a reason why they don't let you order a drink as a triple. But I can't remember it after having a triple made by the Elixer Fixer in K'zoo.

Chapter 44

Season 3, Episode 18

·Grand Rapids

If you haven't been to Grand Rapids in a while,
you'll be amazed when you get there. When it comes
to art, food, shopping, new business and entertainment,
this place has it all. It's a modern cosmopolitan city with a
great history and a brilliant future. It's also a very livable city,
where you can work, play and stay right downtown.

City Flats Hotel
(616) 608-1720
83 Monroe Center St. NW, Grand Rapids, MI 49503
www.cityflatshotel.com/grandrapids

This time in Grand Rapids, we dropped anchor at a place called **City Flats**. It's an ultra modern, extremely progressive and very green boutique hotel that's right in the heart of the city. Believe me, you'll look cool just walking into this place.

If you're looking for an eco-friendly hotel, City Flats is one of the best you'll find anywhere in the world. It was designed to achieve LEED Gold Certification and features twenty-eight conceptually unique guest rooms.

Even though every room is a little bit different, they all help the environment by using cork flooring, black-out curtains to reduce energy use, naturally hypo-allergenic bamboo linens, large windows or architectural light wells to maximize natural lighting, high-efficiency heating and cooling units with occupancy sensors and low-flow faucets and toilets using thirty percent less water than standard fixtures. This place is lean, green and a great place to be seen!

Another neat thing about City Flats is that they're also helping preserve one of Grand Rapids' great historical treasures. After restoring and renovating the historic Michigan National Bank lobby right next door, they turned it into an incredibly classic ballroom. In a couple steps you can go from a hip and ultra modern green hotel to a historically preserved iconic environment, and it works.

So if you're cool and progressive, you might want to stay at the City Flats Hotel. If you're not, don't worry about it. Even I got a little cooler after staying there, and for me that's hard to do!

Kids' Food Basket
(616) 235-4532
2055 Oak Industrial Dr., Grand Rapids, MI 49505
www.kidsfoodbasket.org

What kind of people would work hard for hours every day to help feed hungry kids? I'll tell ya what kind of people. My kind of people!

No matter where you live in the world, it seems there are always hungry kids not too far away. But thanks to one woman's dream and the hard work of dedicated and caring volunteers, that's changing real fast in Grand Rapids.

More than ten years ago, Mary K. Hoodhood heard a story, saw a need and knew she had to do something about it. So she started an organization called **Kids' Food Basket.**

It all started when a friend of Mary K. saw a little girl behind a school searching for something to eat out of a trash dumpster. After hearing the story and having a good cry, Mary K. stocked her kitchen and started making sack suppers for kids that she would give out after school each day so hungry kids in need would have a meal that evening.

Now more than a decade later, Mary K. has assembled an army of caring volunteers who deliver over five thousand handmade, healthy meals every single day. These meals help kids grow, live and learn better at school and ultimately will make a better society for all of us.

You can tell how many caring people live in the Grand Rapids area just by looking around at Kids' Food Basket. Every volunteer autographs the walls there as a sign of solidarity to end childhood hunger. And every sack supper that goes out is covered with loving messages from other school kids who are more fortunate. A lot of healthy food goes into every sack supper, but the main ingredient is love and that's what'll change the world.

If you live near Grand Rapids, I suggest you volunteer a few days at Kids' Food Basket. It will open your eyes and fill your heart with hope. If you live elsewhere, help feed some hungry kids near you.

The People's Cider Company
(616) 322-7805
P.O. Box 6005, Grand Rapids, MI 49516
www.thepeoplescider.com

Let me ask you something. What's the most fun thing you can make with apples? If you said apple pie, you might want to read the next few paragraphs.

Jason Lummen is the CEO, staff and chief bottle washer at **The People's Cider Company**, a brand new business in Grand Rapids that's turning Michigan apples into a party in your mouth.

A little more than ten years ago, Jason Lummen pressed some apples at a local farm to produce his first five-gallon batch of hard cider. After tasting it and thinking to himself, "Hey, this stuff is pretty good," Jason purchased his first fifty-gallon fermenter, which his wife welcomed into the kitchen of their one-bedroom apartment in Heartside.

As the years passed, his friends and family tasted the cider and said, "Hey, this stuff is pretty good." This encouraged him so much that in June of 2011, on his son's first birthday, Jason incorporated The People's Cider Company with the goal of creating a premium dry cider.

Jason loves the fact that he buys his apples locally, ferments his cider locally and sells to locals who love what he's doing. In a way, he's created the classic "circle of cider." I had a chance to sit down, relax and enjoy a bottle of Jason's finest, and I have to say for the record, I don't know why they call it hard cider, because it's so easy to drink!

So expect big things from Jason and The People's Cider Company, because as he grows, it'll be good for the community, good for Michigan and a great addition to your next party.

Anna's House
(616) 361-8500
3874 Plainfield, Grand Rapids, MI 49525
www.annashousegr.com

If you want breakfast, you could come over to my house (not recommended), but if you want a really good breakfast, you should probably go to **Anna's House**.

You won't find an actual Anna at Anna's House restaurant, but what you will find are some of the most inventive and downright delicious morning and midday meal creations this side of the equator. Rean Amato and Josh Beckett worked hard to put together both a menu and a staff whose sole purpose is to get you to leave this place saying one simple word: WOW!

Rean is the heart and soul of the kitchen. She's a self-taught chef who loves to experiment with unusual flavors and food combinations. She loves food so much that she literally dreams about it at night and dreams up some of her best recipes.

All the food at Anna's is made from scratch, and loyal fans of the restaurant describe the food as "ridiculously outstanding." From the eggs benedict to the massive breakfast burrito, everything looked great.

So after we were done looking, we did what we do best on UTR and got down to the business of tasting. And as Rean brought out dish after incredible dish, we suddenly realized that the feeling amongst the crew was absolutely unanimous. When all was said and we were done, what everyone told us was true. This place rocked it!

So, what do I really have to say about Anna's House? Simple: WOW!

Dwelling Place
(616) 454-0928
101 Sheldon Blvd., Ste. 2, Grand Rapids, MI 49503
www.dwellingplacegr.org

If you had a company that created great affordable spaces for all kinds of people to live and work right downtown, what would you call it? I've got an idea. How about **Dwelling Place**?

For over thirty years, Dwelling Place has been making a difference in the communities and neighborhoods where people work and live. As an urban developer, Dwelling Place renovates neglected and abandoned buildings and creates places and spaces where all members of the community can be just that, a community.

Dwelling Place's neighborhood revitalization program infuses neglected neighborhoods with profitable businesses, transforms blighted areas with building façade improvements and rehabilitation efforts and creates a destination with cool attractions and events. For years they've worked hard to improve the quality of housing and to prevent the displacement of downtown Grand Rapids' low-income residents.

Dwelling Place also provides support services to neighbors struggling with issues surrounding homelessness. At any given time, they are helping upwards of three hundred individuals and families reclaim their place in society.

Everyone in our society deserves a sense of place in the community where they live… and the Dwelling Place is just the place to make that happen.

The Great Lakes Pub Cruiser
(616) 319-1199
www.greatlakespubcruiser.com

What do you get when you combine people, pubs and peddling? You get a portable party that's plenty of fun! The Great Lakes Pub Cruiser is like nothing we had ever seen before, and if you're looking for a powerful good time, this one's powered by people and pub juice.

You read right, **The Great Lake Pub Cruiser** is a people-powered, portable pub that the passengers pedal from place to place. It's basically a modernized wagon with seats on both sides, and each seat has a set of bicycle pedals that power the cruiser. As you and your friends pedal away, your tour guide steers the cruiser from pub to pub where you all enjoy some of Grand Rapids finest microbrews.

The people keep the pub cruise powered, and the social lubrication at the pubs keeps the night lively and full of fun. It's a great way to meet new people and discover Grand Rapids' exploding beer scene.

The best part of this crazy excursion is you're not driving, you're actually getting in a bit of a workout and you're getting a chance to work off your buzz before the evening is done. It's the healthiest way I can think of to go drinking with friends and family. So if you're going to partake, The Great Lakes Pub Cruiser is a great reservation to make.

And if you're into exploring a great Michigan City, take a trip to Grand Rapids. Who knows, you might even decide to stay!

Story behind the name:
Pedal Faster!

The pedal-driven pub cruiser in GR gave us the title of this show. Seems that they kept yelling at Tom. Hmmmm. Wonder why.

Chapter 45

Season 3, Episode 19

•West-Side
Mitten Adventure

The west side of Michigan's mitten has so much to offer that we decided to cast our fate to the wind, throw some sandwiches in the car and wander the earth like Caine in Kung Fu looking for cool stuff to feature on the show. And if you've ever been to Michigan, you know it didn't take us long before we just had to stop.

Muskegon Luge & Sports Complex, Muskegon State Park
(877) 879-5843
462 Scenic Dr., Muskegon, MI 49445
www.msports.org

Some people consider themselves winners, which is cool… but me? I call myself a luger. That's right, I'm a luger and proud of it. Why? Because luging is one of the most funnest things you can do in the winter. And believe it or not, you can do it right here in Michigan at the Muskegon Winter Sports Complex. A place where even winners can be lugers!

There are only a handful of luge tracks in the United States, and this is one of only a couple that will let you come in, take a quick lesson and try it for yourself. At the **Muskegon Winter Sports Complex**, they're all about fun, safety and doing things right, so after a brief session on equipment, safety and technique, I grabbed a sled, headed up the steps to the top and let gravity take care of the rest. And, you know me… I went from idiot to expert in the blink of an eye. I'll admit it; I was a little scared at the top. But by the time I got to the bottom, I was hooked.

Aside from the luge run, the Muskegon Winter Sports Complex has more winter activities than you can shake a snow shoe at. You can glide through the woods on groomed ice skating trails, go cross country skiing or even get yourself into a game of hockey. It's a great, healthy place that will cure the whole family of cabin fever in a single afternoon. Heck, this place is so cool, they even use the original Zamboni machine from Madison Square Garden in New York to resurface their ice… classic!

So if you want to feel like a winner this winter, try luging at the Muskegon Winter Sports Complex. Once you try it, you'll be a luger just like me. Only probably better.

Bell's Brewery
(269) 382-2338
8690 Krum Ave., Kalamazoo, MI 49053
www.bellsbeer.com

They were Michigan's first microbrewery and one of the oldest craft beers east of the Rockies... ring a bell? I thought so. If you guessed **Bell's Brewery** in Kalamazoo, you probably already know that Michigan is one of the microbrew hotbeds in the entire USA. There are now more breweries here than wineries. And when it comes to Bell's, they rang the bell for the first round here in Michigan.

Founder Larry Bell went from selling his first home brew in 1985 to now having his liquid gold available in pubs and stores nationwide. He did it the hard way... by using local ingredients, hiring local talent, taking his time and doing it right.

In 2011, Bell's opened the Eccentric Café in Kalamazoo. It's an awesome place to enjoy great food, an array of Bell's best beers and live local music. And in the summer, the Bell's beer garden out back is the place to kick back and enjoy your favorite Bell's brew.

So if you enjoy the occasional frosty cold adult malted beverage... get yourself Oberon over to Bell's and taste the beer that helped get us here... and where's here? Who cares... you're at Bell's!

Herman Miller
www.hermanmiller.com

How did a furniture company in West Michigan become one of the most innovative designers and manufacturers in the entire world? Just ask **Herman Miller**. If you thought Herman Miller just made chairs… well, yeah they do… but they've also helped pioneer the way we work and live for over a hundred years now. When it comes to creative design, they find and make some of the very best.

Herman Miller is one of the most progressive, admired and celebrated companies in the entire world, and they're right here in Michigan. Over one hundred years ago they started off as a small furniture company, and over the years they've become one of the world's most innovative designers of spaces and places where we work and live. Herman Miller has also pioneered and developed some of the most progressive ideas in ways to keep their production facilities green and worker-friendly.

Even though Herman Miller has a global footprint, they stay right here in Michigan because of our talented people and great natural resources. They've rethought and redesigned the modern work space and are responsible for many of us being more productive and comfortable while getting the job done.

So if you're looking for yet another reason to be proud of Michigan, think about Herman Miller. I guarantee they're thinking about ways to make you more comfortable as we speak.

The Gilmore Car Museum
(269) 671-5089
6865 Hickory Rd., Hickory Corners, MI 49060
www.GilmoreCarMuseum.org

If I told you that one of the most incredible car museums you'll ever go to isn't in the Motor City, what would you say? If you said it was in Hickory Corners, you'd be absolutely right. And I'd say… how the heck did you know that?

Hickory Corners is about a half hour northeast of Kalamazoo in the heart of Michigan farm country. And when you get there, you'll think this is some sort of mirage… but it's not. It's **The Gilmore Car Museum**, and it's one of the most extensive collections of vintage cars, motorcycles and just plain cool car "stuff" you'll ever see.

It all started in 1963 when Donald S. Gilmore's wife, Genevieve, gave him an antique car for his birthday—a 1920 Pierce-Arrow "project car." She thought it would be a nice hobby, but it turned into an incredibly wonderful obsession. So Mr. Gilmore purchased ninety acres of farm property, had several historic barns dismantled piece by piece and moved to the site and the rest, as they say, is car history.

Everything about this place is great: the incredible exhibits, the classic barns, the fresh air and beautiful scenery… Oh, and did I mention? There's even a re-created 1930s service station, a small-town train station and the classic Blue Moon Diner that still serves vintage vittles. As for the cars, they are far too numerous to even begin to list here.

If you want to be driven to auto happiness of historic proportions, go to the Internet… find Hickory Corners and get to the Gilmore Car Museum. But just be prepared… there's so much cool car stuff to see there, your brain will need a car-top carrier when you leave.

Water Street Glassworks
(269) 925-5555
140 Water St., Benton Harbor, MI 49022
www.waterstreetglassworks.org

So, how do you teach teenagers teamwork, focus, patience and trust? Well in Benton Harbor, they're doing it with fire and ice. **Water Street Glassworks** is a very unique educational and exhibit space that offers an award-winning after school program called "Fired Up." This program gives teens the skills they need to create, develop, survive and thrive in today's world.

They do it by helping kids develop skills in the fire arts. They learn how to blow and cast molten glass, weld and hammer metal, form glass beads over a torch and create stained glass and mosaics. At the same time, the kids learn responsibility, teamwork and focus, not to mention the fact that they are developing an artistic skill. And research has shown that one of the best ways to help teens mature and grow emotionally and intellectually is through artistic expression.

Water Street Glassworks also teaches these young people how to run a business from top to bottom with their in-house gelato shop. Nothing wrong with a little old fashioned capitalism when it tastes this good.

Through fire, ice and artistic expression, these kids are learning so much more than just how to make something cool out of glass. And speaking of learning and growing, since anyone can take lessons there, I even tried my hand at it. I actually managed not to singe my mustache, and I even made something pretty creative and useful… a paperweight (at least that's what they told me it was when they stopped laughing).

So if you like gelato, cool glass art and helping today's teens, Water Street Glassworks is a great place to check out in Benton Harbor.

And, if you like Michigan beer, classic cars, creative furniture and high speeds on your back on an icy track, give the west side of Michigan's mitten a try. They've got all that and a whole lot more.

Story behind the name:
I'm Such a Luger

Anytime you get to transform a word into a sound-a-like of "loser," you take it. And luging was the perfect opportunity.

Chapter 46

Season 3, Episode 20

Great Lakes Bay Region

If you're looking for a part of Michigan to spend some time in, it's time you looked at The Great Lakes Bay Region, because every time we go there, we have a great time! The Great Lakes Bay Region is the cities, towns and neighborhoods that make up the eastern part of Michigan's palm, right at the base of Saginaw Bay.

W e've been to this part of Michigan a lot on UTR, and for a lot of really good reasons. From the classic, historic cities with their amazing architecture to the beautiful homes and neighborhoods that surround them, this area truly has a sense of place that just makes sense. And if you're in need of green space to help connect you back to Planet Earth and make you feel whole again, you couldn't land your spaceship in a better spot.

Johnny Panther Quest Eco-tours
(810) 653-3859
8065 E. Coldwater Rd., Davison, MI 48423
www.jpqat.com

If you've always wanted to go exploring through the Everglades... guess what? You don't have to go all the way to Florida to do it, because we've got everglades right in the heart of Michigan's lower peninsula. **Johnny Panther Quest Eco-tours** takes you on natural adventures throughout Michigan's wild-water back country for an experience that will blow your natural mind.

When he's not using his superhero name, Wil Hufton is the wild water man who knows and loves every inch of these everglades, and he took us on a journey deep inside one of the most untouched habitats in Michigan: the Shiawassee National Wildlife Refuge.

Book a boat ride with Wil and not only will he tell you how he came up with the cool name Johnny Panther Quest, he'll also show you a natural world I had no idea existed here in Michigan. The passion Wil has for these natural wetlands is powerful, sincere and intensely contagious. The trip we took was filled with good humor, great conversation and some pretty awesome stories. If you're looking to improve your quality of life, just let Wil share some of his life with you. I guarantee; when you're done, you'll wish you were Johnny Panther Quest.

Turkey Roost
(989) 684-5200
2273 S. Huron Rd., Kawkawlin, MI 48631
www.turkeyroostrestaurant.com

Imagine if you could eat Thanksgiving dinner any and every day you wanted to. No questions asked—except maybe what side you wanted with it. Well, stop imagining because at **The Turkey Roost Restaurant**, you can… and we did! This little pink building in Kawkawlin, Michigan is a landmark for people who know what they love, and what they love is a great turkey dinner with all the trimmings whenever they want it.

The owner Todd Ballor eats, thinks, sleeps, serves and even talked turkey with me. He worked there as a kid, came back to buy it and is carrying on the tradition of serving delicious homemade turkey dinners. Not only do the locals love this place, people from all over the Midwest make the pilgrimage there all times of the year. The Turkey Roost is an icon, a tradition for thousands and an anchor to this town. We came real hungry and left real full with a real appreciation for what Todd and the Turkey Roost are all about: friends, family and community. Oh, and a homemade turkey dinner any time you want it… bonus!

Some people say baking is an art. And some say it's a science. But for the person we were about to meet, it's both.

Sweet Sandy B's Bake Shop
(989) 598-0603
801 Columbus Ave., Bay City, MI 48708
www.sweetsandyb.com

If you like sweets, Bay City is the town to head for and **Sweet Sandy B's** is the new place to get 'em. This gourmet throwback bakery is turning heads, creating smiles and making a big difference in this neighborhood. Sweet Sandy B is actually Sandy Bierlein, and she's making her dream come true, one cupcake at a time. She's created a retro-style neighborhood bakery that offers classic favorites that are baked fresh daily with an emphasis on quality, local ingredients.

Her home-style desserts are made in small batches by hand using seasonal ingredients and a whole lot of love. And when you combine Sandy's awesome personality with her great creations, you get a sweet treat that can't be beat.

A lot of young people across Michigan are reconnecting with their cities, starting creative new businesses and driving Michigan's economy and future forward, and Sweet Sandy B is one of those people. It's just that her story is a little bit sweeter than most. Get it?

Frankenmuth Dog Bowl
(800) 600-0105
www.dogfunfest.com

Usually in Frankenmuth, beer and chicken are man's best friends… but not the weekend we were there. That's because that weekend Frankenmuth went to the dogs. It was the seventh annual **Dog Bowl**, and it's the nation's largest Olympics-style event for dogs. Every Memorial Day weekend thousands of humans from across the globe bring their best furry friends to compete in almost every canine event imaginable.

This incredibly fun event was started by the Zehnder family and features just about every breed and event imaginable. What really amazed us was the fact that there were somewhere around three thousand dogs at the event, and we never heard so much as a growl. Good dogs!

Dog Bowl features everything from agility courses, sheep herding and costume contests to doggy disc and aquatic jumping competitions. They even have a huge pet parade and crown the annual canine king and queen. I honestly don't know who has more fun at Dog Bowl, the people or the dogs. As for us, we're total dog lovers, so we had a blast.

So if you're looking for a place where you can explore the everglades, eat Thanksgiving dinner in July, give your sweet tooth a treat and let your dog compete for the gold… take a long look at the Great Lakes Bay Region. When it comes to quality of life, they've got a large quantity.

Story behind the name:
I'll Be Doggone…

1) We were at the Frankenmuth Dog Olympics. 2) It's a Marvin Gaye song. I'll always look for a song title or lyric when it fits.

Chapter 47

Season 3, Episode 21

· Detroit

If you haven't been to Detroit in a while, you're late. There's a lot of cool stuff happening there. But, don't worry... that's why you bought this book. :-) In every direction you turn, there's new business, innovation and creative stuff happening throughout the city. If you had to put a season on Detroit, I'd say it's spring, because new life is popping up everywhere.

Komodo Kitchen
Location varies
www.komodokitchen.com

The **Komodo Kitchen** is what they call a pop-up restaurant and it features the incredible tastes of Indonesia. Now, the great thing about this concept is you never know where they'll be next. And if you're lucky enough to get in, it's an experience you won't soon forget.

This cool culinary collaboration is the brainchild of April Boyle, Deanne Iovan and Gina Onyx. It's an experiment they started a few years back, and they've combined their talents and taste buds to create a unique wandering supper club.

They find an available (often empty) space and transform it into a fully decorated dining experience that serves an array of Indonesian delicacies. I couldn't even begin to pronounce some of the wonderfully aromatic foods I devoured, but I would love to enjoy them again and again and again. It's always wonderful to discover new taste sensations, and these exotic creations were just that... sensational.

Another cool thing about this unique dining experience is that you get to meet other interesting and adventurous people who really appreciate great food. I don't know how interesting I am, but I am interested in finding out where Komodo Kitchen will be next. If you can't find the Komodo Kitchen in your area, seek out and explore other pop-up restaurants. It's a great way to discover new foods and new friends!

The Greening of Detroit
(313) 237-8733
1418 Michigan Ave., Detroit, MI 48216
www.greeningofdetroit.com

If you want to live somewhere that has a great sense of place, you really need green spaces to make you feel alive. And that's why **The Greening of Detroit** is so important to the rebirth of this great city. The Greening of Detroit is more than just a philosophy; it's an actual movement and nonprofit organization that's dedicated to making Detroit a better and greener place to live.

This unique organization plants trees, revitalizes city parks, creates jobs for the community, mentors young people and helps Detroit neighborhoods come alive with people who care and share this experience.

Detroit was once known as "the city of trees," and this green machine is helping make that a reality once again. They're helping to transform the city from a post-industrial urban center into a healthier, safer and greener environment by planting well over eighty thousand new trees.

If you live anywhere near Detroit, the Greening of Detroit is always looking for eager volunteers like you to get involved. If you don't live near Detroit, feel free to find or even start your own community volunteer action group. Getting involved and giving back to your community is one of the most rewarding things you'll ever do. So, if you can… do it!

Redford Theater
(313) 537-2560
17360 Lahser Rd., Detroit, MI 48219
www.redfordtheatre.com

So many people told us that we just had to visit the iconic **Redford Theater** in Detroit that we did just that. And are we glad we did. Describing the theater is easy… I just use the phrase, "Holy Cow, what an incredible place." It's a true Detroit treasure that's been brought back to its glory days by an army of passionate volunteers who keep this classic theater alive and well. This theater totally takes you back to a time when going to the movies was a pretty special event. Everything from the organist who warms up the crowd before the movie to the throwback prices at the concession counter make this theater a great place for the whole family.

The Redford Theater also hosts special events where they feature classic movies and actually bring in some of the stars from that movie to answer questions about the film and sign autographs. The night we were there, the special feature was the classic children's film Willy Wonka and the Chocolate Factory, so we got to meet Peter Ostrum and Paris Themmen… aka Charley and TV Mike. They look a little different now. :-)

Meeting these two guys and the whole evening totally made me feel like a kid again. If you really want to experience some movie magic, take your family to the Redford Theater. And who knows? After the movie, you just might meet a big-time celebrity.

1917 American Bistro
(313) 863-1917
19416 Livernois Ave., Detroit, MI 48076
www.1917americanbistro.com

Next time you're in Detroit and you're in the mood for an American bistro with European flair and a soul-food foundation, have we got a place for you. The **1917 American Bistro** is a Detroit eatery that's sophisticated, casual, funky and a lotta fun to go to. And it's all wrapped up in an artful atmosphere that totally says... oh yeah!

If you like good food, you'll love owners Don and Katrina Studvent. They're an extraordinary couple who followed their dream and opened their arms to a community that's loving everything they do. And what they do is serve some of the best soulful selections this side of the sun. Chef Don's philosophy is simple: keep the food fresh, real and uncomplicated.

The restaurant is filled with incredible aromas, local art, thoughtful Detroiters and a staff that truly cares about your experience. And if you're a jazz lover, beware... jam sessions featuring some of Detroit's finest musicians have been known to spontaneously break out on weekend nights... so be sure to bring your ears. If you're looking for a cool night out with a great hot meal and a warm, friendly environment... 1917 Bistro is... well, oh yeah!

Hamtown Farms
9100 Lumpkin St., Hamtramck, MI 48212
www.hamtownfarms.com

Hamtown Farms is an actual urban farm that sits right next to Kowalski Sausage in the heart of Hamtramck. They grow fresh food there, but they also do a lot more for the people who love to live there.

Michael Davis is the urban visionary who started the farm, and he, Julie Swartz and Jeffrey Doe are growing more than just food... they're growing a better neighborhood. Nothing brings a neighborhood together better than a community farm. People can meet, share ideas, plant food, create a sense of place in their town and the best part: eat healthier foods.

The entire town of Hamtramck vigorously supports what's happening at Hamtown Farms. Even the local fire department helps out by stopping by a few days a week to water the garden with a fire hose. Hamtown Farms is just one of the things that will give Hamtramck a brighter future. And speaking of bright futures, as Detroit gets greener, healthier and more fun and more great restaurants pop-up, don't forget who told you to go there. That's right, your ol' pal Tom at UTR.

Story behind the name:
Yes, I'm Going to Finish ALL My Popcorn

Nothing worse than sharing a bucket of popcorn at the movies with a friend or loved one. Then, just after the opening credits roll, you find that your friend has inhaled two-thirds of the bucket and the important butter layer.

Tom is very protective of his popcorn. Before we can even ask for some, he proudly exclaims, "YES, I'm going to finish ALL of my popcorn."

Chapter 48

Season 3, Episode 22

•Northville Downriver

If you're a half hour from Detroit, fifteen minutes from Ann Arbor, five minutes from a farm and only two minutes from Italy, where are you? Simple. You're in Northville, Michigan. Read on and you'll see what I mean.

I'd heard all about how beautiful Northville was but was still blown away when we got to town. I'm tellin' you, spend an hour there and you just might want to spend a lifetime. The downtown is really comfortable, with great shops, cool spaces and great places to eat.

Genitti's Hole in the Wall
(248) 349-0522
108 E. Main St., Northville, MI 48167
www.genittis.com

Now, speaking of great places to eat, let's get back to that whole two minutes from Italy thing. If you've got a special event coming up and you want to celebrate it with great food, passion, entertainment and a lotta red sauce (you know… like the Italians do) make plans to land at **Genitti's Hole in the Wall**. In one place you can treat your whole party to a great dinner, a night at the theater and a home-style portion of real Italian hospitality.

Genitti's isn't your standard walk in and sit down establishment. It's designed to help you have the most fun possible with your group, party or special event, so please call first and let them fill you in.

Two generations of Genittis are dedicated to making you feel like you truly belong there. So, let me make you an offer you can't refuse… next time you've got a special event and really want it to be special, have it at Genitti's Hole in the Wall in Northville. And who knows? You just might become family, too.

Maybury Farm
(248) 374-0200
50165 Eight Mile Rd., Northville, MI 48167
www.mayburyfarm.org

When was the last time you were down on the farm… or up on the farm, for that matter? Well, it really doesn't matter, because what does matter is that you get yourself down to **Maybury Farm** in Northville. It's a great place for fun, families and hobnobbing with all your favorite furry and feathered friends. From your standard farm stompers like chickens, pigs and cows to your more exotic llamas and peacocks, this is a great chance for your little ones to connect with animals and experience real farm life.

So if you want to warm your heart and renew your faith in the planet, take your kids to Maybury Farm and watch them have a blast interacting with farm animals. Activities at the farm may be dependent on the weather and the time of year, so please remember to call ahead or check their website. Then get ready for some down-home fun on the farm!

Preservation Dental
(248) 348-1313
371 E. Main St., Northville, MI 48167
www.preservationdental.com

Usually when you head to the dentist, it's not a particularly happy occasion. But this time, I was absolutely thrilled to be going. That's because **Dr. Bill Demray** is so much more than a dentist in Northville. He's a big personality with an even bigger heart who genuinely cares about this community. Not only does he cook breakfast for his staff every morning, he puts bling in the town holiday parade with his classic Volkswagen bug collection, raises tons of money for local charities and even makes baby pacifiers a thing of the past with his famous "Binky Tree." When kids are ready, they say goodbye to their pacifiers by hanging them on the Binky Tree covered with hundreds of pacifiers right behind Dr. Demray's office. It's a sight to see and a great symbolic little ceremony to help kids move on to better tooth development.

1

My conversation with Dr. Demray made me realize that just living in a community isn't enough… that you really need to give back to make a difference. He also made me realize that it was finally time to give up my secret binky. It was tough, but I did it. I'll miss you, old friend.

If you're looking for a dentist who's helping put a smile on an entire community, stop by and say hi to Dr. Bill Demray. Even without a cavity, he'll be glad to see you!

Well, you know me, I'm usually up a creek without a paddle. But, this time, I went downriver with a camera crew… bonus! The Downriver area in Southeast Michigan is a collection of cities and towns that are south of Detroit along the western shores of the Detroit River, and we have a blast every time we're there. This time, as soon as we got there, we were hungry—a seemingly perpetual state for us—so we went in search of chow. Now, if you want a good TV dinner, you can go to a number of grocery stores downriver. But if you want a great TV diner, we found just the place.

TV's Deli-Diner
(734) 671-9005
2441 Fort St., Trenton, MI 48183
www.tvsdelidiner.com

In 1995 Tracey and Victor Stroia joined their food forces and opened **TV's Deli-Diner**. It's a cool and casual eatery in Trenton that takes diner food to a whole new level. They'll surprise you with their unique flavor combinations and inventive creations. They also understand the concept of "generous portions." When we were there, the place was packed with passionate people who couldn't wait to tell us how much they love the food. The atmosphere is fun and the staff is awesome.

Believe it or not, I actually found out about TV's Deli-Diner from the guy I buy my cars from. He's also the guy who took our crew for a boat ride up in Boyne City back in Chapter 9. He said we'd love it and we did. Thanks again, Jim Flynn.

So, turn off your TV (unless Under the Radar Michigan is on) and check out TV's Deli-Diner in Trenton. Oh, and you won't need a TV tray; they've got nice tables.

Detroit River International Wildlife Refuge
(734) 692-7608
www.fws.gov/refuge/detroit_river

If you're the kind of person who likes the wild life, Detroit's Downriver area is actually the perfect place to be. That's because it's home to the **Detroit River International Wildlife Refuge**… nearly six thousand acres of islands and coastal wetlands that stretch forty-eight miles along the Detroit River and Western Lake Erie shoreline.

This former industrial area and brown field has been completely transformed back to its pristine and natural condition. Standing there now, you get to experience these coastal forests and wetland just as the Native Americans did hundreds of years ago. It really is an incredibly natural, beautiful and serene place to explore.

After spending some time there, not only will you realize what a great place this is to be, you'll also start to understand why places like this are so important to all of us.

Speedcult
(734) 753-5630
www.speedcult.com

Now, time for a totally different kind of wild life. Time for a little Speedcult in New Boston. And what exactly is Speedcult? **Speedcult** is Len Puch and his wonderfully insane crew of creative metal fabricators. These guys can take any piece of metal and turn it into a great way to soup up your ride, your business or even your home. If you want to make a statement in metal, these are the metal heads to do it for you. Check out their website and get a load of their way cool collection of incredibly creative metal-cut creations.

Speedcult is also an "invitation only" collection of medieval carnie rides, handmade by Len and his merry men of madness. Len calls it his "Abusement Park," and it's a place where he lets his personal friends and clients let loose, have fun and enjoy insanely creative, carnie-like contraptions. From a flame-fired roaster roller coaster and a hydraulic-powered dragster (which by the way launches you straight into an apple orchard) to the insane cage of fire and a wild head-trip tunnel, Len's creativity knows no bounds. You need to know Len to get a ticket, and knowing Len is your ticket to ride and to some of the most creative metal messages you'll find anywhere.

So if you're looking for a wild man to custom cut some metal for you, Len Puch will hook you up, spin you around and make it happen. And if you're looking for some tamer wildlife to enjoy or a TV diner to tune into, Downriver is a great place to be.

Story behind the name:
Abusement Rides?

That term made us laugh the first time we heard it at Lon Von Speedcult's studio. It made us scared when we saw what these rides were.

Chapter 49
Season 3, Episode 23

·Tips of the Fingers

One place in Michigan where I'd never really spent a lot of time was the area at the top of the mitten we like to call "the tips of the fingers." So with provisions packed, we headed north to Michigan's index finger in search of a great place to stay and a good hot meal. And, since this is Michigan, we had no problem finding both.

Manitou Shores Resort
(989) 734-7233
7995 U.S. 23 N., Rogers City, MI 49779
www.manitoushores.com

Just seven miles north of Rogers City we found a place that was so relaxing, it lowered our collective blood pressure the moment we pulled in. If you're looking for laid back log cabin luxury, **Manitou Shores Resort** is the place to kick back and unwind. It's quiet and secluded, and every night the waves rolling in off Lake Huron are your lullaby.

Bruce and Colleen Grant own and operate the resort, and they love making sure you get just what you want out of this relaxing experience. From the fascinating shipwreck just down the beach to nearby Ocqueoc Falls (the largest waterfall in the lower peninsula), Bruce and Colleen will share tons of great information about this wonderful part of the state. Michigan's sunrise side really is a great place to get away from it all and still have all kinds of things to do. And Manitou Shores Resort is a great place to start.

Rosa's Squeeze Inn
(989) 734-2991
16454 U.S. 23, Millersburg, MI 49759

In search of that hot meal, we found a restaurant that's so nice, it's two, two, two restaurants in one! Just eight miles farther north on U.S. 23 in the town of Millersburg, we found a restaurant that's **The Chuck Wagon** by day and **Rosa's Squeeze Inn** by night. The Chuck Wagon serves casual daytime vittles, while Rosa's is a finer Italian diner for evening enjoyment. And since we were feeling festive and Italian, we picked dinner.

Gary, Joan and their son Jeff Yaklin are continuing Rosa's tradition by bringing a little bit of Italy to the sunrise side. This is a great place to unwind, share some home-style Italian cooking and make some new friends. They filled us with good cheer, great food and became friends for life. And that, my UTR friends, is a big part of what life is all about. So, if you're heading up U.S. 23 through Millersburg and the urge for Italian suddenly hits, hit the brakes at Rosa's Squeeze Inn.

The next morning we headed northwest toward Mackinaw City in search of a place that would make us all feel like kids again. And you know us—we totally found it.

Historic Mill Creek Discovery Park
(231) 436-4100
9001 U.S. 23, Mackinaw City, MI 49701
www.mackinacparks.com/historic-mill-creek-discovery-park

If you like Michigan history, nature and adventure, you'll love the **Historic Mill Creek Discovery Park**. It's just five minutes east of the Mackinac Bridge on scenic U.S. 23, and it's a great family place where you can learn about Michigan's past, its wildlife and a whole lot more.

Jeff Dykehouse is the Curator of Natural History at the park, and he spent the entire morning showing us around. We learned about Michigan's native animals and how the pioneers survived and thrived in the Michigan wilderness.

Jeff also took us to a place that would get me even higher on Michigan. It's part observation tower, part climbing wall, part scenic overlook and a completely incredible experience at the park. After you climb the stairs, get ready for your jaw to drop. The view across the straits of the Mackinac Bridge and Mackinac Island is spectacular.

The park also offers an experience called The Adventure Tour. It's a park within the park, and if you're a nature lover, you'll absolutely love this. The Adventure Tour offers a real tree canopy walk where you walk across a rope bridge high above the forest floor. This is something I'd always wanted to do, and I can't even begin to tell you how cool it was.

As part of the Adventure Tour, you also get to walk along beautiful forest pathways with a guide who shares vast amounts of information about this incredible natural landscape. And the best part is, at the end of the tour, you get to zip-line through the trees like an eagle in flight over a cool mountain stream. Bonus!

If you spend a day at the Historic Mill Creek Adventure Park and you find yourself learning, laughing and maybe even launching yourself into the sky like the bird of your choice, just do yourself a favor. Don't pick chicken like I did.

Next up, we went to a place that claims to serve "the best chicken in the world." You know us; we just had to check that place out.

The Dam Site Inn
(231) 539-8851
6705 Woodland Rd., Brutus, MI 49716
www.damsiteinn.com

About twenty miles south on U.S.-31 in the town of Brutus is a place called **The Dam Site Inn**, and not only do they claim to serve the best chicken on the world (and have a haunted table), they just might have one of the coolest retro bars in the world, too. Oh, and if you're wondering where the name came from, you can see an old dam right outside the back windows of the restaurant. Pretty clever!

Four generations of the East Family carry on a tradition at the Dam Site that's brought in the likes of astronaut Buzz Aldrin, our own Michigan rocker Bob Seger, and yes, even the fantabulous Tom Daldin from UTR.

The bar at the Dam Site Inn is like something right out of a Hollywood movie. It's circa 1960s, totally looks like a place George Jetson would stop for a martini after work and was made partly of Naugahyde car upholstery. The groovy chairs in the bar were designed by Eero Saarinen, who also designed the St. Louis Arch and the JFK airport. It's a must see.

The kitchen there is also completely open to all patrons for inspection. And I have to say, it was one of the biggest, cleanest kitchens I've ever encountered.

As promised, they sat us at the haunted table, but to be honest, we were so hungry and the food was so good, I don't remember ever seeing a ghost. I barely saw the food it was so good.

If your dream restaurant has great fried chicken, a funky retro bar, a haunted table, an awesome family and a dam right outside the back window, take a trip to the Dam Site Inn. You'll be darn glad you did… Ha!

You know, last time we drove through the tunnel of trees in northwestern Michigan, we blinked and totally missed the tiny town of Good Hart. But this time, we kept our eyes wide open. Good Hart is little alright, but it's big on both quaintness and creativity. It's nestled halfway between Harbor Springs and Cross Village on Lake Shore Drive, and it's a favorite place for travelers to stop, shop and find something tasty.

Primitive Images
(231) 526-0276
1129 N. Lakeshore, Harbor Springs, MI 49740
www.primitiveimages.com

First we stopped by Ceci Bauer's **Primitive Images**. It's a little log cabin that offers unique antique and rustic furniture as well as creative goods such as hand-crafted wooden bears, hand-loomed rugs and beautifully made jewelry. We had a great conversation with Ceci and managed to browse our way into a state of extreme hunger.

Northern Crepes
(231) 526-1272 or (231) 526-0276
1129 N. Lake Shore Dr., Good Hart, MI 49740
www.primitiveimages.com/northern-crepes

Now, a while back, I mentioned something about finding something tasty to eat… and that's where Ceci's brother Matt Bauer and his **Northern Crepe Cart** comes in. Matt took a French classic, filled it with fresh Michigan ingredients and brought it all the way to Good Hart for everyone to stop and enjoy. These crepes range from a meal packed with fresh local ingredients to decadent dessert crepes. The Northern Crepe Cart Serves breakfast and lunch and is a great spot to take the family and enjoy your crepe on their tea deck with a pot of tea or lavender lemonade. As always, many places in northern Michigan are seasonal, so call ahead first.

Next time you're driving through the tunnel of trees, if you can manage not to blink, stop, shop and roll on up to Good Hart. Matt will be happy to roll up a crepe for ya.

Wilderness State Park
(231) 436-5381
903 Wilderness Park Dr., Carp Lake, MI 49718

What's worth giving up electricity, running water and a bathroom for? **Wilderness State Park**, that's what! You heard right—the UTR crew spent the night in a rustic cabin—and we didn't even mind, because we got to experience one of Michigan's most beautiful places to connect with nature.

Wilderness State Park is one of those iconic parks that almost defines Michigan wilderness. It's the natural world at its best, and it's there for all of us to support and enjoy. The park is only ten miles west of Mackinaw City (almost in the shadows of the Mackinac Bridge) and offers great camping, hiking, beaches and even offers educational nature programs.

I don't remember the last time I breathed air this clean or stared at the lake for so long. This really was a great way to end our "tips of the fingers" adventure. We relaxed on Lake Huron, ate like Italians, flew like birds, dined with a ghost, caught a good crepe and wandered the wilderness. After all that, I give the top of Michigan's mitten a definite high five!

Story behind the name:
Ten MORE Shows?

As season three wrapped up with our expanded season length that took us from thirteen shows to twenty-three, we were actually amazed at how much more work ten more shows created. We like to work hard... but this was a tiny bit insane.

Chapter 50

Season 4, Episode 1

Leelanau Peninsula

If your idea of living right is being in a place surrounded by beautiful blue water, rolling hills, giant sand dunes, inviting vineyards and great places to eat then you already know that the Leelanau Peninsula is pure Michigan heaven. The natural beauty of this place and its warm friendly people will keep you coming back until, well, you just might decide to never leave. And the more you explore it, the more you'll explore it.

On our way up and onto the Leelanau Peninsula, we made a quick stop in Beulah. This beautiful little town is a great laid-back place to stop, shop, relax or even spend your next family vacation! And the best part is, it sits right on the eastern shore of one of Michigan's most beautiful bodies of water: Crystal Lake. The lake stretches almost as far as the eye can see, all the way to the shores of Lake Michigan. And if you love scenic drives, try the drive around Crystal Lake. It just might cure what ails ya.

But, to be honest, there was another very important reason why we just had to stop in Beulah. **The Cherry Hut**!

The Cherry Hut
(231) 882-4431
211 N. Michigan Ave., Beulah, MI 49617
www.cherryhutstore.com

When it comes to Michigan cherries, the Cherry Hut's been doing it right since it started as a little road-side hut in 1922. It's a landmark, a tradition and a big slice of Michigan history. And speaking of slices, the cherry pie there is what they're famous for. It's simple, honest, fresh and full of ripe Michigan cherries—which are, of course, the best cherries in the world!

The Cherry Hut is also a family affair that goes back three generations, and I was lucky enough to sit down with Andy Case and share a little bit of my own Cherry Hut history, because my family has been going there since my kids were small. At the Daldin house, when you turned five, the whole family would pile in the car, drive north to the Cherry Hut, eat tons of pie and you'd get your very first Cherry Hut t-shirt. We'd also bring home a bunch of pies. The pies never lasted very long, but believe it or not my kids still have their original t-shirts.

So if you're driving up north, and you see a big red smiling cherry face: stop, have a slice of Michigan life, start your own family tradition and take home a pie or two of your own. Just remember, the Cherry Hut is red and white—now all it needs is you!

Once we were full and happy, we drove up M-22 to another one of my favorite places in Michigan: **The Village of Empire** (great name for a tiny town!).

It's a walkable little village with cute shops and a great personality and one of the best family-friendly beaches you'll find anywhere. It's actually where my kids learned to swim. On one side you've got the warm and shallow waters of South Bar Lake, and on the other side, the beautiful white sand beach and incredible views of Lake Michigan. It's a classic vacation destination.

Another thing a lot of people don't know is that Empire also has its own tunnel of trees. Just drive south out of town on Lake Street, and you come across an absolutely beautiful canopy-covered road. It's a short drive, and well worth taking. Oh, and speaking of cool things you'll find in Empire... who likes chocolate?

Grocer's Daughter Chocolate
(231) 326-3030
12020 S. Leelanau Hwy., Empire, MI 49630
www.grocersdaughter.com

It's kinda hard to say, but if you're into chocolate, it's real easy to love!

It's the funky green building that grabs your eyes, but when you go inside, it's the aromas that'll melt your mind. That's because DC Hayden and Jody Dotson are making incredible, handcrafted, all natural chocolates. They love what they do and where they are, and they love sharing their chocolates with the world. Not only is all the chocolate there amazing (the hand-dipped truffles are to die for), the work environment DC and Jody have created is wonderful. The staff is one big caring and collaborative family with a single mission: to have fun and make the best darn all natural chocolates in the galaxy.

And at **Grocer's Daughter Chocolates,** not just the building is green. They go out of their way to minimize their impact on the environment. Their chocolates are organic and contain naturally grown ingredients. They even package their chocolates in compostable bags and recyclable/recycled materials when possible. Did I mention that they are also the nicest people EVER!

So if you're looking for a classic little Michigan town where you can kick back, enjoy the views, feel the love and taste some incredible chocolates, roll into Empire, roll out your beach towel and stop by Grocer's Daughter Chocolates. It's proof positive that the Leelanau Peninsula is a sweet place to be.

Secret Beach – North Bar Lake
1030 N. Bar Lake Rd., Empire, MI 49630
www.nps.gov/slbe/planyourvisit/northbarlake.htm

Now, here's a treat for ya—just north of Empire, on a lonely winding country road is a secret beach that only me and the locals know about. I'd tell you where it is, but I've been sworn to secrecy!

When you get there, you walk down a long sandy path that reveals an incredible sand-bottom blue lagoon that's surrounded by beautiful sand dunes. It's almost a tropical place where the sun, surf and sand melt all your cares away. And the best part is it's connected to Lake Michigan by a shallow little river where kids can run and play. Incredible!

So if you ever get the chance, try and make it to this incredible secret beach. Just don't tell anyone else about it! Like I did—oops!

Suttons Bay
(231) 271-5077
P.O. Box 46, Suttons Bay, MI 49682
www.suttonsbayarea.com

Next we headed over and up the bay side of the peninsula to the beautiful northern Michigan town of **Suttons Bay**. If you're looking for a creative community with great art galleries, good food and a certain level of sophistication, you've come to the right place. Suttons Bay's got just enough hubbub to make you feel alive and just the right amount of, "Hey, I'm on vacation" to help you relax. Whether you live or play here, you picked the right spot.

Martha's Leelanau Table
(231) 271-2344
413 N. St. Joseph St., Suttons Bay, MI 49682
www.marthasleelanautable.com

At **Martha's Leelanau Table** they actually have a lot of tables, which is good because the way we eat on this show, we may need a couple.

Martha Ryan took a classic little house right downtown and turned it into a place where everyone can enjoy her home cooking. It's a casual European-style bistro where everything is made from scratch and from fresh Northern Michigan ingredients. Renowned celebrity Chef Mario Batali actually said that Martha's Leelanau Table is one of his favorite places to eat, so this place keeps good company.

Martha takes her culinary consciousness seriously. Every year she leads tours to Europe, and the culinary experiences of her travels are directly reflected in her ever-changing menu. She also strives to create from foods currently available in season. Martha's may close during some of the winter months, so be sure and call ahead.

We filled up on Martha's awesome food and her incredible hospitality and made our usual mess at the table. We also made a new friend, but that's easy to do at Martha's Leelanau Table.

Boskydel Vineyards
(231) 256-7272
7501 E. Otto Rd., Lake Leelanau, MI 49653
www.boskydel.com

The Leelanau Peninsula is known for its many wineries and vineyards, and more are opening all the time. But if you want to find **Boskydel Vineyards**, you've got to wander off the beaten path a bit. It's not what you'd call fancy or shmancy, and you won't find big elaborate signs or luxurious tasting rooms. What you will find is the man and his boys who started it all. This place is refreshingly raw and real and the wines are straightforward.

Way back in 1965, Bernie Rink was a librarian who loved wine. One day when his kids were small, he proclaimed, "Boy, we're gonna dig up your ball diamond and plant some grapes." After a brief protest, Jim and Andy Rink grew up tending to barrels, bottles and bushels of grapes, and they did it all to help their father's dream become a legacy. Today the vineyard is a total family affair, and looking back, they wouldn't have it any other way.

Not only was Boskydel the first vineyard on the peninsula, it was actually the first Michigan vineyard I ever went to, and even back then, Bernie Rink was the man. His passion and quick wit always made visits to the tasting room a social adventure. After all these years, finally going back to Boskydel made me realize that it's more than just about the wine; it's about family, tradition and chasing your dreams. There's a lot of great wine out there, but there's only one Bernie Rink, and to him, I tip my glass.

La Becasse

(231) 334-3944
9001 S. Dunn's Farm Rd., Maple City, MI 49664
www.restaurantlabecasse.com

What do France, the West Indies and Michigan's Leelanau Peninsula all have in common? Guillaume Hazaël-Massieux is the owner and chef at **La Becasse**, an intimate restaurant in Maple City that serves what he likes to call authentic French country cuisine.

Guillaume grew up in France eating the honest and rustic country foods his mother would prepare. After being bit by that illusive culinary bug, he became classically trained, spent time sharpening his palate in the West Indies and is now loving living in the Leelanau Peninsula. As he so eloquently put it, "The wonderful people, beautiful surroundings and the rich agricultural environment make it the perfect place to be."

As is with all enlightened chefs, Guillaume sources locally and creates seasonally. He also goes out of his way to help you match the perfect local wine to go with your meal. The atmosphere is quaint, casual and sophisticated and the food is simply awesome.

Guillaume and I have two out of three very important things in common: we've both been around the world, we both call Michigan our home… but this guy? He can cook!

After tons of great food and fascinating stories, we finished an incredible evening with Guillaume at La Becasse, and with a collective sigh of contentment, it suddenly hit us: we always feature exceptional people, places and things on UTR, but this time, it was just different. On the Leelanau Peninsula, we really made a personal connection with everyone we encountered. I think that says a lot about the people who call Michigan's beautiful Leelanau Peninsula home.

Yep… still one of my favorite places!

Story behind the name:
Fiddy

Our good buddy Gary Galusky relocated to Suttons Bay a few years ago… so when he heard we were coming up to film, he was insistent that we stay with him. He was also insistent that we eat with him, drink with him, play Hendrix SUPER LOUD and pay him to stay with him. He charged us a whopping FIFTY cents to stay with him, hence the show name FIDDY.

About the Authors

Tom Daldin is an Emmy award winning producer, actor and writer who has created programs that have aired across Michigan and the U.S. on PBS. He has also won a number of "best actor" awards in both commercial television and industrial films. When Tom isn't running around exploring cool people, places and things in Michigan, he's either enjoying time with his family, on his mountain bike or playing the drums real loud. Tom has a passion for the simpler things in life like nature, family, a great hockey game and, of course, a reasonably priced chicken salad sandwich. His greatest accomplishments in life are his children, Jeff, Anthony and Andrea, who have all turned out to be exceptional people. His true love is Cathy, his favorite color red, his inseam *34"* and if you ever see him on the street, please make sure to say hello and share what you love about Michigan.

Caryn Taylor Photography

Jim Edelman's main job is the daily care and feeding of Tom and Eric. On the road he makes sure the car is always the right temperature and they have a frosty cold beverage to keep hydrated between shoots. Oh, and he makes sure that there is money in the bank by putting on a sales hat he's worn in numerous media sales jobs around Detroit.

He will tell you that in his entire career, he has loved all his jobs (except the job his mother got him as a kid picking tomatoes. Really, worst job ever, Mom. Thanks.) But UTR is the best thing he's ever been a part of and he is so thankful for the way things work out in life. Well, unless something EVEN better comes along...

Eric Tremonti brought his love for positive storytelling to the UTR Michigan team after fifteen years in advertising production. Joining midway through UTR's first season, Eric wears multiple hats, including director, camera operator, producer, editor and post production manager. Eric will tell you that working on UTR is the second best job he's ever had, because it's given him the opportunity to spend more time on his first bestest job, that of world's greatest dad to his two young daughters. When he's not hard at work on either job, you can find Eric pursuing his passion for all things green in his garden and community farm plot. Eric is also a self-proclaimed super cooker guy and food aficionado... so it's no wonder he fits right in here at UTR World Headquarters.

UTR Shameless Sales Plug

Hello, UTR shoppers. This is the Under the Radar Michigan shopping page. If you visit **www.utrmichigan.com/store**, you can buy really cool UTR merchandise, including…

Hats like Tom wears (not the actual hat that Tom wears).

Cool t-shirts. They come in amazing, stain-hiding black. We subscribe to the Henry Ford school of color selection: you can have any color you want, as long as it's black. By the time you read this in the future, we may have caved in to demand and started offering different colors. This is a book, and it's likely we won't do a reprint just because we started selling white or yellow t-shirts.

DVDs—new UTR store item! Everywhere we went you can go anytime you want, from the comfort of your couch, in rich, full mustache-enhancing color. Now you won't have to deal with a DVR that's ninety-nine percent full because you needed to save all the UTR episodes; buy all the seasons of the show on handy DVDs. (And if you're reading this in the future… we probably now offer your preferred storage/playback device… including for seasons that haven't been filmed as of this printing! How did we do that?!)

Look around and see what you like. Our professional and courteous sales staff is there to help you… email them at **iwantahat@utrmichigan.com** with any questions.

Have a nice shopping day.

Index by Category

Salons/Barbershops

Wineries, Breweries & Distilleries

General Index

State Theater, The, *141*
Stonehouse, The, *236*
Stormy Kromer, *73*
Studio *1219*, *12*
Suttons Bay, *285*
Swedish Pantry, *235*
Sweet Sandy B's Bake Shop, *264*
Sweet Tooth Candy Shop, The, *164*
Sweetie-licious Bakery Café, *77*
Symons General Store, *61*
Tall Ship Manitou, *98*
Tap Room, The, *120*
Tashmoo Biergarten, *221*
Tawas, *47*
Tawas Bay Beach Resort, *48*
Telway Hamburgers, *199*
Thatcher, Becky, *178*
Third Coast Surf Shop, *90*
Thomas, Andy, *114*
Thumbfest, *138*
Thunder Bay Marine Sanctuary, *25*
Tip-up Town, *71*
Tollgate Farm, *242*
Tom's Mom's Cookies, *210*
Top of the Lake Snowmobile
Museum, *72*
Tour America Bike Shop, *115*
Tower of History, The, *37*
Toy Town, *10*
Traffic Jam & Snug, *96*
Traverse City, *29*
Trenton, *273*
Troy, *202*
Tunnel of Trees, *210*
Turkey Roost, *264*
Turkey's Café & Pizzeria, *209*
TV's Deli-Diner, *273*
Twilight Walking Tour, *27*
U.P. 200, *74*

U.S. Coast Guard Cutter
Bramble, The, *13*
U.S. Ski and Snowboard
Hall of Fame and Museum, *144*
Ugly Dog Distillery, *208*
USS Badger, *113*
USS Silversides, *102*
Valley of the Giants, The, *122*
Van Dam Custom Boats, *57*
Van Landschoot & Sons Fish House, *42*
Village at Grand Traverse Commons, *30*
Voodoo Choppers, *201*
Warren Dunes State Park, *89*
Water Street Coffee Joint, *92*
Water Street Glassworks, *261*
Weirdsville Records, *229*
West Texas Barbeque Company, *216*
Whitehouse Restaurant, The, *170*
Wilderness Sports, *144*
Wilderness State Park, *281*
Willard Street Roasting House, *92*
William Mitchell State Park, *10*
Willi's Sausage Company, *68*
Wurst Bar, The, *241*
Wyandotte, *77*, *201*
Yale, *156*
Yesterdog, *133*
Yooper Bars, *145*
Your Nesting Place, *248*
Ypsilanti, *119*
Ypsilanti Summer Beer Festival, *155*
Zehnder's Inn, *69*
Zingerman's Deli, *44*
Zumba Mexican Grille, *4*